THE HINDU TRADITIONS

THE HINDU TRADITIONS

 A CONCISE INTRODUCTION

Mark W. Muesse

Fortress Press / Minneapolis

THE HINDU TRADITIONS

A Concise Introduction

Cover image: Hindu sculpture of Vishnu at Perumal Temple in Singapore, photo: © Ted Streshinsky/CORBIS
Cover design: Kevin van der Leek Design, Inc.
Book design: Zan Ceeley, Trio Bookworks

Library of Congress Cataloging-in-Publication Data
Muesse, Mark W. (Mark William), 1957–
  The Hindu traditions : a concise introduction / Mark W. Muesse.
    p. cm.
  ISBN 978-0-8006-9790-7 (alk. paper)
  1. Hinduism. I. Title.
  BL1202.M84 2011
  294.5—dc22

                    2010044876

Manufactured in the U.S.A.

16   15   14   13   12   11   1   2   3   4   5   6   7   8   9   10

For Ariyana Prabashwari Muesse

CONTENTS

Part IV — Modern Challenges 169

ILLUSTRATIONS AND BOXES

Figures

Boxes

PREFACE

Of all the world's religions, Hinduism is probably the most difficult to present in a concise introduction. The sheer dimensions of this cluster of traditions point to the challenges of the task. Reckoned by number of practitioners, it is the world's third largest, exceeded in size only by Christianity and Islam. Calculated by age, it is arguably the world's oldest, with roots reaching back at least five thousand years. In terms of influence, it is undoubtedly one of the most prominent, directly shaping the worldviews of millions who are not even Hindus, namely, Buddhists, Jains, and Sikhs. And measured by diversity of belief and practice, it is certainly the richest and most complex. This diversity, more than anything else, makes it hard to reduce the Hindu traditions to a compact introductory text. Any brief treatment of these traditions always runs the risk of omitting important features, neglecting important texts, and slighting important eras. A short introduction, moreover, risks making Hinduism seem more coherent and systematic than it actually is.

But despite the obvious hazards, there is a real need for texts to present the Hindu traditions in a concise and introductory way. In an age in which it is increasingly necessary to understand the perspectives of our neighbors, books such as this one are essential to provide a basis for appreciating worldviews other than our own. And in some cases, these texts are useful to introduce us to our *own* worldview, especially when we have been raised within a tradition without knowing its history and breadth. Those who desire a rudimentary knowledge of Hinduism will find here a clear presentation of the fundamental components and dynamics of the Hindu traditions informed by the latest scholarship. And those who wish to develop a deeper understanding of Hinduism will discover here a solid basis for the pursuit of topics that can only be mentioned briefly.

Approach of This Book

This book is by no means comprehensive. Specific choices have been made to emphasize certain aspects of the Hindu traditions to the exclusion of others. Such decisions are essential to present Hinduism in a succinct, introductory format. I can only hope that others familiar with the breadth and depth of the Hindu traditions will consider these decisions to be well informed and judicious. Undoubtedly, others would have chosen to highlight different aspects of the traditions and to present them in a different manner. The richness of Hinduism itself makes possible a wide variety of introductory texts. Just as the Hindu traditions admit many valid approaches to the divine, there are many valid approaches to Hinduism.

The approach adopted here has been governed principally by the needs of the college classroom, although the text will serve well in other contexts. *The Hindu Traditions* will be valuable in courses for which a short overview of Hinduism is desired, particularly when no previous knowledge is assumed. Instructors teaching courses in the history of India or Asia and survey courses on the religions of Asia or world religions should find the approach and scope of this volume especially attractive. The book may also serve as a foundational text for introductory courses in Hinduism. The number of chapters corresponds closely to the number of weeks in an average college semester. Each chapter can be used to provide a topic of study for an entire week when supplemented by other resources such as films and primary texts.

Features in This Book

To facilitate the use of this volume in collegiate courses and other educational venues, *The Hindu Traditions* provides a number of important features to supplement and enrich the narrative. Each chapter begins with a preview, presenting in summary form its principal points and topics. The end of each chapter contains a list of key words, all of which are defined in the glossary. (For more information about these terms and how they are presented, please consult "A Note about Terminology" on pages xix–xx.) Each chapter also concludes with sets of questions for review and further reflection and a selected bibliography for those interested in pursuing topics in greater depth.

Throughout the book is also an array of illustrations and text boxes. Because the Hindu traditions are intensely visual, the images are an

www.fortresspress.com/muesse

Further information about the use of *The Hindu Traditions* in educational settings may be found at **www.fortresspress.com/muesse**. Both instructors and students will find additional materials to assist with their teaching and study of this book and of Hinduism generally. Included on the website are course syllabi, sample test questions, pedagogical suggestions, web resources, and an audio guide for pronouncing technical terms.

essential component of the volume. They both augment the written text and provide a vital dimension to understanding Hinduism that cannot be gained simply by reading. To help situate the Hindu traditions in time and space, several key maps and graphs as well as a timeline have been furnished. The textboxes offer additional information of a variety of sorts. Some of the boxes present material that allows the Hindu traditions to be compared and contrasted with other world religions. Other boxes contain passages from the primary sources of Hinduism, including excerpts from the Vedas, the Bhagavad Gita, and poetry composed by great Hindu practitioners. Still other boxes relate interesting sidelights and more detailed information about particular subjects.

Overview of the Chapters

The Hindu Traditions seeks to mediate between a strictly historical (diachronic) approach and a thematic (synchronic) one. To meet this objective, the book follows a basic chronological format, beginning with the earliest known expressions of Indian religion and moving through its classical manifestations to its responses to modernity. Along the way, salient aspects of Hindu life are discussed and placed in context. The overarching structure is such that a reader should be able to have a clear sense of the development of the major Hindu traditions as well as a good understanding of how these traditions inform Hindu life today.

But the story of Hinduism begins not in ancient history, but rather in the modern era, when the idea of "Hinduism" was first proposed. For this reason, the introduction opens this study with a brief analysis of the concept of Hinduism and its problematical nature.

Although the term *Hinduism* is useful, I argue that the expression "Hindu traditions" is a more adequate way of referring to this vast and multifaceted cultural complex.

Beginning with chapter 1, we start our journey through five thousand years of Hindu history with an examination of the early cultures that most significantly shaped the development of what came to be known as Hinduism. We make a brief visit to the indigenous culture of northern India, the Indus Valley Civilization, and consider the elements of its religious practice that may have influenced the Hindu traditions. Then we introduce the Indo-Aryans, who bequeathed to the Hindus their most sacred and authoritative scripture, the Vedas. Today, the origin of Indo-Aryan culture is the subject of a vigorous debate. We briefly examine the issues involved in that debate, although ultimately we take the view of the majority of scholars by presenting the Aryans as arriving in the Indian Subcontinent from Central Asia. From this point of view, we are able to discuss the close connections of the Indo-Aryans with their cousins, the Irano-Aryans. Chapter 2 sets the stage for exploring Indo-Aryan religion by considering its oldest beliefs and practices, as we can best reconstruct them. Considering Aryan culture in its Central Asian and Iranian contexts is one way in which this introduction to Hinduism differs from others. Even though the origin of the Aryans is a source of contention, their influence on subsequent Indian religion is not. In chapter 3, we examine the religious world of the Indo-Aryans as disclosed through the Vedas.

Chapter 4 discusses the transformations that began in the first millennium B.C.E. and that precipitated the development of the "classical" Hindu worldview, which included the decisive concepts of rebirth and karma. To indicate the connections between Hinduism and other religious and philosophical developments beyond the Indian Subcontinent, we situate these transformations in the context of the Axial Age, a broad cross-cultural movement that ultimately produced the major world religions. Analyzing the emergence of the classical Hindu traditions within the framework of the Axial Age is another feature that distinguishes the present introduction from others. In chapters 5 and 6, we continue to present the components of the classical traditions with a study of the principal social arrangements of Hindu culture, namely the caste system and the ideal life patterns for men and women.

Building on the foundations of the classical transformations, the remaining chapters explore the diverse religious and philosophical features of the Hindu traditions. This part of the book follows the traditional typology of the *Trimarga*, the three pathways to spiritual liberation, and explains the three major Hindu religions, Shaivism, Vaishnavism, and Shaktism. Chapter 7 outlines the way of action, the spiritual discipline pursued, at least in part, by a majority of Hindus. This path aims to improve an individual's future births through meritorious actions such as participating in religious rituals, festivals, and pilgrimages. Chapter 8 describes the way of knowledge, a rigorous and less-traveled pathway to ultimate salvation. Although relatively few Hindus are inclined to seek liberation by means of knowledge, this tradition offers a profound vision of the self and ultimate reality that has influenced almost all other Hindu traditions and perspectives. Chapter 9 focuses on the different ways

Hindus conceptualize the divine reality, providing a transition between discussions of the way of knowledge and the way of devotion. In this section of the book, we explain how Hinduism can be both monotheistic and polytheistic, and we discuss the function of images in Hindu worship. In chapter 10, we explore the way of devotion through one of the most important and best-loved Hindu texts, the Bhagavad Gita. Chapter 11 concerns devotion to the goddess and surveys her many manifestations in the Hindu pantheon. Finally, the book concludes in chapter 12 with a discussion of Hinduism in the modern era, particularly its sometimes ambiguous relationship with the West. We will explore the Hindu-Muslim relationship, the British Raj and the Indian independence movement led by Mohandas K. Gandhi, and the movement of Hinduism into the West.

Because this book is introductory rather than comprehensive in nature, it has its limitations. But even if it were a comprehensive text, I would feel compelled to acknowledge that no written work can do justice to Hinduism, or, for that matter, to any living religious tradition. We always distort Hinduism—and any religion—by trying to bring it into the classroom or discuss it in a text. There is simply no way adequately to describe the lived reality of nearly a billion people. In the classroom and in books, we deal mainly in ideas and concepts. But Hinduism, like all religions, is vastly more than that. To understand Hinduism, it should be not only thought about but also—and perhaps especially—seen and felt and tasted and heard and smelled. For that, no book can suffice.

ACKNOWLEDGMENTS

I have many to thank for helping bring this book to fruition. Let me start at the beginning.

Diana L. Eck, Professor of Comparative Religion and Indian Studies at Harvard, provided me with a most compelling entry into the study of the religions of India. It was so compelling, in fact, that my professional and spiritual pathways were indelibly altered. Since then, she has remained my teacher and continues to nourish my understanding of religion through her scholarship.

A crucial part of my understanding of the Hindu traditions came during an extended stay in India twenty years ago as a visiting faculty member at the Tamilnadu Theological Seminary (T.T.S.) in Madurai. I am grateful to that institution and especially to three former professors at T.T.S. who made that experience so meaningful: M. Thomas Thangaraj, now professor emeritus of Candler School of Theology at Emory University; Chellaian Lawrence, now minister of religion for the Methodist church in England; and Vedanayagam Devasahayam, now Bishop in Madras for the Church of South India. I want also to acknowledge two T.T.S. students—and now dear friends—Lutz Meyer, pastor of the evangelisch-lutherische Kirchengemeinde St. Nicolai, Altenbruch, Germany, and I. P. Job Gnanaiah, pastor of the Tamil Evangelical Lutheran Church in Pollachi, Tamilnadu, who shared much of that time with me.

Over the last decade, The Teaching Company has become a valued partner in the publication and distribution of my work. I am thankful for its confidence and support, and I am particularly grateful to Lucinda Robb for providing me with the opportunity to develop further the lectures on which this book is based. My student Margaret Love was my editorial assistant during that project, and I wish to express my appreciation to her as well.

I am grateful to my colleagues at Rhodes College, especially the members of the Department of Religious Studies, as well as David Mason in the Department of Theatre, Lynn Zastoupil in the Department of History, and David Sick in the Department of Greek and Roman Studies. My friend and colleague Bob Patterson, now professor emeritus at Rhodes, shared many experiences with me in India, Sri Lanka, Nepal, Thailand, and China. I am appreciative of his companionship and insight. Special thanks go to my former students at Rhodes: Christopher Johnson, now in the Department of Religious Studies at the University of Alabama, Matt Wilson, and my editorial assistant, Scarlett D'Anna.

My editors at Fortress Press have been a great delight to work with. I am especially indebted to Ross Miller, senior acquisitions editor, and Michael West, former editor-in-chief, as well as Zan Ceeley, the book's designer and project manager, of Trio Bookworks.

For kind support from two important institutions, I am grateful to Vinod Jain, President and CEO of the India-US World Affairs Institute and Prashad S. Duggirala, chair of the Executive Committee of the India Cultural Center and Temple in Eads, Tennessee.

My family is fortunate to have many good friends who have in many small ways enriched my understanding of South Asian religions and culture. Not all of them are Hindu, yet they have all provided me something that has deepened my appreciation for the Hindu traditions. They are Chhabil and Asha Dass; Manoj and Sunita Jain, Rakesh and Sarita Goorha, Gopal and Aruna Murti, Aditya Gaur and Nehali Patel, and Nikhil Mundra. In the same vein, but for different reasons, I am grateful to Peggy and Hal Bishop for their friendship over many years.

Most of all, I thank my wife, Dhammika Swarnamali, and our daughter, Ariyana Prabashwari, for providing me with the love and support that has become the staple of my life.

A NOTE ABOUT TERMINOLOGY

Like all cultural traditions, the Hindu religions use certain technical terms and expressions. This technical vocabulary presents some challenges for the English-speaking reader, especially for one not previously acquainted with the Indian context. These terms derive from many different languages (see box Intro.2) and can be transliterated into English in several ways. My approach to this terminology for this book has been to make the technical language of the Hindu traditions as accessible as possible while preserving the sense of its richness in its native context.

When technical terms are introduced for the first time, they will appear in **boldface** type. For convenience, these terms are listed at the end of each chapter and defined in the glossary at the end of the book.

Some technical terms will appear in *italics* and others will not. The basis of this distinc-tion is simple: familiarity. Certain Hindu words have been adopted into English and are recognizable to most English speakers. Accordingly, words like karma, samsara, and dharma will appear in plain type in recognition of their status as English words. Other terms, however, are not so familiar and therefore always appear italicized, such as *rishi*, *sannyasin*, and *puja*. By the same token, the titles of some texts will be italicized while others will appear plain. References to collections such as the Vedas and the Upanishads are not italicized, much like similar conventions for the Bible and the Qur'an. But most texts, such as the *Gita Govinda* and the *Ramayana*, will be italicized in the standard way for such documents.

The scholarly transliteration of the languages of the Hindu traditions involves certain standard diacritical marks. To avoid creating unnecessary distractions, however, I have chosen to keep the diacritical markings of these words to a minimum. The glossary provides the full transliteration of terms including diacritics in parenthetical marks. For direct quotations from other texts, I have reproduced the transliteration and capitalization scheme of the original, even though it might be at slight odds with my own.

The diacritics are helpful for anyone interested in pronouncing the technical terms of Indian religions. The brief guide below will assist in the pronunciation of these transliterated terms. Consonants are usually pronounced in the same way as English, with a few exceptions noted below.

a	like the *u* in cut
ā	like the *a* in father
i	like the *i* in hit
ī	like the *ee* in feet
u	like the *u* in put
ū	like the *u* in rule
e	like the *ay* in may
o	like the *o* in hope
ṛ	like the *r* in pretty
g	like the *g* in give
h	always pronounced
c	like the *ch* in chill
j	like the *j* in joy
ñ	like the *ny* in canyon
ś, ṣ	like the *s* in sugar

TIMELINE OF THE HINDU TRADITIONS

B.C.E.*

3300–1500	Indus Valley Civilization
2300–1200	Composition of the *Rig-Veda*
1600–1000	Migration of Aryans into Northwestern India
1200–900	Composition of the *Yajur-Veda*, *Sama-Veda*, and *Atharva-Veda*
1000 (?)	Birth of Zoroaster, Iranian prophet
1000	Migration of Aryans into the Gangetic Plains
800–400	Composition of the principal Upanishads
540–468	Vardhamana Mahavira, 24th Tirthankara of Jainism
490–410	Siddhattha Gotama, the Buddha
400 B.C.E.–400 C.E.	Composition of the *Mahabharata*
327–325	Campaign of Alexander the Great in India
200 B.C.E.–200 C.E.	Composition of the Laws of Manu
200 B.C.E.–200 C.E.	Composition of the *Ramayana*
200 B.C.E.–100 C.E.	Composition of the Bhagavad Gita
4 B.C.E.–29 C.E.	Jesus of Nazareth, Christian messiah

C.E.

300–1700	Composition of the *Puranas*
400–700	Appearance of the Tantras
570–632	Muhammad, Last Prophet of Islam
710s	First Muslim invasions of northwest India
788–820	Shankara, Vedanta philosopher
800	Parsi immigration to western India

timeline continues on following page

*Many of the early dates are approximate and subject to scholarly debate.

TIMELINE OF THE HINDU TRADITIONS *(continued)*

C.E. *(continued)*

1077–1157	Ramanuja, Vedanta philosopher
1100s	Composition of Jayadeva's *Gita Govinda*
1192	Muslim capital established at Delhi
1320–1392	Lalla, Kashmiri poet
1440–1518	Kabir, mystic and poet
1469–1539	Guru Nanak, First Guru of Sikhism
1486–1533	Caitanya Mahaprabhu, Vaishnavite saint
1498	Vasco da Gama lands on India's west coast
1526–1707	Mughal Rule in India
1540s	Portuguese missionaries arrive in India
1542–1605	Akbar, Jalal ud-Din Muhammad, Mughal emperor
1718–1770	Ramprasad Sen, Bengali Shakta poet
1757–1947	British Rule in India
1774–1833	Rammohun Roy, Brahmo Samaj founder
1824–1883	Dayananda Sarasvati, Arya Samaj founder
1828	Founding of the Brahmo Samaj
1836–1886	Ramakrishna, Bengali sage
1863–1902	Vivekananda, Hindu sage and representative to the West
1869–1948	Mohandas K. Gandhi
1875	Founding of the Arya Samaj
1876–1948	Muhammad Ali Jinnah, President of the Muslim League
1891–1956	B. R. Ambedkar, Dalit leader
1893	World's Parliament of Religion, Chicago
1896–1977	A.C. Bhaktivedanta, ISKCON founder
1914–2008	Maharishi Mahesh Yogi, Hindu guru
1931–1990	Bhagwan Sri Rajneesh, Hindu-Jain guru
1947	Indian Independence and Partition
1950	Constitution of the Republic of India
1966	International Society for Krishna Consciousness founded

Introduction: Hinduism in Time and Space

PREVIEW

As a phenomenon of human culture, Hinduism occupies a particular place in time and space. To begin our study of this phenomenon, it is essential to situate it temporally and spatially. We begin by considering how the concept of Hinduism arose in the modern era as a way to designate a purportedly coherent system of beliefs and practices. Since this initial construction has proven inadequate to the realities of the Hindu religious terrain, we adopt "the Hindu traditions" as a more satisfactory alternative to "Hinduism." The phrase "Hindu traditions" calls attention to the great diversity of practices and beliefs that can be described as "Hindu." Those traditions are deeply rooted in history and have flourished almost exclusively on the Indian Subcontinent within a rich cultural and religious matrix.

As strange as it may seem, most Hindus do not think of themselves as practicing a religion called Hinduism. Only within the last two centuries has it even been possible for them to think in this way. And although that possibility now exists, many Hindus—if they even think of themselves *as* Hindus—do not regard "Hinduism" as their "religion." This irony relates directly to the history of the concept of Hinduism. A brief overview of this history will help prepare us for our study of the diverse array of phenomena that we include in that concept. Appreciating the origin of the idea of Hinduism and the context in which Hinduism thrives will allow us to approach our subject in the proper frame of mind, with expectations appropriate for a cultural reality that is considerably different from that to which most Westerners are accustomed.

The Temporal Context

Through most of the millennia of its history, the religion we know today as Hinduism has not been called by that name. The word *Hinduism* (or *Hindooism*, as it was first spelled) did not exist until the late eighteenth or early nineteenth century, when it began to appear sporadically in the discourse of the British missionaries and administrators who occupied colonial India.[1] Within a few decades of its creation, *Hinduism* became more widely accepted by both Westerners and Indians. But before the word was invented, there was no specific name in any language to refer to the religion of the Hindus. The indigenous phrase that most closely approximates what is now called Hinduism is **sanātana dharma**, a Sanskrit expression that might be translated as "eternal religion." But this translation is not completely satisfying because the word *religion* as used in the West is not an adequate equivalent to the Indian concept of *dharma*. The indigenous languages of India, in fact, lack a word equivalent to the English word *religion*.

The Hindus

Although there was no special term for their religion, there had long been people known as Hindus. *Hindū* was an Old Persian word that initially appeared around the twelfth century C.E. to identify the inhabitants of the area flanking the Indus River, which was called the **Sindhu** in Sanskrit. This region, in what was once northwestern India and is now Pakistan, was known as **Hindustan**.[2] Eventually, *Hindustan* became a common name for all of northern India and, later, for India and the subcontinent

as a whole (figure Intro.1). Thus, in its original sense, *Hindu* had no religious connotations at all; it meant nothing more than what we today would mean by "Indian."

Sometime between 1200 and 1500 C.E., however, the word *Hindu* also came to refer to a person with a particular religious orientation.[3] It was almost always used to identify those inhabitants of India who were not Muslims. Even so, the meaning of *Hindu* was ambiguous. It was sometimes used to indicate religious identity, sometimes geographical identity, and sometimes both. Yet even when intended in a religious way, the specific meaning of the term was far from clear. Because it was primarily a way to distinguish non-Muslim Indians from Muslims, what it meant to be "Hindu" was not readily apparent, even to those who might be identified in that way. There was no central core of teachings, scriptures, creeds, communities, or

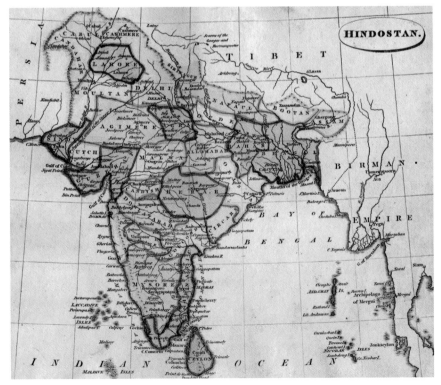

Fig. Intro.1
Indian Subcontinent in the nineteenth century. This early nineteenth-century map displays the political divisions of what was then called Hindustan. Today, this region comprises the modern nations of India, Pakistan, Afghanistan, Nepal, Bangladesh, Bhutan, and Sri Lanka. (Photo courtesy of http://commons.wikimedia.org/wiki/File:Hindostan_1814.jpg.)

practices that could be specified as forming the essence of Hindu identity. As other terms—particularly the word *Indian*—came to designate geographical identity, *Hindu* came to be an exclusively religious designation. But the specific meaning of *Hindu* as a religious identity remained no clearer.

The Invention of "Hinduism"

As Western cultures developed greater interest in India—especially as the British sought control of India's commerce beginning in the eighteenth century—understanding the Hindus and their religion became more important to the West. Both Western administrators and Christian missionaries considered it necessary to their work to describe and comprehend this religion. By the nineteenth century, efforts were under way to ascertain the essential nature of Hindu beliefs and practices. The British relied on their own observations, as well as information provided to them by upper-caste Hindus, to shape their conception of this "religion." Lacking a suitable indigenous word, they began to refer to *Hinduism*, an English neologism formed by adding the anglicized Greek suffix *-ism* to the Persian *Hindū*. Hinduism thus joined Judaism as one of the only world religions named for a place.

The British tended to think of this "Hinduism" in much the same manner as they thought of their own religion. Christianity, especially its Protestant manifestation, thus served as the largely unconscious prototype for the way they imagined Hinduism. From the British point of view, a religion was fundamentally a unified set of doctrines pertaining to belief in god and a code of behavior based on this belief. Religions had sacred books on which these doctrines were founded and creeds in which they were set out

systematically. A clearly identifiable clergy was responsible for interpreting these texts to the laity, who gathered at temples for meetings to understand and express their faith.

With these assumptions, the British and other Europeans involved in studying and managing colonial India created a conception of Hinduism that met their expectations. They identified a system of thought that constituted what they took to be the core of Hinduism. That essential philosophy was **Advaita Vedanta**, a highly influential system formulated by the great south Indian **pandit Shankara** (see chapter 8). They identified a sacred set of texts, the **Vedas**, which they took to be the scriptural source of this philosophy. And they identified an ecclesiastical hierarchy, the **Brahmins**, members of the priestly and intellectual caste, whom the Europeans considered Hinduism's religious authorities and interpreters.

The Hindu Adoption of "Hinduism"

Once created, this conception became widely influential, governing the way not only Westerners but also many Hindus thought about Indian religion. Indian adoption of the idea of Hinduism meant that, to some degree, Hindus relied on Europeans to tell them what Hinduism was. For instance, before the eighteenth century, only a small number of upper-caste Indians had much acquaintance with the Vedas, the Upanishads, or even the Bhagavad Gita, some of the most important texts in Indian history. But when these texts were translated by Europeans and heralded as Hindu scripture, other upper-caste Hindus became aware of these books for the first time and accepted them as the sacred sources of their religion. With these texts in hand, they began to take pride in the historically ancient but newly identified Hinduism—at least as they believed these books presented it.

In an important step toward solidifying the concept, some Hindus began to present to Western audiences an interpretation of Hinduism that was substantially informed by the British construction. The foremost symbol of this act was the renowned appearance of Swami **Vivekananda** at the 1893 **World's Parliament of Religions** in Chicago.[4] In his keynote address to this assembly of representatives of religions from around the world, Vivekananda declared Hinduism to be "the mother of religions," the faith that taught universal tolerance and acceptance to the world. Following his warmly received speech, Vivekananda subsequently toured the United States and England, teaching a particular Hindu tradition—Advaita Vedanta—as the authentic form of Hinduism. Advaita Vedanta fit the Western expectation of a religion very well: it was a systematic exposition of ideas about the one god. Vivekananda was so successful that many Westerners—as well as Hindus—accepted his interpretation as the expression of genuine Hinduism. Vivekananda's view did in fact describe a genuine form of Hinduism, but in presenting it as the *essence* of Hinduism he neglected the great diversity of Hinduism, omitting those aspects of the ancient traditions that Western audiences might have found less attractive. Nevertheless, Hindu intellectuals who adopted this negotiated, homogenized conception of Hinduism became its global representatives, teaching to the West a version of indigenous Indian religion that was substantially articulated by Westerners.

The Problems with "Hinduism"

What we have begun increasingly to appreciate is how impoverished—and distorted—this original conception is when compared to the vast empirical reality of the Hindu religious terrain. As we begin our study of this territory, it is vital for us to examine the ways in which this initial construction of Hinduism skews the actual religious experience of Hindus. Exploring the distortions of this construct will not only provide us with key information about the history of Hinduism in the modern era; it will also help dispel problematic expectations we ourselves may have as we approach a religious complex that defies our expectations at virtually every turn.

Perhaps the most troubling aspect of the Western construction of Hinduism was the way it imagined the Hindu traditions as a system of beliefs or doctrines about god. Conceiving of religion in this manner was a legacy of the Enlightenment, which was reaching its zenith among European intellectuals near the time the British were first colonizing India. So influential was this view that even today many still define religion as a set of beliefs about god. Whether or not this characterization is suitable for other religious traditions, it is clearly inappropriate for defining Hinduism. This is not to suggest that the Hindu traditions *lack* beliefs about god. On the contrary, Hindus believe almost everything that is possible to believe about the ultimate reality. From various points of view, Hinduism contains elements of **monotheism**, **polytheism**, **henotheism**, **animism**, **pantheism**, **panentheism**, **monism**, and even **atheism**. But as this list suggests, these beliefs do not comprise a uniform set or integrated system that can be defined as the essence or foundation of Hinduism. An individual Hindu or a particular Hindu community may hold a reasonably coherent set of views about the divine, but no such system or coherence characterizes the entirety of the Hindu religious structure.

There are, therefore, no creeds or statements of faith to which all Hindus would subscribe.[5] It is hard to overstate the tremendous range of ideas and practices embraced by the Hindu traditions. One scholar calls India a "veritable laboratory of religion: everything imaginable seems to have been tried out, and nothing ever completely rejected."[6] There is probably no theological conception or religious observance that cannot be found in Hinduism. Traditions and ideas are preserved and incorporated into the larger whole without an attempt to make the various parts consistent with one another. Hinduism is highly individualistic and encourages its practitioners to structure their spiritual lives in ways that best suit their individual needs and temperaments.

It would be misleading to think, furthermore, that the Hindu traditions are essentially concerned with belief and doctrine. While belief and doctrine have been extremely important for practitioners of the **Abrahamic traditions**, this is not the case with the traditions originating in India. Hindus not only *believe* many different and sometimes contradictory things, but the significance they assign to belief itself also varies widely. For some Hindus, belief is an impediment to the complete realization of life's ultimate reality. For these Hindus, beliefs must be transcended altogether if one is to attain the highest level of spiritual awareness.

Nor do the Hindu traditions have a sacred, canonical scripture that functions like the Tanakh, the New Testament, or the Qur'an of the Abrahamic religions. True, there are sacred texts in Hinduism—indeed, more texts than one finds in Judaism, Christianity, and Islam. But these books are not read by the vast majority of Hindus, and those for whom these texts are meaningful—mainly the Brahmins—do not function principally as interpreters for the laity. The Brahmins often serve as priests and ritual specialists, particularly in temples. They are chiefly concerned with the sacred texts for the purpose of ceremonial recitation, not exegesis and explanation. Furthermore, Brahmins are not the only ones who serve as priests. In homes, the center of religious life for most Hindus, the senior woman of the family usually functions as *pujari*, or ritual leader.

Since the Hindu traditions lack a single scripture or ecclesiastical hierarchy, admit no single creed, and embrace an immense array of beliefs and practices in an unsystematic fashion, discovering an essence of Hinduism—something that characterizes all Hindus—seems well-nigh impossible. Novelist E. M. Forster said it well: "The fissures in the Indian soil are infinite: Hinduism, so solid from a distance, is riven into sects and clans, which radiate and join, and change their names according to the aspect from which they are approached."[7]

Yet Hinduism's conservatism and pluralism have produced (or perhaps have been produced *by*) an attitude that is possibly as close to a characteristic Hindu quality as we may find. That outlook is the belief that there are many *valid* viewpoints, each partially correct. A justly famous passage from the oldest Hindu scripture makes this point: "The wise speak of what is One in many ways," states the *Rig-Veda*.[8] Hindu traditions, at their best, honor all seekers after this truth and recognize that different persons require different ways of relating to and thinking about ultimate reality.

Hinduism Today

Today in India, the concept of Hinduism is increasingly accepted by the communities who were identified religiously by the West as Hindu. In the last several decades, there has been an increase in the use of the word *Hindūtva*, which translates as "Hinduness." We might call this a rise in Hindu consciousness, and it has been accompanied by an upsurge of participation in Hindu festivals, rituals, and pilgrimage.

But the idea of Hinduism by no means enjoys universal acceptance in India. Rather than regarding themselves as practicing Hinduism, most Hindus consider themselves as devotees of a particular god or goddess, such as **Shiva**, **Vishnu**, or **Durga**, or as members of a community dedicated to a specific deity. They are more likely to classify themselves as "Shaivite" (a follower of Shiva), "Vaishnavite" (a follower of Vishnu), or "Shakta" (a follower of Devi, the goddess). Devotion to a particular god rather than to a religion called "Hinduism" is symbolized by forehead markings called *tilaks*, which are frequently one of the first things Westerners think of when they hear the word *Hindu* (box Intro.1; figure Intro.2). Yet thinking of Hinduism as comprising these many religions is potentially misleading if we conceive of these forms of devotion as discrete entities. Vaishnavites might on occasion worship the goddess or Shiva, and Shaivites might venerate the spirits of a sacred tree, Jesus Christ, or a Muslim saint. As these examples indicate, on the everyday level of practice, many Hindus are simply not much concerned about precisely defining their religious identity.

Although a case can be made for retaining *Hinduism* as an umbrella term for these religions and philosophies, throughout this book we shall prefer the expression "Hindu traditions." By this phrase we mean the complete array of religious communities, systems of belief, spiritualities, mores, ethics, and social structures related to and constituent of the historical complex that has come to be known as Hinduism. The term *Hinduism* may be fine as long as its problematical character is kept in mind. But "Hindu traditions" is more forthright in drawing attention to the pluralistic nature of Hindu practices and serves to disrupt any temptation to assume that Hindus share a core set of doctrines and practices.

The Spatial Context

While the salient features of some religious traditions can be grasped with little or no reference to their geographical contours, such is not the case with the Hindu traditions. Just as the study of Judaism requires appreciation of the land of Palestine and its meaning for Jews, an adequate understanding of the Hindu traditions must include acquaintance with its South Asian context and, most especially, the land of India. The best way to acquire this familiarity, of course, is travel. Literary descriptions of India, no matter how accurate and beautifully written, cannot substitute for the experience of being there. The colors and forms, the sounds and textures, the tastes and smells that are vital components of the Hindu traditions simply defy language. E. M. Forster understood this when he wrote of Hinduism, "Study it for years with the best of teachers, and when you raise your head, nothing they have told you quite fits."[9] But short of a journey, we can still provide some essential impressions for understanding the Hindu context.

Where Hindus Live

One of the reasons India is so important to the Hindu traditions is that 95 percent of all Hindus live there. Most of the remaining 5 percent live in the other countries of South Asia, the areas immediately adjacent to India (figure

Box Intro.1   SYMBOLIZING RELIGIOUS IDENTITY

A *tilak* is a special marking frequently used to indicate religious identity in Hinduism. Many Hindus wear the *tilak* for worship only, but some wear it every day. Its basic function is to symbolize the "third eye," the organ of spiritual insight. Particular markings may further symbolize the deity to whom one is especially devoted. Devotees who apply horizontal stripes across the forehead using *vibhuti*, or sacred ashes, indicate their allegiance to the god Shiva. They may also apply a dot made with sandalwood paste or *kum-kum* (colored turmeric or saffron powder) to the center of the forehead. The *tilak* for Vaishnavites, those dedicated to the worship of the god Vishnu, comprises thin vertical lines connected at the bridge of the nose in a U shape. Clay from a sacred river or sandalwood paste is used to make this design. Worshipers of Devi wear a single red dot or a vertical line made of *kum-kum*. The *tilak* is principally a religious marking that should not be confused with the *bindi*, a forehead emblem wore by women for ornamentation (see chapter 6). Although Hindus may principally identify with devotion to a specific deity, this identification does not preclude their worship of other gods.

Fig. Intro.2   Tilaks. These Brahmin priests wear forehead markings to indicate the deity to which they are devoted. (Photo courtesy of India Cultural Center and Temple, Eads, Tennessee.)

Fig. Intro.3
India in the twenty-first century.
The Indian Subcontinent is home
to the overwhelming majority
of Hindus. This map displays the
current political divisions of the
region, including the states of the
Republic of India. (Mapping Specialists.)

Intro.3). Approximately twenty million Hindus live in Nepal, the only nation where Hinduism is the state religion. Although Indians are perhaps the most religious people on earth, the Republic of India is officially a secular nation and prides itself on being the world's largest democracy. There are about fifteen million Hindus living in the Muslim states of Pakistan and Bangladesh. On the island of Sri Lanka, just south of India, Hindus make up about 15 percent of the total population and number nearly two million. Beyond the Indian Subcontinent, smaller populations of Hindus may be found across Southeast Asia, especially Thailand, Burma, Cambodia, Laos, Vietnam, Malaysia, the Philippines, and Indonesia. Over 90 percent of the inhabitants of the Indonesian island of Bali are Hindu and practice a religious form quite different from varieties of Hinduism elsewhere. Immigrants from India have also established Hindu communities in the West. At the end of the twentieth century, the Hindu population in the United States and Europe was estimated at two million, and the vast majority of these were Indian immigrants. Because the Hindu traditions generally lack a proselytizing impulse, they have not, as yet, taken root in a major way outside the land of their origins, unlike other major religions such as Christianity, Islam, and Buddhism.

Today, the term *India* is usually taken to refer to the political entity known as the Republic of India, which came into existence in 1950. But prior to that time, *India* included not only the Republic of India but also the nations now known as the Republics of Pakistan and Bangladesh. Throughout most of this book, the India we shall study is the India prior to its partition into separate states. Interestingly, although the name *India* has gained wide currency among the English-speaking population of the subcontinent, the older, indigenous term for India—**Bhārata**—is still very common.[10]

Box Intro.2   OFFICIAL LANGUAGES OF INDIA

At present, the Republic of India lists twenty-two official languages. English, which has become a lingua franca for many Indians, is not one of them.

Assamese	Konkani	Sanskrit
Bengali	Maithili	Santali
Bodo	Malayalam	Sindhi
Dogri	Manipuri	Tamil
Gujarati	Marathi	Telugu
Hindi	Nepali	Urdu
Kannada	Oriya	
Kashmiri	Punjabi	

People

With more than one billion people, the Republic of India is the second most populous country in the world, next to China. If current trends continue, India will surpass China by 2030.[11] Indians derive from a host of racial and ethnic stocks. Accordingly, there is no standard Indian appearance. Indians manifest many different colors of skin and many different physical characteristics.

Languages

The many languages spoken in India further compound and complicate this cultural richness. According to the government of the Republic of India, there are twenty-two official languages with at least one million native speakers each (box Intro.2). In addition, there are hundreds of dialects, which raise the count to an estimated 850 languages in daily use. These languages, furthermore, do not all derive from the same language groups.[12] Consequently, basic communication between Indians from different regions is often difficult at best. Increasingly, English is often used as a lingua franca among educated Indians.

Religions

When it comes to religion, the Republic of India is one of the most pluralistic of all places in the world. Besides the Hindus, who currently comprise about 80 percent of the population, Indians profess a wide variety of religious traditions and practices. Each of these non-Hindu traditions has a historical relationship with Hinduism. Sometimes that relationship has involved friction and conflict; sometimes it has been one of competition; sometimes it has been a relationship of mutual enrichment.

Muslims make up about 13 percent of the Indian population. The Republic of India has the world's third-largest Muslim population, next to Indonesia and Pakistan. In many ways, Islam is diametrically opposed to Hinduism theologically, and this difference has been the source of much conflict between practitioners of those religions. When we study modern Hinduism, we shall explore the relationship between Hinduism and Islam in greater detail (chapter 12).

Concentrated in the region known as the **Punjab**, **Sikhism** is a religious tradition that

Fig. Intro.4 **Tomb of Jesus.** Some believe this tomb in Kashmir is that of Jesus of Nazareth. (Photo courtesy of http://en.wikipedia.org/wiki/File:Rozabal.jpg.)

brings together elements of both Hinduism and Islam. Founded in the fifteenth century in an area that has seen a great deal of Hindu-Muslim conflict, Sikhism initially sought to reduce those frictions. Today, Sikhs constitute about 2 percent of the Indian population.[13]

Many are unaware that Christianity is a tradition long established in India, especially in the southern part of the subcontinent. According to legend, the Christian faith was brought to India by "Doubting" Thomas, one of Jesus' twelve apostles. Thomas was martyred and buried near the city of Chennai. Other legends suggest that Jesus himself studied in India with Buddhists and Hindu sages before his public ministry in Palestine; after his crucifixion (which he survived, according to some accounts), Jesus returned to India with his mother, Mary, and died there. There is even a tomb in Kashmir reputed to be that of the Christian messiah (figure Intro.4). Presently, Christians comprise about 2 percent of the total Indian population.

Although founded in India, **Buddhism** has only a small following there today (figure Intro.5). Buddhism arose during a time of intense religious ferment in the middle of the first millennium B.C.E., the same cultural upheaval that precipitated the formation of the classical Hindu traditions and Jainism (chapter 4). In the late ancient and early medieval periods of Indian history, Buddhism flourished and even threatened to eclipse Hinduism as the dominant religion of the country. But in the late medieval period, Buddhism's following on the subcontinent was brought nearly to the point of extinction. Although Indian Buddhists number around only three or four million today, there has long been a close relationship between Buddhism and Hinduism, such that distinguishing the two is not always easy. The two traditions share common ideas and practices. Many Buddhists pray to Hindu gods (although Buddhists

Fig. Intro.5 **The Buddha.** This image from the Gupta period (fifth century C.E.), now on display at the Sarnath Museum, recalls the important role played by Buddhism in the religious history of South Asia. (Photo courtesy of Creative Commons, Tevaprapas.)

do not consider the gods "Hindu"), and some Hindus revere the Buddha as a manifestation of god and regard Buddhism as a denomination of Hinduism.

Jainism is not as widely known in the West as Buddhism, but it has much in common with it—and with Hinduism. Some Hindus think of Jainism, like Buddhism, as another Hindu religion. Though small in numbers (about two million), the Jains significantly influenced Indian life in general and Hindus in particular. The Jain practice of absolute nonviolence (*ahimsa*) helped foster the customs of cow protection and vegetarianism in the Hindu traditions and had a profound effect on Mohandas Gandhi's philosophy.

To round out this picture of religious diversity in India, let us mention the Jews and the **Parsis**, practitioners of the ancient Iranian religion known as **Zoroastrianism**. Both religious traditions developed in India as their followers fled persecution in their homelands. Small Jewish communities have existed in India for at least 2,500 years. India's high toleration of religious diversity has meant that Indian Jews have suffered almost none of the anti-Semitism they have experienced in other parts of the world. There are more than thirty synagogues throughout India, although not all of them are active. The Parsis began to leave for India in the eighth century C.E. to avoid Muslim control in Iran. Zoroastrianism is based on teachings very closely related to the foundations of Hinduism (see chapter 2). Today, several hundred thousand Indians belong to the Jewish and Parsi communities.

By considering the development of the idea of Hinduism and its problematic aspects, and by introducing the cultural contexts of the Hindu traditions, we are better prepared to discuss how and what these traditions came to be. We have seen that we should not too readily assume that the Hindu traditions fit Western expectations of what a religion ought to be. Most importantly, we should resist the temptation to impose a coherence and consistency on these traditions as a whole. Such a "Hinduism" would not be Hindu.

◆ **KEY TERMS**

Abrahamic traditions

ahimsa

animism

atheism

Bhārata

Brahmins

Buddhism

Durga

henotheism

Hindustan

Hindūtva

Jainism

monism

monotheism

pandit

panentheism

pantheism

Parsis

polytheism

pujari

Punjab

Rig-Veda

sanātana dharma

Shankara

Shiva

Sikhism

Sindhu

tilaks

Vedas

Vishnu

Vivekananda

World's Parliament of Religions

Zoroastrianism

◆ **QUESTIONS FOR REVIEW**

1. Explain the development of the idea of Hinduism.

2. Why is "Hinduism" a problematic concept? Why might "the Hindu traditions" be considered a more adequate alternative?

3. Why do most Hindus live in India?

4. What aspects of Indian culture may have contributed to (or been produced by) the Hindu appreciation of diversity and tolerance?

◆ **QUESTIONS FOR FURTHER REFLECTION**

1. Why might persons interested in controlling others be concerned with understanding their religion?

2. Why might Hindus have lacked a specific word for their religion prior to the creation of the word *Hinduism*?

3. What is the value of determining a religion's "essence"?

4. Can a single religion embrace monotheism, polytheism, and atheism?

◆ **FOR FURTHER STUDY**

Inden, Ronald. *Imagining India*. Oxford: Blackwell, 1990.

King, Richard. *Orientalism and Religion: Postcolonial Theory, India and "the Mystic East."* New York: Routledge, 1999.

Lorenzen, David. "Who Invented Hinduism?" *Comparative Studies in Society and History* 41:4 (Oct. 1999): 630–59.

Sugirtharajah, Sharada. *Imagining Hinduism: A Postcolonial Perspective*. New York: Routledge, 2003.

PART I

INDIA'S
EARLY CULTURES

1. The Indus Valley Civilization

PREVIEW

What came to be called *Hinduism* was an amalgamation of beliefs and practices from several sources. This chapter focuses on the first of the two major contributors: the Indus Valley Civilization. In subsequent chapters we will focus on the second: the Indo-Aryans. The discovery of the Indus Valley Civilization in the nineteenth century revealed a sophisticated and long-forgotten ancient culture that appears to have contributed to the development of the Hindu traditions. In this chapter, we examine the architectural ruins and artifacts left by this civilization and contemplate their import for its inhabitants and for subsequent Hindu history. This examination reveals that Indus Valley religion focused on maintaining ritual purity and appropriating divine powers to assist in reproduction and the maintenance of life. Finally, we introduce the Indo-Aryans with a brief discussion of their relationship to the dwellers of the Indus Valley.

Two major cultural streams contributed to the development of what later came to be called Hinduism. The first was an intriguing and sophisticated ancient culture known today as the **Indus Valley Civilization**. The second source was a nomadic people called the **Indo-Aryans**, whom most scholars believe migrated into India from Central Asia and bequeathed to Hindus their most sacred texts and rituals. In this and the next two chapters, we will study each of these cultures and explore their respective influences on the evolution of the Hindu traditions.

The Indus Valley Civilization

In the nineteenth century, British engineers searching for ballast for a railway line in what was then northwestern India and is now **Pakistan** stumbled upon the remains of an ancient city known only to locals. The engineers were only interested in the well-fired bricks from the ruins, and they proceeded to quarry the city for that resource. It was not until the early twentieth century, as other similar sites were uncovered, that archaeologists appreciated the full significance of this unwitting discovery. They determined that the ancient city, now reduced to railroad ballast, was part of a vast network of villages and towns constituting an entire civilization long forgotten by the rest of humanity. The discovery of this ancient culture, one of the most remarkable archaeological finds of modern times, compelled scholars to revise their understanding of the earliest history of India and has in recent years sparked a heated debate about the original inhabitants of the Indian Subcontinent.

The Indus Valley Civilization, so named because many of its settlements were situated along the Indus River, turned out to be one of the great cultures of the ancient world.[1] What has come to light since the first excavations suggests that the Indus Valley Civilization was as impressive as ancient Egypt and Sumeria. While many Hindus today do not regard the Indus Valley Civilization as part of their sacred history, the evidence suggests that this culture contributed significantly to the grand complex known to many as Hinduism (box 1.1).

Box 1.1 TWO VIEWS OF TIME

A Hindu View of Time

Traditional Hindus regard the passage of time as cyclical rather than linear. According to an ancient Hindu cosmology developed after the Vedic era, the universe undergoes a series of four successive ages, or *yugas*, of varying lengths before it is destroyed and re-created. The world's destruction at the end of the final yuga marks a new beginning, initiating a whole new cycle of yugas. This pattern has had no beginning and will have no end.

The first period, known as the Satya Yuga, is a golden age in which the gods maintain close relationships with human beings, who are naturally pious and live an average of a hundred thousand years. The later yugas—the Treta, Dvapara, and Kali (the current period)—are characterized by the decline of human piety and morality and evinced by cruelty, discord, materialism, lust, and shorter life spans. According to a common method of reckoning, the four yugas make one *Mahayuga*, lasting for a period of 4,320,000 human years. One *Mahayuga* is a single day in the life of Brahma, the creator god according to many traditions. A period of 360 Brahma-days equals one Brahma-year, and a Brahma lives one hundred such years. Thus, a Brahma lives 155,520,000,000,000 human years!

The Periods of Hindu History

Although most Hindus would not think of their history in a linear fashion, the following scheme is one way to view the stages of Hindu history.

3300–1400 B.C.E.	Indus Valley Civilization
1600–800 B.C.E.	Vedic Period
800–200 B.C.E.	Classical Period (coincident with the Axial Age)
200 B.C.E.–500 C.E.	Epic and Early Puranic Period
500–1500 C.E.	Medieval and Late Puranic Period
1500 C.E.–present	Modern Period

What is known about the Indus Valley culture comes exclusively from archaeological evidence, because its cryptic script has never been completely deciphered. We do not even know what the citizens of this civilization called themselves. The archaeological data indicate that the Indus Valley culture was established around 3300 B.C.E. and flourished between 2600 and 1900 B.C.E. Around 1900 B.C.E., it entered a period of decline and ultimately disappeared around 1400 B.C.E. At its height, the Indus Valley Civilization covered most of present-day Pakistan, the westernmost part of present-day India, and parts of Afghanistan, in an area estimated to be over five hundred thousand square miles (figure 1.1). Over fifteen hundred Indus Valley sites throughout this region have been unearthed so far, and most have yet to be fully excavated. Several hundred of these sites are large enough to be classi-fied as villages or towns. The largest and most important are cities known as **Mohenjo-daro** and **Harappa**. These names are post–Indus Civilization designations that refer to towns built much later on the ruins of the ancient urban centers. In their heyday, Mohenjo-daro and Harappa may have each hosted a population as large as forty to fifty thousand, which was immense by ancient standards. Harappa appears to have been the capital, and accordingly the culture is sometimes referred to as the Harappan Civilization.

All of the Indus Valley municipalities were highly organized and carefully planned, displaying remarkably similar features. The uniformity of these cities suggests a centralized authority and code enforcement, since many of the settlements were over fifty miles apart. The remains of buildings and the layout of the towns indicate that their inhabitants prized order and

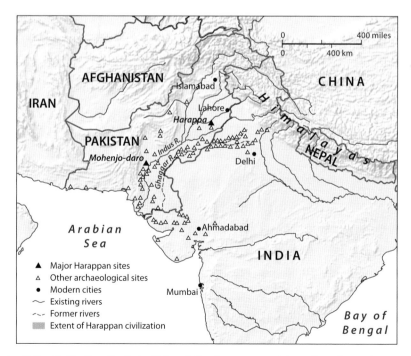

Fig. 1.1   The Indus Valley Civilization. The Indus Valley Civilization was spread throughout the northwestern part of the Indian Subcontinent in an area roughly the size of Texas. (Mapping Specialists.)

organization. But aside from the urban consistency that indicates central administration, we know very little about the way Indus dwellers governed themselves or structured their society. We also know little about their economy except that village life focused on agriculture and cattle herding and life in the larger cities centered on the production of arts and crafts. The discovery of Indus Valley artifacts as far away as Mesopotamia and Central Asia suggests that trade played a significant role in the Harappan economy.

Although the archaeological data do not tell the complete story of this society, they do reveal enough for scholars to make informed judgments about its worldview and religious practices. Yet, since literary sources are unavailable for corroboration, and because the artifacts are often ambiguous, these judgments remain conjectures and are frequently debated by experts. We will consider the archaeological discoveries that appear to have religious import and attempt to comprehend what they tell us about the Indus culture and its possible impact on the development of the Hindu traditions.

Purity and Pollution

One of the most obvious and intriguing features of the Indus cities is the evidence that points to an intense concern with cleanliness. Private homes were furnished with sophisticated indoor bathing and toilet facilities that were plumbed and lined with ceramic tiles in a relatively modern way. The plumbing and sewer systems were superior to those found in other cultures of the time and even to facilities found in many Indian and Pakistani homes today. Not only did individual homes feature advanced lavatories, but municipalities did as well. Mohenjo-daro and Harappa each had a large central bath with public access (figure 1.2). These public baths predate similar facilities in ancient Rome by many centuries. The ubiquity of the baths, their central locations, and the care with which they were constructed all point to a deep preoccupation with purity and cleanness.

Almost certainly, this concern was more than a matter of bodily hygiene. Like many premodern cultures, and like Hindus today, the Indus dwellers were probably anxious about

Fig. 1.2 The Great Bath of Mohenjo-daro. The prominence of this bathing facility in Mohenjo-daro suggests the centrality of ritual purity for the inhabitants of the Indus Valley Civilization. (Photo: © DeA Picture Library / Art Resource, N.Y.)

ritual purity. Ritual purity, as compared to hygiene, involves more than removing the sweat and grime that accumulate on the body and avoiding germs that cause disease. In its most basic sense, ritual purity is the state of cleanness that is required for approaching what is **sacred**, or holy. It often concerns what and how one eats, the kinds of clothes and ornamentation one wears, the flow of one's bodily fluids, and the great mysteries of life: birth, sex, and death. What counts as pure and impure varies greatly from culture to culture and time to time (box 1.2). Observant Jews and Muslims regard pork as unclean, for example, but others consider it a great delicacy. Traditional Christianity once considered childbirth to be an occasion requiring ritual purification, but most contemporary Christians no longer regard it as such. In some societies, including Hindu India, one may become ritually contaminated simply by coming into contact with someone who is impure.

Despite the wide variation in practices, all purity regulations essentially involve maintaining a community's order, its sense of what is right and appropriate. Purity regulations are not always explicit or written into law. Unspoken taboos are often laid upon those areas of life where one may run the risk of violating order. Societies impose these restrictions out of the shared belief that they prevent personal and social disorder, and for this reason many cultures enforce taboos with harsh punishments for violations. Whenever order has been violated, it must be restored to ensure social and personal well-being. Cultures therefore develop methods for reestablishing ritual purity.

We do not know what specific things the Indus dwellers regarded as ritually impure. Whatever the cause of impurity, the baths most likely served to remove contaminants and reinstate the order of things, just as public and private baths do in contemporary Hindu practice. In modern India, the first religious act of the day for most Hindus is bathing, a ritual that brings the individual into the appropriate bodily and mental states for relating to the gods and other persons. Today, many Hindu temples have tanks or reservoirs that function as ritual baths. Many natural bodies of water, such as the river Ganges, serve this purpose as well (figure 1.3).

**Fig. 1.3
Bathing in the Ganges.**
Bathing for ritual purification is still an important aspect of the religious practice of most Hindus.
(Photo courtesy of Creative Commons, Ilya Mauter.)

Box 1.2 **RITUAL IMPURITY**

The kinds of activities considered to be ritually polluting vary from culture to culture and from time to time. There is often great variation within cultures as well. The following list delineates some of the activities that different religious traditions (or parts of those traditions) have regarded as unclean.

Judaism

- Eating pork, shellfish, catfish, amphibians, reptiles, bats, birds of prey, and snails
- Eating meat that has not been slaughtered in a prescribed manner
- Eating with non-Jews or using utensils used by non-Jews
- Drinking wine made by non-Jews
- Touching a dead body, a human bone, or a grave
- Touching someone with leprosy
- Menstruation
- Abnormal bodily discharges
- Childbirth
- Sexual intercourse
- Masturbation

Islam

- Touching a pig or dog
- Menstruation
- Eating pork, amphibians, reptiles, bats, and birds of prey
- Consuming alcohol
- Eating meat that has not been slaughtered in a prescribed manner
- Defecating
- Touching a corpse that is unwashed and has become cold
- Sleep or other forms of unconsciousness
- Flatulence

Shinto

- Sickness
- Contact with blood
- Death, especially that of one's father
- Speaking taboo words
- Wearing shoes in a home
- Wicked thoughts

Zoroastrianism

- Contact with dead bodies
- Coming into contact with snakes, flies, ants, or wolves
- Sickness
- Body waste such as excrement and clipped hair or nails
- Menstruation
- Miscarriage or stillbirth

Hinduism

- Tanning and leatherwork
- Eating meat
- Death
- Contact with dead bodies
- Scavenging
- Menstruation
- Eating food prepared by a person of a lower caste
- Childbirth
- Eating with the left hand
- Touching or seeing someone who is unclean

There, devout Hindus restore the pristine order that might have been disrupted by inappropriate behavior or thoughts, or by contact with a person who is deemed unclean. What we find in the sophisticated baths and lavatories of the Harappan Civilization is probably the earliest expression of religious practices that run throughout Hindu history.

Artifacts

In addition to architectural ruins, the excavation of the Indus Valley cities has revealed a host of intriguing artifacts. Some of the most interesting of these relics are the hundreds of tiny soapstone seals that were used to stamp designs into soft clay. These seals were probably used to mark property in the merchant trade, as one might use a signet ring. Similar seals have been found as far away as Mesopotamia, suggesting a commercial connection between these two civilizations. While the practical use of the Harappan seals is not so mysterious, the significance of the images on the seals is still a matter of speculation and debate.

The great majority of the seals portray male animals with horns and massive flanks and legs (figure 1.4). Indeed, throughout the artifacts found in the Indus Valley ruins, the male sex is almost exclusively represented by animals; artistic representations of the human male are rare. Many of the animals are easily recognizable: buffaloes, elephants, rhinoceroses, bulls, tigers, and antelopes. But other seals display strange creatures that appear to be products of the imagination, such as a three-headed antelope and a bull with a single horn protruding from its forehead, like a unicorn's. This "unihorned" bull is one of the most common images on the seals. The bull often appears along with what seems to be a brazier or censer, either of which may have been used for ritual purposes. Braziers can be used for cooking sacrificial meat, and censers are receptacles for burning incense.

The soapstone images raise many questions. Why do they depict only *male* animals? Why

Fig. 1.4   Seals. Steatite, or soapstone, seals provide archaeological evidence for much of our understanding of Indus Valley religious practices. (Four on left: Scala / Art Resource, N.Y. Four on right: Borromeo / Art Resource, N.Y.)

is the male sex represented almost exclusively in animal rather than human form? Why do the images accentuate the animals' horns and flanks? Do the animals have religious importance, as suggested by what appear to be ritual objects on some of the seals? If the seals have religious meaning, why would they have been used for commercial purposes, such as marking property for trade? Why are some of the animals realistic and others imaginary? Efforts to answer these questions will be speculative, of course, but not necessarily uninformed. What we know of other ancient cultures and later Hindu beliefs and practices can help guide our hypotheses. But because answers cannot be certain without confirmation from literary or other sources, they must be held tentatively and kept always open to revision.

With this caveat in mind, let us try to elucidate the meaning of these unusual images. To begin, we may reasonably conclude that the images express an intense fascination with, and perhaps anxiety about, sexuality and reproductive functions. That the seals portray only male animals, with their genitals on obvious display, supports this supposition, as does the strong emphasis on the animals' horns and flanks. Still, we must wonder why animals rather than humans are taken as symbols of male sexuality. Perhaps these depictions are associated with the human appropriation of animal powers. Throughout the world, human beings have often sought to incorporate certain qualities they admired in animals. In some cultures, for example, eating the heart of a powerful animal was believed to allow a human to incorporate the animal's courage and strength, which were thought to reside in the heart. The animal images of the Indus Valley seals may represent a symbolic attempt to obtain such powers. By creating and using visual representations of

sexually potent animals, the dwellers of the Indus Valley may have intended to acquire that potency for themselves. Furthermore, it is possible that the animals themselves were regarded as sacred because of their sexual prowess. If so, they may have been worshiped and made the objects of cultic practice. Its frequent appearance in these designs might indicate that the bull was the principal object of veneration.

Further underscoring the Indus Valley culture's captivation with sexuality is the discovery of numerous terra-cotta figurines depicting women with exaggerated hips, full thighs, bare breasts, and elaborate hairstyles. While men seemed somehow insufficient to symbolize male sexuality in this society, the same was not true of women (figure 1.5).

Whether these images signify human women or goddesses (or different manifestations of a single goddess) cannot be ascertained by examining the figurines alone. But two factors support the argument that the images are goddesses. First, the Hindu traditions assumed to have roots in the religion of the Indus Valley do not always make sharp distinctions between the divine and the human domains. The gods and goddesses, as we shall see in subsequent chapters, can assume human forms, and individual human beings can come to be regarded as divine.[2] Because of the permeability between these two realms, the fact that the figurines appear unremarkably human does not rule out the possibility that they symbolize the divine. Second, similar representations of females from the same time period have been unearthed in many parts of the world (figure 1.6). These comparable figurines are almost certainly symbols of divine females.[3]

The widespread discovery of such images has led some scholars to theorize the existence of a vast **mother goddess** religion that long

Fig. 1.5 Female figurine from the Indus Valley.
Images such as this terra-cotta statuette from the Indus
Valley Civilization were perhaps representations of
goddesses who were worshiped for their life-giving powers.
(Photo: Bildarchiv Preussischer Kulturbesitz / Art Resource, N.Y.)

Fig. 1.6 The Venus of Willendorf. This figurine from
Northern Europe is one example of an ancient goddess
that some believe may have been at one time the object
of worldwide devotion. (Photo courtesy of Creative Commons, Matthias
Kabel.)

antedated the worship of male gods.[4] That
hypothesis has been controversial and does
not enjoy universal acceptance among scholars. But whether or not such a wide-reaching
cult ever existed, it is quite likely that the
dwellers of the Harappan Civilization venerated a mother goddess. The worship of a divine
mother figure has a long, deep-rooted tradition in Hindu history, and thus it is at least
plausible that the Indus Valley images are the
vestiges of what may be the earliest form of
that tradition. Even if the figurines are not
goddesses per se, it seems evident that in the
Indus Valley culture, the reproductive powers
of women were revered and celebrated, and

women themselves were perhaps regarded as
sacred.

Sexuality and the Sacred

The intimate connection between sexuality and
the sacred may strike some modern persons,
particularly those living in the West, as odd.
For many today, religion seems more involved
in suppressing sexuality rather than encour-
aging and celebrating it. To understand the
correlation of sex and divinity in the ancient
world, we must appreciate several things about
the way early humans viewed the world and
their role in it. First, we must bear in mind

that the reproductive process was the object of awe. How new human beings were produced by the sexual union of males and females was a fundamental mystery. The idea that new life was created by the merger of sperm and egg did not arise until the late eighteenth and early nineteenth centuries, little more than two centuries ago. That reproduction was controlled by powers beyond the reach of human beings was for millennia a reasonable assumption. Second, although the ancients thought reproduction was governed by forces greater than themselves, they often believed it was necessary to cooperate with and assist these forces in certain ways. One of the functions of sacrifice, for example, was to provide the gods with the nourishment and raw materials (in the form of meat and blood) they required to produce (or reproduce) life. In this sense, the divine and human realms were dependent on each other.

Third, most ancient peoples believed in the power of what we would call magic. Magic, in this sense, is the process of achieving a desired effect through the use of rituals, words, thoughts, and other technical means. For example, many societies believed ceremonial dancing could induce rain. Because reproduction, both human and animal, was so vital to human survival, it was often made the object of magical practices. The mythologies of some cultures told how the world and its inhabitants were produced by the sexual union of a god and goddess. In such cultures, men and women might perform ritualized sex acts to ensure the fecundity of the land and its people. A magical performance imitating the primordial act of the gods was thought to provoke them to re-create or to harness the same creative and procreative powers in the service of human reproduction. In the Harappan culture, the creation and usage of the soapstone seals and terra-cotta figurines depicting aspects

of sexuality may have been a way of magically petitioning and assisting the divine forces in the crucial matter of continuing life.

Proto-Shiva

Another bit of Harappan archaeology worth our attention is a seal illustrating a person sitting in what appears to be the lotus posture, a fundamental pose in the Hindu practice of yoga and meditation (figure 1.7). This seal raises the intriguing possibility that the earlier dwellers on the Indus—or at least some of them—were practitioners of meditation. If true, then India has had an interior-looking, contemplative spirit throughout its history. There are other tantalizing features to this seal as well. The individual is surrounded by various kinds of animals, including a tiger, an elephant, a rhinoceros, and a bull or buffalo. The seated figure seems to have three faces looking in different

Fig. 1.7 Pashupati, Lord of the Animals. This soapstone seal from the Indus Valley displays a figure in a posture associated with meditation in the later Hindu traditions. (Photo courtesy of http://commons.wikimedia.org/wiki/File:Shiva_Pashupati.jpg.)

directions. For Hindus today, multiple faces or heads are an iconographic convention symbolizing divine omniscience. On the figure's head is a headdress. Some who study this seal believe the figure is male and sporting an erect phallus. As with other artifacts from the Indus Valley, it is not exactly clear who or what this image represents. Many scholars believe this figure may be an early likeness of the god later known as Shiva. They have dubbed this particular seal **Pashupati**, "Lord of the Animals," one of the many titles for Shiva.

Comparing the Indus Valley imprint with a modern image of Shiva helps substantiate the contention that the seal depicts this popular Hindu god. The corresponding modern image is called **Mahayogi**, "Great Meditator" (figure 1.8). Juxtaposing the two images reveals numerous similarities. Both figures assume the lotus position for meditation. Both are surrounded by animals. In the modern image, Shiva wears and sits on a tiger or leopard skin and is accompanied by his animal companion, the bull Nandi. The motif of the horned headdress in the soapstone seal seems to be replicated in the modern Shiva's trident or the horns of Nandi. Although not so represented in the Mahayogi image, Shiva is described in later Hindu texts as having an erect phallus.

Yet despite these comparisons, not all scholars are convinced of the argument. Some are not even persuaded that the Indus Valley image is intended to represent a human figure; they see it as a buffalo head attached to a human body. To some it is not evident that the figure has three faces and an erection. These latter features are not associated with Shiva in later Hindu iconography, but the dispute about their appearance in the image illustrates how even experts in the field may come to vastly different conclusions when presented with the same

Fig. 1.8 **Shiva as Mahayogi.** Some scholars think the modern image of Shiva, the god of ascetics, may be rooted in the iconography of similar figures from the Indus Valley Civilization. (Photo courtesy of Creative Commons, Luna Park.)

artifacts. Again, the evidence leaves us with no definitive conclusion.

A second seal similar to the Pashupati image portrays another figure sitting in the lotus position (see figure 1.4, bottom row, third seal from left). Like Pashupati, this figure appears to have more than one face and to wear a horned headdress, but these features are even less clear than on the Pashupati seal. What is intriguing about the second seal, however, is the tree design that appears to grow out of the headdress. Most scholars agree that the design is a stylized version of the pipal tree. The pipal tree (*ficus religiosa*) is easily recognized by the distinctive shape of its leaves. This motif has been found on a large number of Indus seals. In some images, people surround the tree, apparently in the act of venerating it. In another, a woman, or perhaps a goddess, appears within the tree (see figure 1.4, top row, third seal from left). In view of the role trees play in later Hindu history, it is reasonable to conclude that Indus Valley dwellers regarded the tree as auspicious and probably sacred. If subsequent Hindu practice can be taken as a guide, the Harappans may have considered the pipal tree to be a home for spirits or the manifestation of a goddess. Interestingly, the pipal is the same tree under which the Buddha sat on the night of his awakening, centuries after the dissolution of the Indus Civilization.

The Absence of Evidence

Perhaps as important as what archaeologists have uncovered around the Indus River is what they have failed to find. The Indus Valley was apparently a relatively peaceful culture, since few real weapons have been discovered; archaeologists have found no traces of spears, swords, or arrows. And as yet, no temple or house of worship that can be positively identified as a sacred precinct has been found. It may be that the central place of worship in this culture was located in the home, as it is for present-day Hindus. In any event, the absence of clearly recognizable temples underscores an important fact of ancient existence in many parts of the world: that the sacred and secular, or the holy and profane, were not sharply distinguished. There was no separate domain of life that could be identified as "religious."

To conclude our sketch of life in the ancient Indus Valley, let us sum up the conclusions that seem best supported by the evidence currently available. Harappan culture was deeply concerned with procreation and purity. Its citizens

likely worshiped certain male animals, perhaps foremost the bull. Representations of male sexuality may have been the focus of veneration and may have been used magically to enhance fertility. Female powers of reproduction were regarded as sacred and perhaps revered through the symbol of the goddess. Ritual practices and the production of images may have centered on ways to incorporate the sexual powers of animals and divine figures. Purification rites, evidence of meditative practice, and well-organized cities suggest the Indus dwellers placed a premium on order and restraint. To the extent that this is an accurate sketch of Indus culture, it indicates that beliefs and practices were oriented toward the present life here on earth and not toward a life hereafter. There is little in the ruins to indicate that Indus dwellers thought much about an afterlife or even wondered about what might be in store for the individual after death. Ritual practices seem to have been chiefly—if not exclusively—for the purposes of sustaining and renewing life in the here and now. Religious beliefs and practices in this culture served a conservative function: to keep things as they were and to maintain the world by honoring and harnessing its powers and respecting its boundaries. And throughout its history, the Indus society was quite successful in its efforts. Little seems to have changed in this civilization during its life span.

The Demise of the Indus Valley Civilization and the Advent of the Aryans

After the discovery of the Indus Valley Civilization, modern scholars were faced with the task of explaining the demise of the great culture and its relationship with the Indo-Aryans, a people with whom the Hindu traditions had long been associated. The theory that came to prominence in the early twentieth century suggested that the Indus Civilization declined near the middle of the second millennium B.C.E. when bands of light-skinned **Aryans** ventured into the Indian Subcontinent from Central Asia and conquered the dark-skinned Indus dwellers. Many members of Harappan society were killed off, and the survivors were subjugated and assimilated into the Indo-Aryan culture. This theory was not an unreasonable conclusion, given the Aryans' documented love of war and conquest. The idea of such a military invasion and conquest, in fact, informed Adolf Hitler's creation of the myth of Aryan superiority and his appropriation of the **swastika**, an ancient Aryan symbol (figure 1.9).

Fig. 1.9   The swastika. The swastika is an ancient Indian symbol, long antedating its appropriation as a Nazi emblem. Its modern association with Adolf Hitler has not diminished its usage in India. (Photo courtesy of Creative Commons, Vivek Joshi.)

Today, however, most scholars of ancient India think the Aryans' arrival in South Asia was well short of an invasion. The invasion theory is now generally acknowledged as heavily influenced by the ideology of Western colonialism. Other evidence paints a different picture of the Aryan movement into India. We know, for example, that the Indus Civilization was already in serious decline by 1600 B.C.E., when the Aryans supposedly subdued the region by military means. Recent satellite photography has shown that between 1900 and 1600 B.C.E. the Indus River changed course, leaving the region desiccated. Archaeology confirms that cities of the Indus Civilization were being abandoned during this period. Furthermore, there is no evidence, archaeological or otherwise, to suggest a massive Aryan conquest. The Aryans' own extensive writings never mention wars or hostilities against peoples who can be positively identified as indigenous to India. In all likelihood, the Indo-Aryans migrated slowly and relatively peacefully into the Indus region beginning around 1600 B.C.E. and may have coexisted for a time with the remaining citizens of the native culture.

But there is another theory to explain the relationship between the Indus dwellers and the Aryans. According to this idea, the Aryans were actually indigenous to India, not Central Asia, and migrated *from* the subcontinent to other locations throughout the world. This perspective is known as the **Out of India theory**. According to this hypothesis, Aryan culture was actually an outgrowth of the Indus Valley Civilization. An upshot of this theory is that the foundations of the Hindu traditions are wholly the product of Indian culture with no influences from outside sources.

In recent years, the Out of India theory has been revived by Hindu communalists, who seek to promote Hindu interests and traditions in Indian politics, and by some Indian and Western scholars. Hindu nationalists believe the idea that the Aryans came from anyplace other than India, whether by invasion or even by a milder form of migration, denigrates Hindu and Indian culture. The proponents of the Out of India position use Aryan literature and the absence of archaeological evidence to support their point of view. Because the issues at stake are highly charged in the current political climate of India, the so-called **Aryan question** has now become the subject of great debate. The issue has become as much a matter of politics as of history.

In the next chapter, we will begin our study of Aryan culture and its impact on the development of Hinduism. Our examination adopts the theory that the Aryans began moving rather peacefully into the subcontinent from Central Asia around 1600 B.C.E. This is the perspective held by most scholars of the history of the Hindu traditions. In the opinion of this scholarly majority, the hypothesis of a relatively quiet migration makes the greatest sense of all the available evidence. But as we have seen in our consideration of the Harappan Civilization, the data relating to ancient cultures is often subject to multiple interpretations, and those who study these data must always keep an open mind about the larger significance of what they study. Our presentation of the Aryan migration is therefore set forth with the understanding that future discoveries and scholarly arguments may require that we revise that position or discard it altogether.[5] We turn now to explore that hypothesis in greater detail.

◆ **KEY TERMS**

Aryan question

Aryans

Harappa

Indo-Aryans

Indus Valley Civilization

Mahayogi

Mohenjo-daro

mother goddess

Out of India theory

Pakistan

Pashupati

ritual purity and pollution

sacred

swastika

◆ **QUESTIONS FOR REVIEW**

1. What is ritual purity and how does it differ from physical hygiene?

2. Which aspects of the Indus Valley Civilization's religious practice may be present in the later Hindu traditions?

3. How did the Indus Valley dwellers depict male and female sexuality?

4. What evidence suggests that the Harappans venerated a mother goddess?

5. What are the possible causes of the Indus Valley Civilization's decline?

6. How have the Harappans' and Indo-Aryans' ambiguous origins been used to support the objectives of modern political movements?

◆ **QUESTIONS FOR FURTHER REFLECTION**

1. Why do you think sexuality—whether it is being restrained or celebrated—is so important in religious practice?

2. What social, political, and religious functions do symbols serve? Can a symbol itself become powerful, apart from the reality it represents? Consider the origin of the swastika and the meaning it attained as an emblem of the Nazi Party.

3. Why is it important to theorize about an ancient culture, even when there is too little evidence to reach definite conclusions? What are the dangers of such theories?

◆ **FOR FURTHER STUDY**

Bryant, Edwin. *The Quest for the Origins of Vedic Culture: The Indo-Aryan Migration Debate.* Oxford and New York: Oxford University Press, 2001.

Eisler, Riane. *The Chalice and the Blade: Our History, Our Future.* New York: Harper, 1988.

Fairservis, Walter A., Jr. *The Roots of Ancient India.* 2nd ed. Chicago: University of Chicago Press, 1975.

Kenoyer, Jonathan Mark. *Ancient Cities of the Indus Valley Civilization.* New York: Oxford University Press, 1998.

Sjöö, Monica, and Barbara Mor. *The Great Cosmic Mother: Rediscovering the Religion of the Earth.* New York: Harper, 1987.

2. The Noble Ones

PREVIEW

Linguistic and textual analysis has conclusively shown that the people who occupied northwestern India (present-day Pakistan) and eastern Iran prior to the Axial Age (800–200 B.C.E.) were closely related, spoke similar languages, and held common religious beliefs. Most scholars think that these Indo-Iranians descended from the pastoral nomads who originated in the Central Asian steppes. A small minority, however, believe that these people were indigenous to India. Following the view of the majority of scholars, this chapter explores the culture and religion of the Indo-Iranians prior to their split into two separate groups. The *Rig-Veda* and the Avesta, which later became foundational scriptures of Hinduism and Zoroastrianism, respectively, give us a glimpse of the Indo-Iranians' gods, their social and moral structures, their cosmology, and their ritual practices. Essentially, the Indo-Iranians' religion provided them the means to attain the goods necessary for a prosperous and stable life on earth. The gods were entreated for help in maintaining productivity and harmony in the here and now rather than to secure otherworldly salvation.

The story of the **Indo-Aryans**, according to the migration theory held by most Hindu scholars, begins in Central Asia in an area now known as the Pontic-Caspian steppe, just north of the Black and Caspian seas. Today, this region roughly corresponds to the area stretching from Ukraine, across a portion of southern Russia, to west Kazakhstan (figure 2.1). Six thousand years ago, this area was mostly a barren desert that suffered bitterly cold winters and harsh summers. It was not an easy place in which to live.

We do not know a great deal about the inhabitants of this region during this period. But most scholars believe that many of the original occupants of this area and their descendants gradually migrated to other parts of the world, including the northern Mediterranean, northern Europe, west as far as Ireland, and southward into Iran and the Indian Subconti-

nent. This hypothesis suggests that many of the historical and current residents of these regions derive from a common ancient stock. The basis of this theory is principally linguistic. Careful analysis of languages as diverse as Icelandic, German, Gaelic, Latin, Greek, Russian, Persian, Sanskrit, Sinhalese, and English has determined that they evolved from what was once a single language known today as Proto-Indo-European (PIE) (figure 2.2). Because it fell into disuse before writing was invented, there is no direct evidence of the existence of this original language. But by analyzing the dozens of existing languages believed to have developed from it, linguists have been able to reconstruct much of Proto-Indo-European. This reconstruction, along with some archaeological and archaeogenetic evidence, has given scholars the means to hypothesize the migratory patterns of the Cen-

Fig. 2.1   Current political map of Central Asia. According to the prevailing theory, the ancestors of the Aryans once lived in the area represented by the upper-left quadrant of this modern political map of the Caucasus and Central Asia. (Mapping Specialists.)

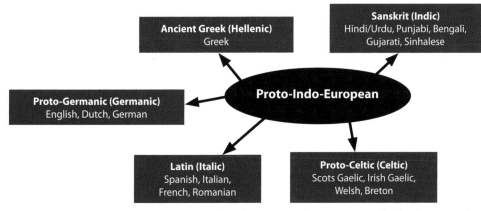

Fig. 2.2   Indo-European family of languages. Linguists think that many modern European and Indian languages derive from a single Proto-Indo-European language no longer in existence.

tral Asians. While some of the specific details of these patterns are still the subject of debate, there is general (but not universal) agreement among scholars about the main features of these movements (figure 2.3).

The Indo-Iranians

Of the many groups that migrated from Central Asia to other locations, the most important for the study of the Hindu traditions are those who migrated southward into the regions now occupied by Iran, Pakistan, and India. To differentiate the members of this group from other Indo-European peoples, scholars refer to them as the **Indo-Iranians**. These people did not think of themselves as Indo-Iranians, of course. They referred to themselves as the Aryans, a name that derives from *ariya*, which translates into English as "noble." Thus, their self-designation was "the Noble Ones."

This group remained unified until about four thousand years ago, when it too slowly split and moved in separate directions. Those who settled in present-day Iran are referred to as the **Irano-Aryans**. Those who migrated further into Afghanistan and then into the Indus Valley and across northern India are called the Indo-Aryans. As the Indo-Iranians divided, their languages began to evolve away from one another, although they were similar enough that communication was possible for some time. The Iranian tribes spoke a dialect we call

Avestan, because it now exists only in a collection of sacred writings known as the **Avesta**. The group that migrated to India spoke a form of the language now known as **Sanskrit**.

When each group arrived at its final destination, they called their new territory the "Land of the Noble." The Indo-Aryans knew their new home not as India, but rather as *Aryavarta*, and the Irano-Aryans called theirs *airyana waējah*, an expression that later evolved into the name *Iran*.

Society and Economy

Almost all of what we know of the Indo-Iranians comes from two sources: the *Rig-Veda*, the oldest extant Indo-European text, taken to India in oral tradition, and the Avesta, a slightly later text from Iran, also preserved orally for much of its history. Because they were composed before the final division of the Aryans, the *Rig-Veda* and the Avesta tell us a good bit about Indo-Iranian

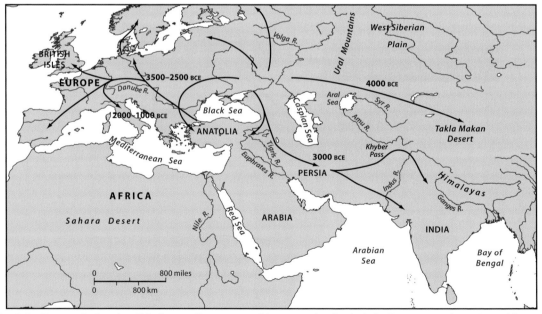

Fig. 2.3 Routes of migration. This diagram illustrates possible routes taken by the Indo-Europeans as they migrated from Central Asia, according to the dominant theory. (Mapping Specialists.)

life. The two texts make it clear that the Aryans were nomadic and seminomadic shepherds and cattle herders who wandered in relatively small areas, seeking pastureland for their animals. Since the Central Asian steppes were arid and barren, the Indo-Iranians were not great agriculturalists. The principal source of their food was the domesticated animals they kept and the wild animals they hunted.

Their society was divided into two classes: the priests and everyone else. Members of the secular class were simply called "producers" because of their occupations. The Aryans arranged themselves loosely into tribes with little to no formal governing structure. Early Indo-Iranian society appears to have been relatively peaceful and probably quite static, as it seems to have existed for centuries with few significant cultural changes.

The Religion of the Indo-Iranians

The religious life of the early Indo-Iranians, inasmuch as it can be reconstructed from our limited resources, suggests a commonsensical worldview for a people living in the harsh environment of Central Asia. Like all ancient groups, the Indo-Iranians had their gods, their beliefs about the nature of the world, and rituals to help them understand and influence those gods and that world.

The Gods

The gods were of various sorts, each related to a different aspect of everyday life. Especially important to the ordinary people were the deities who controlled the natural world. These included gods of the sky and the earth, the sun and the moon, and the winds. Although not considered gods as such, trees were also venerated, especially those growing beside rivers or

streams, probably because the bark and fruit were thought to have healing properties. In India today, certain trees growing by rivers are still seen as highly auspicious and often mark the sacred site of a temple or shrine.

At one time the Indo-Iranians worshiped an overarching sky god. This king of the gods was known in the Iranian dialect as **Dyaoš**, and in the Indian dialect he was called **Dyaus-Pitr**. But over time he became so remote and distant from everyday life that he simply became irrelevant, and the Aryans effectively forgot about him. The names Dyaoš and Dyaus, by the way, are cognates of Zeus, the chief sky god of the ancient Greeks. Pitr is a cognate of Jupiter, the chief god of the ancient Romans.

In addition to nature deities, there were gods associated with ritual practices. Particularly important among these were the gods of fire and water and a deity called **Geush Urvan**, or "Soul of the Bull." Geush Urvan was the spiritual energy of a primordial bovine that had once lived on earth, but had died and ascended to the heavens, where its powers continued to replenish the animal world. A vision-inducing substance called **Haoma** in the Avestan dialect and **Soma** in the Sanskrit was also deified. Because of their importance in religious ceremonies, these divinities were especially significant to the priests.

A third category of divine beings were the *ahuras*, in Avestan, or *asuras*, in Sanskrit (names that simply mean "lords"). In this class, three gods were of greatest significance. The first two—**Varuna** and his assistant **Mitra**—were associated with oaths and promise-keeping (box 2.1). The third and greatest was **Mazda**, the lord of wisdom.[1] As the Iranian tradition evolved, Ahura Mazda became the most important god of all; he played no role, however, in the development of the Indian traditions.

> **Box 2.1 OATHS AND PLEDGES**
>
> Making and keeping oaths and pledges is vital to any culture. Ancient societies, however, did not always have the human means to enforce such covenants and agreements. It was therefore not uncommon for oath-makers to beseech gods to punish those who failed to live up to their oaths. A vestige of this practice survives in modern legal proceedings in which a person swears to tell the truth and concludes by saying "so help me god." In other settings, one might say, "As god is my witness." The ancients might have added an additional clause: "and may I be smitten by god if I fail to honor my word."

Finally, there were numerous lesser divinities known as **devas** in Sanskrit and **daevas** in Avestan. These words are ordinarily translated as "gods," but a more literal rendering would be "shiny ones." These Sanskrit and Avestan words have obvious cognates in other Indo-European languages. *Deus* in Latin, *divine* in English, and *diva* in Italian are three examples. The shiny ones initially represented such qualities as courage, friendship, justice, obedience, and "glory," a charisma-like quality that dwelled in gods and heroes. In the later Indo-Aryan tradition, *deva* and its female form, *devi*, became the terms for the most important class of divinities, although that was not the case in Iran. In the theological developments associated with **Zoroaster**, the Avestan word *daeva* was used to designate deities linked with the forces of evil, a connection not made by the Aryans in India. The English word *devil*, although related to the Sanskrit *deva*, derives from Iranian usage and hence retains its association with wickedness (figure 2.4).

Fig. 2.4 The devil. The English word *devil* derives from *daeva*, Zoroaster's term for an evil spirit. (Illustration by Gustave Doré from John Milton's *Paradise Lost*.)

Morality and Order

In addition to this complex world of spirits and gods, the Indo-Iranians believed in an abstract, impersonal principle of order. The Sanskrit speakers called it **rita**, and those who spoke Avestan referred to it as **asha**. Both words designated a natural law that maintained cosmic order, keeping the astral bodies on their paths and the seasons turning in proper sequence. *Rita* or *asha* had moral as well as cosmological aspects, and in this sense it was a principle of appropriate human and divine behavior; the deities, like humans, were subject to it. Adherence to this moral law promoted harmony and well-being for the individual and for society.

Ritual Practices

The Indo-Iranians performed sacrifices to maintain the cosmic and moral order and to ensure that new life properly replaced the old. (Sustaining the right order of things seems to have been the chief purpose of Aryan ceremonies.) To accomplish this end, the Indo-Iranians performed a wide variety of rituals, from the simple to the complex.

Among the simplest were the offerings of **libations** to the deities of water and fire. In the arid and cold steppes, the importance of—indeed, the very sacredness of—these two elements is readily evident. Worshipers gave the water deity offerings of milk and two plant leaves, representing the animal and vegetable realms. These libations returned to the divine powers the vital elements required to maintain productivity and harmony. The water goddess was strengthened by these gifts.

Fire was of great importance not only for providing warmth but also for cooking meat, the staple of the Indo-Iranian diet. Because starting a new fire was difficult, fires were kept continually lit in fireplaces and terra-cotta pots. Like the libations to water, offerings to the fire deity came from the two kingdoms: incense and wood from plants and animal fat from cooked meat. The melting fat made the flames blaze, visibly fortifying the fire.

More complex rituals required the creation of sacred spaces and the guidance of professional priests. Because of their nomadic life, the Indo-Iranians' ritual precincts were temporary and their sacred implements portable. Sacred space was marked out with lines drawn on the ground as prayers were uttered to keep out evil spirits. Ritual fires burned in sacred vessels and pits dug in the ground.

The most sacred of these ceremonies were the fire rituals, which often involved the blood sacrifice of goats, sheep, horses, or cattle. The Avestan word for "sacrifice" was *yasna*, almost identical to the Sanskrit *yajña*. The Indo-Iranians were awed by the act of taking life and did so with solemn respect. "We reverence our [own] souls," relates one Avestan text, "and those of the domestic animals which nourish us . . . and the souls of useful wild animals."[2] Animal sacrifices were performed with special prayers to enable the animal's spirit or life force to become part of the Soul of the Bull, the divine being comprising the life energy of the animal world. Blood from the sacrificial victim was believed to nourish this divinity. By thus providing food for the Soul of the Bull, the Indo-Iranians assisted in its care of the animals and guaranteed their abundance. Consecrated and cooked meat was also offered to the other gods and then eaten by the participants in the ritual. Because of their respect for animal life, the Indo-Iranians sanctified the meat they ate from domesticated animals. Before killing a wild animal for food, hunters said prayers to ensure the safe return of its spirit to the Soul of the Bull.

Priest-led rituals also involved the sacred beverage called Soma in Sanskrit and Haoma in Avestan. Like fire and water, this substance was regarded as a god. It was extracted from a plant species whose identity is unknown to us today and was probably unknown to the Indo-Iranians after their departure from Central Asia. The liquid essence of these plants was pressed out and mixed as a golden drink resembling honey.

Soma caused those who imbibed it to feel ecstatic, transported out of the ordinary world into the realm of the gods. This passage from the *Rig-Veda* captures a sense of the experience of consuming Soma:

I have tasted the sweet drink of life, knowing that it inspires good thoughts and joyous expansiveness to the extreme, that all the gods and mortals seek it together, calling it . . . [ambrosia].

When you penetrate inside, you will know no limits, and you will avert the wrath of the gods.

We have drunk the Soma; we have become immortal; we have gone to the light; we have found the gods. What can hatred and the malice of a mortal do to us now, O immortal one?

The glorious drops that I have drunk set me free in wide space. . . . Let the drops protect me from the foot that stumbles and keep lameness away from me.

Inflame me like a fire kindled by friction; make us see far; make us richer, better. I am intoxicated with you, Soma, I think myself rich. Draw near and make us thrive.

Weakness and diseases have gone; the forces of darkness have fled in terror. Soma has climbed in us, expanding. We have come to the place where they stretch out life-spans.[3]

By ingesting Soma, the Indo-Iranians achieved what they considered the apex of existence: the sense of immortality (which may have simply meant a long life), freedom from suffering and fear, communion with gods and the spirit world, and intense pleasure. Little wonder that Soma was so highly prized and zealously protected! Its chief downside, however, was that it provided only temporary ecstasy. Eventually the effects wore off and ordinary life reasserted itself. But the experience of divine communion was important in confirming the existence of the gods and expanding the mind to consider the deepest possibilities of human life. Soma allowed the Indo-Iranians to imagine a life free from suffering and fear. In the centuries to come, the heirs of these traditions would seek similar experiences through meditative introspection and ascetic practice, without the ingestion of physical substances.

The Raiders

At some point near the end of the third millennium or the beginning of the second millennium B.C.E., the Indo-Iranians learned to build and use war chariots. The advent of the chariot and other more sophisticated implements of war completely disrupted the once stable culture of the Aryans. A new form of livelihood now emerged to supplement the tending of sheep and cows: *stealing* sheep and cows. Many of the Indo-Iranians became rustlers. Raiding and pillaging became a new way of life, initiating a restless, heroic age not unlike those of the Old Norse and pre-Islamic Arabian cultures. Those who took up a career in raiding found a new purpose in life: to gain wealth and glory. Cattle and sheep had long been the measure of prosperity among the Indo-Iranians. Besides providing meat and milk, these animals were the source of leather for clothing and tents, bones for tools, dung for fuel, and even urine for the consecration of sacred utensils.

Raiding not only altered the economy of the Indo-Iranians; it also disrupted moral concerns and respect for the rule of law. The cattle rustlers showed little regard for the weak and defenseless; whole villages might be wiped out in an afternoon just to enhance another clan's livestock holdings. Might rather than right ruled the day. A third class of individuals came to stand alongside the priests and producers: the warlords and professional warriors. This emergent class soon became identified with their love for rough living, hard drinking, and gambling. They were similar in many ways to the Hollywood image of the old American West, with its outlaws, gunslingers, and saloons. There was an excitement and a thrill to living on the edge, outside the restraints of conventional society.

The Religious Transformation

By no means were all Indo-Iranians cattle rustlers and outlaws, but the raiding and looting life still had ramifications for those who wanted nothing to do with it. New gods more acceptable to the growing warrior class began to appear in and at times even dominate Indo-Iranian religious life. Many turned to worship **Indra** (figure 2.5), the brave new deity of the heroic age. By the time the *Rig-Veda* reached India, Indra was already the ascendant divine being. Over one-quarter of the *Rig-Veda*'s thousand hymns of praise are addressed to him alone.

Indra was a macho god, to be sure. He was valiant in combat, reckless to the point of being foolhardy, largely amoral, but deeply loyal to those who revered and made offerings to him. In return, he was a giver of many gifts to his followers. And he loved Soma, the drink that fueled his passion and reckless spirit. As we noted earlier, the Aryans imbibed Soma to commune with the gods, to feel themselves immortal, to imagine a life free of distress, and to inspire poetry. Now, in the heroic age of raiding, quaffing Soma seems to have acquired another purpose: to produce a frenzy conducive to war and lawlessness. The *Rig-Veda* extols Soma's capacity to whip up a frenetic mental state:

This, yes this is my thought: I will win [i.e., steal] a cow and a horse. Have I not drunk Soma?

Like impetuous winds, the drinks have lifted me up. Have I not drunk Soma?

The drinks have lifted me up, like swift horses bolting with a chariot. Have I not drunk Soma?

The five tribes are no more to me than a mote in the eye. Have I not drunk Soma?

In my vastness, I surpassed the sky and this vast earth. Have I not drunk Soma?

Yes! I will place the earth here, or perhaps there. Have I not drunk Soma?

I am huge, huge! flying to the cloud. Have I not drunk Soma?

I am going to a well-stocked house, carrying oblations to the gods. Have I not drunk Soma?[4]

While Soma enabled the priests to see visions of the gods and poets to utter sublime words, the warriors now felt themselves invincible and powerful, beyond worldly limits.

Fig. 2.5 **Indra, Aryan god of war.** By the time the Aryans had migrated to the Indian Subcontinent, the war-loving Indra was the ascendant deity. (Photo courtesy of http://commons.wikimedia.org/wiki/File:Indra,_a_Vedic_God_in_Hinduism.jpg.)

As devotion to Indra increased, some of the other gods began to suffer decline, which is to say they were not given as much attention in ritual and cultic celebration. Deities such as Varuna, the venerable old *ahura* sitting up in his palace in heaven, keeping order in the world, seemed to many to be a little too tame. For a nomadic people now equipped with the horse and chariot, the adventurous life of the daring Indra was more appealing.

The Indo-Iranian Divide

It is possible that the two branches of the Indo-Iranian family began to diverge in the third millennium B.C.E., but the split was definitely under way by the middle of the second millennium. Precise dates are notoriously difficult to establish for nomadic peoples because they leave very few archaeological artifacts behind. The division was gradual, of course, and the concomitant religious developments were incremental in nature. As the two branches parted, their relatively homogenous religion slowly evolved into the separate traditions much later called Zoroastrianism and Hinduism. Interestingly, many Zoroastrians would later join the Hindus in India; beginning around the eighth century C.E., they migrated to the subcontinent to escape Muslim persecution in Iran. In India, these descendants of the Aryans and practitioners of Zoroaster's religion are now known as Parsis, another tradition that makes up the rich and colorful religious landscape of this land.

◆ **KEY TERMS**

ahuras

airyana waējah

ariya

Aryavarta

asha

asuras

Avesta

Avestan

daevas

devas

Dyaoš

Dyaus-Pitr

Haoma

Indo-Aryans

Indo-Iranians

Indra

Irano-Aryans

libation

Mazda

Mitra

Rig-Veda

rita

Sanskrit

Soma

Soul of the Bull (Geush Urvan)

Varuna

yajña

yasna

Zoroaster

◆ **QUESTIONS FOR REVIEW**

1. What was Soma or Haoma, and what was its role in Indo-Iranian religion?

2. In what ways are warrior-god Indra's ascendance and popularity related to cultural changes in Indo-Iranian society?

3. Consider the societal structure of the early Indo-Iranians. How did this structure change as the peaceful, nomadic culture gave way to the heroic age of raiding?

4. What was *rita* or *asha*, and what role did this principle play in the Indo-Iranian worldview and religious practice?

5. What was the Soul of the Bull, and what function did the Indo-Iranians believe it played in animal sacrifice? What does this divine being's place in Indo-Iranian theology suggest about the Aryans' relationship with animal life?

◆ **QUESTIONS FOR FURTHER REFLECTION**

1. Does morality play an inherent role in religion? Why or why not?

2. Why is ritual such an important aspect of the world's religions?

◆ **FOR FURTHER STUDY**

Anthony, David W. *The Horse, the Wheel, and Language: How Bronze-Age Riders from the Eurasian Steppes Shaped the Modern World.* Princeton, N.J.: Princeton University Press, 2007.

Boyce, Mary. *Zoroastrians: Their Religious Beliefs and Practices.* London: Routledge, 2001.

Bryant, Edwin. *The Quest for the Origins of Vedic Culture: The Indo-Aryan Migration Debate.* Oxford and New York: Oxford University Press, 2001.

Doniger, Wendy, trans. *The Rig-Veda: An Anthology.* London: Penguin, 1981.

Foltz, Richard C. *Spirituality in the Land of the Noble: How Iran Shaped the World's Religions.* Oxford: Oneworld Publications, 2004.

Malandra, William W., trans. and ed. *An Introduction to Ancient Iranian Religion: Readings from the Avesta and Achaemenid Inscriptions.* Minneapolis: University of Minnesota Press, 1983.

Mallory, J. P. *In Search of the Indo-Europeans: Language, Archaeology, and Myth.* London: Thames & Hudson, 1989.

3. The World of the Vedas

PREVIEW

Although the idea of an Aryan conquest of India is now disputed, the influence of the Aryans on Indian religion is undeniable. In this chapter, we begin to explore the Aryan contributions to the emergence of the Hindu traditions. Our guide to these investigations is the rich collection of Aryan texts known as the Vedas, today regarded by Hindus as their most sacred and authoritative scripture. We can learn much about the Aryans' beliefs and practices by examining how these ancient texts envisioned the world and its creation, portrayed the functions of the gods and goddesses, and explored the nature and destiny of human beings. For a full understanding of the Vedic world, we must also discuss the different kinds of ritual practices and consider the relationships among ritual, myth, and caste.

The Indo-Aryans probably entered north-western India around 1600 B.C.E. as the Indus Valley Civilization was nearing its end. By this time, they were skilled in horsemanship, the use of chariots, and the manufacture of bronze, all of which helped facilitate a passion for battle and heroic ideals, at least for many Aryans. As newcomers to the subcontinent, the Aryans continued to live as pastoral nomads for some time before finally settling down to engage in agriculture. Their society was now stratified into three classes: the priests, the warriors, and the producers. They were loosely organized into clans led by chieftains and often referred to themselves as the **Five Tribes**.

As the Indo-Aryans parted company with the Irano-Aryans during the centuries preceding their entry into India, the religious practices and beliefs of the two groups evolved in separate ways, much as their languages did. The Irano-Aryan religion experienced a radical transformation when the prophet Zoroaster proclaimed that Ahura Mazda was the chief deity aligned with *asha*, the principle of goodness and order. The other gods of the pantheon, he declared, were actually demonic and associated with the forces of evil. Accordingly, he envisioned existence as the grand battlefield between Mazda and the malevolent powers of darkness. Zoroaster's reformation of the Aryan tradition moved Iranian religion closer to monotheism and probably influenced the development of Judaism and Christianity through its concepts of the devil, angels, an apocalyptic savior, and a day of judgment (box 3.1).

But in India, Aryan religion progressed in another direction. Whereas in Iran the tradition was simplified by Zoroaster's call to wor-

Box 3.1 ZOROASTER'S REFORMS AND INFLUENCE

Zoroaster—or Zarathustra, as he is sometimes called—is one of the most obscure founding figures in the history of the world's religions. Researchers usually date his birth to sometime between 1500 and 800 B.C.E. Most agree that he lived in the eastern area of present-day Iran, but a few scholars would place him in Central Asia in the Proto-Indo-European homeland. Tradition tells us that Zoroaster was a priest who was troubled by the violence and lawlessness of the land and who at age thirty experienced a luminous, life-altering vision that led him to reform his own religious tradition. His efforts were enshrined in the eponymous religion of Zoroastrianism. By the sixth century B.C.E., his teachings had power enough to function as the state religion of the Persian Empire and two subsequent Iranian empires until the seventh century C.E., when it was finally displaced by Islam.

In terms of its effects on *other* religions, Zoroastrianism may well have had the greatest impact of any single religion in history. Zoroaster's theology advocated the worship of Ahura Mazda as the foremost deity and assigned clear moral qualities to the gods: all the spirits—the *ahuras* and the *daevas*—were now either good (*asha*) or evil (*druj*), respectively. Because *daevas* like Indra were honored by rustlers and outlaws, Zoroaster reserved the word *daeva* exclusively for the wicked gods and the word *ahura* for the ethical gods.

Zoroaster also suggested the existence of an independent evil deity, a chief god among the *daevas*, commonly called Ahriman. Zoroaster thus envisioned two superior beings—one completely good, the other completely evil—locked in mortal combat since the beginning of time, each struggling for the triumph of his principles and power. People were obligated to align themselves with one deity or the other, and their ultimate destinies depended on the choice they made.

This kind of personal commitment was novel in religious history, but is part and parcel of every major religion today. What ultimately becomes of you—whether you go to heaven as in Christianity or paradise as in Islam, or find *nibbana* in Buddhism or *moksha* in Hinduism—is contingent on moral and theological choices made in the here and now. Prior to the first millennium B.C.E., such a belief was not widely accepted, if at all.

Zoroaster believed that individuals would be judged on the fourth day following their death, atop a sacred mountain where the great *ahuras* had their palaces. If they were found to be good, individuals were led across a wide bridge to the heavens, accompanied by a beautiful maiden. Those who were judged evil had to cross an extremely narrow bridge—the texts say the width of a razor's edge—and were led by a revolting hag. Inevitably, they fell while crossing and landed in the abyss of hell, where they suffered painfully for their sins in the realm ruled by the Evil One.

Leading monotheistic traditions contain elements that parallel aspects of Zoroastrian theology. Direct influence, however, is difficult to document and prove. But in the sixth century B.C.E., during the formative period of Judaism, Jews came into contact with the Persian Empire during and after their exile in Babylonia, and new ideas, curiously like Zoroaster's, began to appear in Jewish and then Christian writings. These ideas were significantly different from the theology of earlier Hebrew writings and bear the traces of outside influences, notably concepts such as the day of judgment, paradise and perdition, and a divine savior figure.

ship Ahura Mazda alone, the evolving religion of the Indo-Aryans preserved the many gods of the ancient pantheon and became even more complex and diverse. This tendency to preserve old beliefs and observances while simultaneously embracing new ideas and practices became characteristic of the family of Hindu religions influenced by the Aryan tradition. In this chapter, we will explore in more detail the elements that comprised Vedic religion, the term we use to designate the Indo-Aryan worldview prior to the classical period in Hindu history.

The Vedas

Because the Indo-Aryans were migratory and left little that might be accessible to modern archaeology, almost everything we know about them comes from a compilation of writings now called the Vedas. The *Rig-Veda*, to which we referred in our study of the Indo-Iranians, belongs to this collection.

The Vedas are the oldest and most sacred of Hindu scriptures. According to traditional belief, the Vedas have no author and existed prior to this world's creation. They were revealed by reality itself to certain ancient **rishis**, or seers, who were extraordinarily skilled in the practice of meditation and the use of language. The custodians of this precious wisdom were **Brahmins**, members of the priestly class of the Aryans. Most Hindus today believe the Vedas embody an eternal knowledge that contains the deepest secrets of the universe. Some Hindus have suggested that the Vedas contain *all* knowledge, even the principles of nuclear physics and the distances between heavenly bodies. A few have even claimed that the West climbed so quickly to technological and scientific prominence because Westerners translated the scrip-

tures and appropriated Vedic knowledge in the eighteenth and nineteenth centuries.

The term *veda* usually translates as "wisdom," but it derives from the Sanskrit root *vid*, which means, simply, "to see." English cognates of the Sanskrit root include *video* and *vision*. Seeing is an extremely important dimension of Hindu religious experience, as we will discover later when we discuss the function of images of the gods and goddesses. One of the principal reasons Hindus go to temple is to receive ***darshan***, that is, to glimpse the divine in physical manifestations.

The Vedas are classified as **shruti**, a category designating the highest level of sacred literature in the Hindu traditions. *Shruti* literally means "what is heard" and is often translated as "revelation" to underscore the mode by which this form of knowledge was imparted to humans. The *rishis* of old heard the divine truth revealed to them directly as they attained the highest states of consciousness through contemplative practice. *Shruti* is distinguished from **smriti**, another category of sacred literature. *Smriti* refers to scriptures that have secondary authority and are not considered to be of divine origin, a point emphasized in the word's common translation as "commentary" or "tradition." The more well-known examples of *smriti* include the *Mahabharata*, the *Ramayana*, the *Puranas*, the Bhagavad Gita, and the *Dharma-Shastras*.

Interestingly, the *smriti* texts are far more important to the daily life of most Hindus than *shruti*. Despite their paramount status, the Vedas have never been widely read in India. The vast majority of Hindus have never read a fragment of them, although most have heard parts of the Vedas recited at weddings and temple ceremonies without comprehending their meaning. Very few Hindus today understand Sanskrit. But even in translation, the Vedas lack the concrete relevance to ordinary life that one finds in *smriti* literature. The Vedas are not a narrative, like the Bible or the *Iliad* and the *Odyssey*; they tell no grand story of the gods and humans. They are more like liturgy manuals such as the Book of Common Prayer or a Roman Catholic missal. They include hundreds of hymns addressed to various deities, many of whom are no longer worshiped, having been superseded by other divine figures later added to the Hindu pantheon. The Vedas also contain myths, incantations and spells, and a bit of philosophical speculation. It is clear that the Vedas were concerned primarily with rituals and were probably composed to be recited at sacrifices. Their relevance, therefore, was much greater for those of the priestly class than for the other classes in the Vedic and Hindu cultures.

Originally, and for thousands of years, the Vedas existed only in oral tradition, preserved by the Brahmins' special memorization techniques. The Vedas were never intended to be written down, and doing so was considered by many priests to be a sacrilege. Their reluctance to commit the Vedas to writing stems from the Aryan view of the Sanskrit language. The Aryans believed spoken Sanskrit to be the perfect linguistic embodiment of reality. Words were neither mere labels attached to objects nor ideas that could be altered by whim or social agreement. For the Aryans, the spoken Sanskrit word had an intrinsic ontological connection to the reality it indicated. The oral word, as contrasted with the written word, was extremely powerful and potentially dangerous. Only the Brahmins, by virtue of their training and purity, were competent enough to recite the Vedas effectively without grave danger. An old Hindu law even stated that if

a *Shudra*—that is, a low-caste person—was to hear the Vedas, his ears should be filled with molten lead. Initially, horrible punishments were also prescribed for Brahmins who divulged the contents of the Vedas to outsiders. Eventually, in the post-Vedic period, the Vedas that existed for hundreds of years only in the oral tradition were written down.

The Vedas divide into four collections, or **samhitas**, each concerned with a particular aspect of Aryan ritual. The *Rig-Veda* is the oldest and most important of these collections. It contains the **mantras**, or sacred words, to be chanted during rituals. For the most part, these mantras are flattering songs addressed to various gods and goddesses. The word *rig* means "praise," so this collection is aptly named. The other three *samhitas* are the **Sama-Veda**, which consists of melodies as well as mantras, since the sacrificial songs had to be chanted at just the right pitch to be effective; the **Yajur-Veda**, which provides instructions and mantras for sacrifices; and the **Atharva-Veda**, which offers magic spells and incantations for healing and the **apotropaic** rituals performed to ward off evil.

The World of the Vedas

The Vedic writings are not systematic theology. Some ideas in the Vedas are in tension with, or even contradict outright, other ideas presented in the complete collection. The meaning of some passages is obscure and lost to time. In one hymn, one god is praised as the deity of the sun; in a different hymn, another god is given the sun as his province. These overlaps and inconsistencies often confuse modern readers.

To provide some order to this highly unsystematic material, we will explore the Vedic worldview with three essential questions in mind:

- How do the Vedas characterize the natural world?
- How do they portray the world of the divine?
- What do they say about human beings?

Answering these questions requires extrapolation from the texts and risks making the Vedas seem more consistent and systematic than they actually are. But such an analysis will detail the chief components of the Indo-Aryan view of the world in a way more comprehensible to our modern understanding.

The Natural World

Like many ancient cultures, the Indo-Aryans thought of the world as divided into three levels. They used the term *triloka*—literally "the three places"—to refer to the cosmos. The first level was the earth, inhabited by humans and other animals. Above the earth was the atmosphere, or "mid-space" as it was sometimes called. Finally, the highest level was **Svarga**, or heaven, the home of the gods and the ancestors.

As we recall from an earlier chapter, the Indo-Iranians believed the world to be governed by an abstract, impersonal principle of harmony and order called *rita*, the Sanskrit counterpart to the Avestan term *asha*. *Rita* kept the universe intact and preserved unity. It was similar to the Greek idea of Logos. Even the gods were subject to *rita*. The concept of *rita*, however, had more than just cosmological significance. It also regulated moral order and the order of ritual. In fact, two of the most important words associated with morality and ceremony are derived from the same root syllable as *rita*. The words *right* (as in "right and wrong" and "human rights") and *rite* (as in "ritual") intimate the way the Vedas connected cosmic structure, morality, and ritual activity. The significance of these connections will become evident as we study the role of ritual in Aryan life.

Like all cultures, the Aryans pondered how the world came into being, and the Vedas offer several different explanations. The fact that these creation stories were often at odds with one another does not seem to have been a problem. Even today, the Hindu traditions contain dozens of differing accounts of creation.

One of the most intriguing Vedic cosmogonies is a short hymn that seems intended to astound and confuse rather than to explain. It has been the subject of dozens of commentaries throughout Hindu history.

There was neither non-existence nor existence then; there was neither the realm of space nor the sky which is beyond. What stirred? Where? In whose protection? Was there water, bottomlessly deep?

There was neither death nor immortality then. There was no distinguishing sign of night nor of day. That one breathed, windless, by its own impulse. Other than that there was nothing beyond.

Darkness was hidden by darkness in the beginning; with no distinguishing sign, all this was water. The life force that was covered with emptiness, that one arose through the power of heat.

Desire came upon that one in the beginning; that was the first seed of mind. Poets seeking in their hearts with wisdom found the bond of existence in non-existence.

Their cord was extended across. Was there below? Was there above? There were seed-placers; there were powers. There was impulse beneath; there was giving-forth above.

Who really knows? Who will here proclaim it? Whence was it produced? Whence this creation? The gods came afterwards, with the creation of this universe. Who then knows from whence it has arisen?

Whence this creation has arisen— perhaps it formed itself, or perhaps it did not—the one who looks down on it, in . . . the highest heaven, only he knows—or perhaps he does not know.[1]

Other creation stories from the Vedas are not always so modest in their conclusions. These stories develop other creation themes that have parallels in many other cultures. According to them, the world came into being through such things as a cosmic egg, the union of the earth and sky, a cosmic battle, and, as we shall see later in this chapter, the ritual dismemberment of a primordial giant (figure 3.1; box 3.2).

The *Devas* and *Devis*

God and *goddess* are the English words most frequently used to translate *deva* and *devi*, the most common Sanskrit terms for divine beings. *Devas* and *devis* are beings with powers and qualities beyond those of humans, but they are not necessarily omniscient or omnipotent. They are not lawgivers like Yahweh and Allah in Western religions and are usually not regarded as moral exemplars or as models for human behavior. Because they were created after the world's creation, the *devas* and *devis* are themselves subject to its laws, including the principle of *rita*. *Devas* and *devis* differ in many respects from Western understandings of divinity, and we must bear in mind these distinctions when we call them gods and goddesses.

An ancient tradition says there are thirty-three different gods and goddesses mentioned in the Vedas, although that is not the actual number. The *devas* and *devis* were believed to dwell throughout the *triloka*: on earth, in

Fig. 3.1   Vishnu and Laksmi on Shesha. According to one Hindu myth, the creator Brahma emerged from the navel of the god Vishnu as he was attended to by his wife, Lakshmi. (Photo courtesy of http://commons.wikimedia.org/wiki/ File:Vishnu1.jpg.)

Box 3.2 **ANOTHER HINDU CREATION STORY**

The Vedas contain several stories of the world's creation, and later Hindu traditions add even more, including this cosmogony involving Lord Vishnu, a minor *deva* in the Vedas, and Brahma, a god who does not appear in the Vedas at all (although later traditions identify him with the Vedic god Prajapati). As Vishnu reclines on the remains of the previous universe, the creator Brahma emerges from his navel, sitting on a lotus, to begin the cycle once again.

Prior to creation, the Lord was engrossed in yoga nidrā [conscious sleep] on the primeval waters, absorbed in his own bliss. The subtle bodies of all the beings who had existed in the previous cycle were with the Lord in their atomic state. Only time was awake and time had been endowed with the power to arouse the creative faculties within the Lord at the time allotted by him.

When the moment arrived, time illumined the nature of all the beings resting in the Lord in their atomic state. The Lord saw countless worlds within his own being. These worlds were stirred by the quality of activity, impelled by time. The subtle matter which issued from the navel of the Lord as a result of this stirring looked like a lotus, and it illuminated the primeval waters like the sun. The Lord himself entered this lotus; and the creator [Brahmā] appeared on it. Brahmā looked around in the four directions and thus came to have four heads. He asked himself: "Who am I? What is my support? Who supports this lotus which seems to be my support?"

Brahmā dived into the primeval waters, looking for his own source. A long period of time elapsed. Time is the Lord's discus [*sudarshana*] and frightens people by consuming their life-span. Brahmā gave up the search and returned to his own abode to practice deep meditation. After a hundred years of deep meditation the light of wisdom dawned on him and he saw.

On the primeval waters in which the whole universe was submerged lay the Lord on the body of Shesha [the residue of the previous cycle, visualized as a serpent]. He shone with a splendour that had no comparison. The worlds with all their animate and inanimate objects were hidden within him. He was inaccessible even to the sun, moon and stars; his own divine weapons devoutly went around him. At that very moment the creator, intent on bringing the universe into being, beheld the lotus which supported him, the primeval waters, the cosmic blast, space and himself. He then fixed his mind on the Lord and began to praise him.*

*Swami Vankatesananda, trans., *The Concise Srimad Bhagavatam*, vol. 3, bk.10 (Albany: State University of New York Press, 1989), 45–46.

heaven, and in the space between them. Most of them were associated with specific functions or realms. We will examine a few of the most important in more detail here.

Indra

In terms of the sheer number of hymns addressed to him, Indra was the most important *deva* in the *Rig-Veda*. His popularity reflects his importance to the Aryan community. Like the biblical god Yahweh, Indra was a god of war, leading the Aryans into battle and serving as the model soldier. Indra's love of conflict, in fact, is what prompted the prophet Zoroaster to classify him as one of the principal *devas* associated with chaos and evil, although the Indo-Aryans did not view him in that way. Indra's domain, however, was not limited to the battlefield. Like other *devas*, he also ruled a province of nature: the waters of heaven that brought the rains. One of the myths of the *Rig-Veda* tells how the heroic Indra slew Vritra, the demonic dragon that controlled the primordial waters, thus allowing the rivers of earth to flow freely.

Agni

Next to Indra in popularity was the *deva* **Agni**, the divine fire. Nearly one-fifth of the songs of the *Rig-Veda* are addressed to him. The name *Agni* is etymologically related to the English word *ignite*. Agni was unique among *devas* because he dwelled in all three levels of the world: in heaven, as the fire of the sun; in midspace, where he was lightning, the "child of the waters"; and on the earth, where he lived in plants, wood, and the fires of altar and hearth. Because of his mobility, Agni served as mediator between the gods and humans. Through the ritual fires, he carried sacrifices to the gods and ancestors, and through the fires of cremation,

he transported the dead to Svarga. Agni could even dwell in the bodies of spiritual adepts as *tapas*, the creative energy associated with religious austerities. It is not surprising that the Aryans felt closer to Agni than to other gods.

Varuna and Mitra

The *deva* Varuna was the guardian of *rita*, the principle of cosmic, moral, and ritual order. Varuna enforced *rita*, but he did not create it. The Aryans imagined Varuna seated in a large palace in Svarga, from which he watched the world and punished those who violated the world's order. The Vedas describe him as the "thousand-eyed one," probably an allusion to the stars, his empirical manifestation. Because of Varuna's role as custodian of *rita*, sinners sought to appease him through pleasing ritual sacrifices.

Like Varuna, Mitra was one of the deities associated with covenants and oaths in Indo-Iranian religion. In the Vedic tradition of ancient India, Mitra retained this association and was regarded as the patron of friendship and honesty. He was one of the seven *adityas*, the celestial gods who were the sons of Aditi and regarded as benevolent protectors of all beings.

Rudra

Rudra was known as "the Howler." He had no friends among the other gods and preferred to dwell in wild and terrifying places. Rudra had matted hair and dressed in animal skins. He despised human beings and often afflicted them with sickness and misfortune. Aryans usually left their offerings to Rudra outside their villages and implored him to stay away. But, paradoxically, Rudra was also a healer. We will encounter this paradox frequently when we study later Hindu gods such as Shiva and Kali.

Fig. 3.2 Surya, the sun god. Surya, the Vedic god associated with the sun, is still a popular god among many Hindus. (Photo courtesy of Creative Commons, JJ Harrison.)

Many scholars, in fact, believe that the Vedic *deva* Rudra may have provided a prototype for the god later known as Shiva.

Other *Devas* and *Devis*

In addition to the *devas* noted here, the Vedas mention a coterie of other gods and goddesses who appear to have played important roles in Aryan life. Among these were the sacred plant, Soma, as already mentioned; **Yama**, the god of justice and ruler of the dead; **Ushas**, the goddess of the dawn; **Kubera**, the *deva* of wealth and prosperity; **Surya**, god of the sun (figure 3.2); **Sarasvati**, a river goddess; and a host of other lesser divine beings of different ranks and qualities, including the *asuras*, whom the Indo-Aryans considered evil and in opposition to the *devas*. (In Iranian religion, however, the *ahuras*—the Avestan form of *asuras*—were associated with the forces of good.)

At different times in the Vedic period, different *devas* took center stage. Generally, the Aryans worshiped the *deva* or *devi* whose favors were needed at the moment. As Aryan interests and needs evolved, so did their worship practices. The war *deva* Indra, for instance, was much more important in the early Vedic period than later, when the Aryans had settled and were more concerned with agriculture and ranching than raiding. Although there were many gods, the Aryans often worshiped one god or goddess as the supreme deity. Max Müller, one of the first Western scholars to study the Vedas, coined the term *henotheism* to describe this practice. Henotheism is a synthesis of polytheism and monotheism in which one god is worshiped without denying the existence of other gods. This approach to divine worship continues throughout the Hindu religions today. Unlike contemporary Hindu practice, however, none of the gods of the Vedic period, apparently, were represented by human-made images.

Humanity

Later in this chapter we will investigate how the Aryans related to their gods, but before we do, let us take a moment to consider how they viewed themselves and their own place in the universe. One of the most telling observations about Aryan views on human nature and destiny is that the Vedas have very little to say on the subject. We must therefore rely on inference. Apparently the Aryans did not spend much time analyzing themselves and developing a systematic self-understanding. This point comes into relief when we compare the scanty Vedic speculations on human nature with the incredible energy spent on self-scrutiny in the post-Vedic era, after 800 B.C.E. The Vedas are by far more focused on the praise of the gods and the performance of sacrifices and other rituals than on understanding what it means to be human. It may be more accurate to say that it is *through* ritual that the Aryans understood the meaning of being human.

We get some sense of the Aryan perspective on human beings in the few hymns of the *Rig-Veda* that concern death. This is not surprising: in the face of death—whether that of ourselves or of others—we humans almost reflexively raise questions about the essential nature of who we are and the real significance of our lives. In the Vedic hymns we discover fairly wide-ranging speculation about what occurs at death. In one hymn alone, several fates for the human individual are mentioned as possibilities.[2] In one verse, the individual is believed to travel on the smoke of the cremation fires to heaven, where he or she joins the gods and ancestors in a pleasant postmortem existence. In another verse of the same hymn, the deceased individual dissolves into the elements of the natural world. Addressing the dead person, the hymn says:

> May your eye go to the sun, your life's breath to the wind. Go to the sky or to the earth, as is your nature; or go to the waters, if that is your fate. Take root in the plants with your limbs.[3]

Still later, the same hymn suggests that perhaps the corpse is "cooked" by the funeral pyre to make it a fit sacrifice to be consumed by the gods. Other Vedic hymns suggest that the soul descends to the **House of Clay**, the underworld ruled by the god of death, Yama. Obviously, the Vedas do not take a single view on the ultimate destination of human beings.

Furthermore, these hymns offer no consensus about what exactly makes up the human spirit or about what determines a human's final destiny. Sometimes the hymns refer to the *atman*, often identified with the breath, as the seat of the self or personality; others point to the *manas*, a somewhat vague concept denoting the mind, the heart, or the life-spirit that animates the body. The Vedas are likewise in conflict about what determines one's destiny. Sometimes it appears that the correct performance of sacrifices and other rituals decides fate; at other times it seems that other deeds—like fighting in battle or giving gifts to the priests—make this determination. Frequently it seems as if one's ultimate fate has no relationship at all to how one lived his or her life. One thing is clear: the Vedas make no unambiguous pronouncements that individual destiny—if there is one—is related to moral choices, a viewpoint that the later Hindu traditions adopt.

The Aryans did regard death as an occasion for grief and sadness, because life on earth was valuable and something to hold on to for as long as possible. Yet there is no indication in the Vedas that death was terrifying to the Aryans, nor is there any suggestion that life after death—if indeed there was one—might be torturous or extremely unpleasant. The *Rig-Veda* says nothing explicit about reincarnation, the notion that the spiritual essence of the person resumes life in a new body an infinite number of times. Reincarnation does not appear as a clearly defined and widely accepted belief in India until after the Vedic era.

Vedic Ritual

It is evident that the Aryans regarded ritual as far more important than doctrine and belief. The Vedas were a manual of religious *ceremony*, not of creedal statements or theology. To complete our understanding of the Vedic tradition, therefore, it is essential that we investigate its ritual practices. We will examine next the kinds of rituals the Aryans practiced, the purposes for which they were intended, and the persons who performed them.

Our first glimpse into the religious environment of ancient India revealed a world of gods and goddesses controlling the various aspects of existence of particular concern to the inhabitants of the Indus Valley and to the Aryans. The Aryans and Indus dwellers focused on the ways these powerful beings could help sustain and improve human life on earth. Gods and goddesses might be called upon to render aid in battle, stave off disease, or facilitate reproduction. The essential means for making such appeals to the divine was ritual.

The practice of ritual brings together the three dimensions of the Vedic worldview: its conceptions of the world, divinity, and humanity. To impose order on material that is quite unsystematic, let us consider a typology for discussing the kinds of rituals conducted by the Aryans. Like all typologies, of course, this schema is a simplification. In practice, Aryan ritual was more complex than any typology could represent. We will first consider the *griha* rituals conducted in the home at the hearth; then we will turn to the *Atharvan* rites, the rituals for healing and life transitions; and finally we will examine *shrauta* rites, which were conducted on special occasions.

Griha Rites

We actually know very little about the **_griha_**, or home, rituals. The Vedas were more concerned with the other types of ceremonies. Home rituals were probably simple sacrifices at the domestic fires, where the senior male served as priest by offering food—usually milk or **ghee** (clarified butter)—to *devas* such as Agni in the morning and again in the evening. These domestic practices probably derived from the libation offerings rooted in ancient Indo-Iranian culture. The purpose of such rites was to honor the gods, to acknowledge one's dependence on them, and to beseech them to continue to be generous.

Even today, the home is the center of Hindu devotion. Virtually every residence has some sacred space, whether small or large, dedicated to one or more of the *devas* and *devis* (figure 3.3).

Fig. 3.3 **Shrine in a Hindu home.** Most Hindu homes have a special space devoted to the family's favorite gods and goddesses. (Photo: Dushi-Yanthini Kanagasabapathipillai, http://www.passionparade.blogspot.com. Used by permission.)

rites involving incantations, herbs, and fire. But the *Atharvan* could do more than heal. He also provided protection from demons, snakes, and the **evil eye**; promoted good luck in gambling; and could cause misfortune for one's enemies and rivals. The *Atharva-Veda* is the text that contains the mantras used to bring about these desired outcomes (box 3.3).

The kinds of rituals enacted by the *Atharvan* priest are still important in Hinduism today, even though the *Atharvan*, as such, is no longer a familiar figure. There are many persons—including many who are not Brahmins—who conduct similar sorts of rituals for healing, providing protection from devils, and foretelling the future through astrology and other means.

Atharvan Rites

Aryan families called upon a ritual specialist known as an ***Atharvan*** to provide help during times of crisis (such as sickness), during times of transition (such as birth, naming, initiation, or death), or on auspicious days (such as the new moon or harvesttime). *Atharvans* were members of the Brahmin caste who might be compared to what we today call **shamans**. *Shaman* is a term from ancient Siberian culture now used cross-culturally to refer to those persons who have special access to the spirit world and who are able to use that connection for the benefit of others. In some African traditions, a shaman might be called a witch doctor; in some native American traditions, he or she might be known as a medicine man or woman. As these names suggest, one of the principal functions of the shaman is healing the sick. Like shamans in other cultures, the *Atharvan* priest cured with

Shrauta Rites

Although they were performed with less frequency than other ceremonies, information concerning the **shrauta** rites make up a large portion of the Vedas. *Shrauta* rites were conducted for unusual occasions, such as coronations. Wealthy persons could also pay to have the rites performed on their behalf. The *shrauta* rituals required great skill, and only Brahmins, who were experts in the recitation of the Vedas, were empowered to enact them. As the *shrauta* rituals grew in importance, the Brahmins gained power and prestige.

A typical *shrauta* sacrifice involved a team of Brahmins, each charged with different responsibilities. Setting up and performing the sacrifice might take several days or even weeks. Under Brahmin supervision, workers created an outdoor sacred space by erecting a temporary canopy using very precise measurements,

Box 3.3 SPELLS AND INCANTATIONS FROM THE *ATHARVA-VEDA*

The *Atharva-Veda* is a large assortment of hymns, prayers, incantations, and spells, ranging from the sublime to the mundane. The following excerpts are examples of religious magic from the latter category.

　　With this prayer, the Indo-Aryans sought relief from constipation and the inability to urinate.

　　We know the father of the shaft [arrow], Parjanya strong with hundred powers: By this may I bring
　　　　health unto thy body: let the channels pour their burthen freely as of old.
　　We know the father of the shaft, Mitra, the Lord of hundred powers: By this may I bring health unto
　　　　thy body: let the channels pour their burthen freely as of old.
　　. . . .
　　Whate'er hath gathered, as it flowed, in bowels, bladder, or in groins: Thus, let the conduit, free from
　　　　check, pour all its burthen as of old.
　　I lay the passage [penis] open as one cleaves the dam that bars the lake: Thus, let the conduit, free
　　　　from check, pour all its burthen as of old.
　　Now hath the portal [bladder] been unclosed as, [*sic*] of the sea that holds the flood: Thus, let the
　　　　conduit, free from check, pour all its burthen as of old.
　　Even as the arrow flies away when loosened from the archer's bow: Thus let the burthen be
　　　　discharged from channels that are checked no more.*

In the following passage, a woman seeks revenge on her unfaithful lover by making him impotent. To do so, she (or a priest acting on her behalf) chanted these words and smashed a plant (probably a root that resembled the penis). A nineteenth-century translator rendered the last stanza into Latin so as not to offend the Victorian sensibilities of his audience, but I have provided a translation of his translation.

　　O Plant, thy fame is spread abroad as best of all the herbs that grow.
　　Unman for me to-day this man that he may wear the horn of hair.
　　Make him a eunuch with a horn, set thou the crest upon his head.
　　Let Indra with two pressing-stones deprive him of his manly strength.

　　I have unmanned thee, eunuch! yea, impotent! made thee impotent, and robbed thee, weakling!
　　　　of thy strength.
　　Upon his head we set the horn, we set the branching ornament.

Box 3.3 continues on the following page

Box 3.3 (*continued*)

The two vas deferens, made by the gods, in which a man's virility resides,

I cleave (them) in the testicles with a wooden stick on account of that woman of yours.

As women about to make a mat split a reed with a stone,

so do I cleave your member with the testicles on account of that woman.[†]

The quest for the cure for baldness is ancient. The following charm to promote the growth of hair is around three thousand years old. Like all other baldness "cures," this one, regrettably, does not work.

Over a magic stone, beside Sarasvati, the Gods ploughed in this barley that was blent with mead.

Lord of the plough was Indra, strong with hundred powers: the ploughers were the Maruts, they
who give rich gifts.

Thy joy in hair that falleth or is scattered, wherewith thou subjectest a man to laughter. To other
trees, far from thee will I drive it. Grow up, thou Samī, with a hundred branches.

Auspicious, bearing mighty leaves, holy one, nurtured by the rain,

Even as a mother to her sons, be gracious, Samī, to our hair.[‡]

*Ralph T. H. Griffith, trans., *The Hymns of the Atharvaveda*, Book 1, Hymn 3 (1895–6) (accessed at http://www.sacred-texts.com/hin/av/av01003.htm).

[†]Ibid., Book 6, Hymn 138 (1895–6) (accessed at http://www.sacred-texts.com/hin/av/av06138.htm).

[‡]Ibid., Book 6, Hymn 30 (1895–6) (accessed at http://www.sacred-texts.com/hin/av/av06030.htm).

a practice harkening back to Indo-Iranian religious practices. Under this cover, four earthen altars were fashioned to contain the sacred fires. Three of the altars corresponded to the components of the *triloka*: earth, mid-space, and heaven; a fourth received the sacrifices (figure 3.4). The ritual performance began with the purification of the sacrificer, who was not one of the Brahmin priests, but rather the person who paid to have the ritual conducted on his behalf. Sacrifices were not cheap, often costing at least a cow. The sacrificer's wife's presence was necessary for success, although she did not have a specific role in the rituals.

Once the ritual was under way, the gods were invoked and invited to attend. Soma—or more likely, a Soma substitute—was imbibed. (By the time the Aryans had reached India, the identity of the Soma plant had probably been forgotten.) A goat or other animal was sacrificed and cooked; the sacred food was then offered to the gods and later eaten by the participants. The most important aspect of the sacrifice, however, was the hymns and prayers sung by the Brahmin priests. These were verses from the Vedas, and it was essential that they be chanted correctly. One priest's sole responsibility was to ensure that the sacred words were

Fig. 3.4   Vedic fire sacrifice. The altar of fire received offerings that were conveyed to the gods by Agni. Fire is still a central component in many Hindu rituals. (Photo courtesy of http://commons.wikimedia.org/wiki/File:Yajna1.jpg.)

accurately uttered; he corrected any mistakes made by the others. Mistakes rendered the ritual ineffective and perhaps even dangerous; thus, the Brahmins placed great importance on exact memorization of the Vedas.

Shrauta rituals were performed for a variety of reasons, but their primary goals were of this world. Sacrificers sought to improve their relations with the gods to achieve greater success in business, to breed more and heartier livestock, to produce "manly sons," and to promote health and longevity. The attainment of a pleasant afterlife in heaven might also be included in this list, but that goal was viewed as secondary to the others. As we observed earlier, the Aryans held a wide array of views on the fate

of humans after death. The practice of Aryan religion thus seemed oriented more toward the practical concerns of the here and now than toward the hereafter.

In the early Vedic period, the Aryans believed the *shrauta* sacrifices effectively urged the gods to act on behalf of the sacrificer. In return for pleasing songs sung in a *deva*'s or *devi*'s honor and offerings of meat, Soma, and other sumptuous foods, the gods were believed to grant the sacrificer's wishes. Over time, however, the ritual itself—rather than the gods—came to be regarded as the agent of transformation. By manipulating the objects of the sacrifice, and especially by uttering powerful mantras, the Brahmins believed that they themselves were controlling the cosmic powers associated with the elements of the ritual. The creative power of the Vedic sacrifice even acquired a technical name, **Brahman**, a word meaning "that which makes great." By virtue of their skills at chanting Vedic mantras, the Brahmins came to see themselves as the custodians of Brahman (box 3.4). So important was the spoken word that the later Vedic tradition personified voice as the goddess **Vak**, reflecting the belief that language had a divine origin and embodied spiritual power.

In the Vedic view, sacred words were the manifestation of an eternal, meaningful, and inexhaustible reality. One Vedic creation myth even suggests that the ancient *rishis* brought the gods into existence by naming them. Later sources tell how the entire universe was created from the primordial mantra, **aum** (or om). Aum is the **Prāvnava**, the most potent of mantras. It is not a concept; it does not denote anything. It is the All-Word; it embodies all things in the form of sound. Recitations of scripture usually begin and end with *aum* (figure 3.5).

Today, Hinduism retains much of this emphasis on the spoken word. Throughout India, scriptures are often recited in villages and towns over loudspeakers, sometimes beginning at four in the morning! Even if no one hears or listens to the recitation, it is meritorious and generates communal blessings.

Myth and Ritual

We have observed that the Aryans did not have a highly developed or consistent self-understanding. The Vedas offer no clear picture of how the Aryans understood human nature and the ultimate destiny of the individual. But we should not infer from this that they were somehow incapable of sophisticated or systematic thought. Our study of Vedic ritual practices makes it clear that the Aryans were able to think in complex and highly abstract ways. It is amazing, in fact, to consider the intense intellectual energy the Aryans devoted to understanding and practicing their rituals.

To illustrate this sophistication and also the Vedic understanding of the relationships

Fig. 3.5 **The Prāvnava.** Aum, written here in the Devanagari script, is the syllable from which the whole of reality emerges. (Photo: Mark W. Muesse.)

among the ceremonial, divine, and social worlds, let us examine a *Rig-Veda* cosmogony more closely. The passage is a well-known story that describes the ritual dismemberment of a primordial person. Although this myth is a late addition to the Vedic corpus, it clearly echoes a very ancient creation theme: the idea that the world was created by the gods through sacrifice.

In the Vedic story, the sacrificial victim is a massive cosmic man called the **Purusha**, who is described as having "a thousand heads, a thousand eyes, [and] a thousand feet." He is larger than the physical universe itself. The *Rig-Veda* relates the details of this divinely performed ritual:

When the gods spread the sacrifice with the Man [Purusha] as the offering, spring was the clarified butter [ghee], summer the fuel, autumn the oblation.

They anointed the Man, the sacrifice born at the beginning, upon the sacred grass. With him the gods ... sacrificed.

From that sacrifice in which everything was offered, the melted fat was collected, and he[4] made it into those beasts who live in the air, in the forest, and in villages.

From that sacrifice in which everything was offered, the verses and chants were born, the metres were born from it, and from it the formulas were born. [That is, the Vedas themselves—including this very story—came from this sacrifice.]

Horses were born from it, and those other animals that have two rows of teeth; cows were born from it, and from it goats and sheep were born.

When they divided the Man, into how many parts did they apportion him? What do they call his mouth, his two arms, and thighs and feet?

His mouth became the [Priest]; his arms were made into the Warrior, his thighs the [Producer], and from his feet the Servants were born.

The moon was born from his mind; from his eye the sun was born. Indra and Agni came from his mouth, and from his vital breath the Wind was born.

From his navel the middle realm of space arose; from his head the sky evolved. From his two feet came the earth, and the quarters of the sky from his ear. Thus they set the worlds in order.[5]

One important aspect of this hymn is the way it established reciprocal relationships among the sacrifice, the act of creation, and the elements of the world. Because sacrifice was the primordial mode of creation, sacrifice became the method for the periodic re-creation and necessary maintenance of the world. The priests who performed sacrifices—and this was clearly the way the Aryans understood it—were re-enacting creation itself, thus making themselves tantamount to gods.

It may be difficult for those of us in the modern world to grasp completely the ancient need to participate in the process of cosmic regeneration. We think the world proceeds on its own. We do not usually perform ceremonies to help the sun come up in the morning or make sacrifices to coax seeds to sprout and produce an abundant crop. But ancient societies often viewed the human relationship to the natural world quite differently. For many ancients, the powers responsible for the well-being of life often needed human assistance. In the discussion of the Indo-Iranian tradition, we observed how pouring libations of milk into water, or animal fat into the fire, was understood to fortify the gods. The human and divine worlds maintained a symbiotic relationship. Each relied on the other for the maintenance of life.

The formation of the world out of the dismembered pieces of the Purusha also implies a system of relationships between the ritual and the greater reality beyond. If, as the story suggests, the seasons are identified with the components of the sacrifice (as demonstrated in that cryptic phrase, "spring was the clarified butter, summer the fuel, autumn the oblation"), then by manipulating these aspects of the ritual, the priests were effectively controlling the seasons themselves. The technical term for this belief is **sympathetic magic**. Sir James George Fraser, one of the early theorists on magic and religion, explained it this way: "Things which have once been in contact with each other continue to act on each other at a distance after the physical contact has been severed."[6] Because everything that exists was once connected to the Purusha, and because the Purusha is sympathetically connected to the ritual, the performance of ritual sacrifice was understood to have effects in the world beyond. One might liken this manner of thought to the belief that sticking pins in a voodoo doll will harm the person it represents.

Finally, the myth of the Purusha has implications for the understanding of caste, which is mentioned for the first time in the Vedas in the passages quoted above. Previously we witnessed the gradual evolution of the caste system among the Aryans, beginning with the simple distinction between priests and producers among the earliest Indo-Iranians. Then we saw the expansion of the warrior caste as the cattle-rustling and village-raiding life became more popular, creating a three-tiered society. The fourth and lowest tier in the Aryan system, the servants, was probably made up of remnants of the indigenous people of the old Indus Civilization.

The story of the Purusha suggests that the stratification of humanity into priests, warriors, producers, and servants—the basic structure of what came to be known as the *varna* system—is both intended by the gods and embedded in the very fabric of the cosmos. This account of the divine origin of caste is part of the ideological structure that has kept the system in place for over three thousand years. In other words, caste is not regarded as a mere social construction, but rather as a fundamental element of reality. To challenge the system would be like challenging the gods or gravity, and the consequences would be dire.

Now let us take a moment to summarize some key points about Vedic ritual. First, ritual was immensely important in Vedic religion. The Aryans, like most ancient peoples, were not terribly anxious about belief and doctrine. But they were greatly interested in the correct performance of specific religious acts because these ceremonies and sacrifices were integral to their well-being on earth and possibly to their fate after death. These ritual practices came to be regarded as the special province of Brahmins, the experts trained to enact these ceremonies in precise ways. As religious practices were developed and refined, the Indo-Aryans came to believe that the rituals themselves were powerful. The rites were no longer performed to persuade or prompt the gods to act on human behalf; rather, the rite itself—and especially the words of the ritual—came to be seen as the true agent of control.

◆ KEY TERMS

Agni

apotropaic

Atharvan

Atharva-Veda

atman

aum

Brahman

Brahmins

darshan

evil eye

Five Tribes

ghee

griha rites

henotheism

House of Clay

Kubera

manas

mantra

Prāvnava

Purusha

rishis

Rudra

Sama-Veda

samhitas

Sarasvati

shamans

shrauta rites

shruti

smriti

Surya

Svarga

sympathetic magic

triloka

Ushas

Vak

Yajur-Veda

Yama

◆ QUESTIONS FOR REVIEW

1. Why have the Vedas never been widely read in India?

2. How do the Vedic *devas* and *devis* differ from the god described by Abrahamic religions (Judaism, Christianity, and Islam)? What features do they share?

3. What role does the concept of *rita* play in Vedic religion?

4. Which aspects of Hindu theology suggest great reverence for oral language?

5. What do the Vedas suggest about the Aryans' beliefs on life, death, and the afterlife?

6. What are *shrauta* rituals, and what did sacrificers wish to accomplish by having these rites performed?

◆ QUESTIONS FOR FURTHER REFLECTION

1. How do the Vedas compare and contrast with other scriptural traditions in the world's religions?

2. What purposes are served by conceiving the great forces in life as personal beings?

3. Why do you think creation and destruction are often linked together in cultural myth, as in the story of the Purusha?

4. What makes a place sacred? Does the location's privacy or publicity affect this?

◆ FOR FURTHER STUDY

Edgerton, Franklin. *The Beginnings of Indian Philosophy*. Cambridge, Mass.: Harvard University Press, 1965.

Mahony, William K. *The Artful Universe: An Introduction to the Vedic Religious Imagination*. Albany: State University of New York Press, 1998.

O'Flaherty, Wendy D., trans. *The Rig-Veda: An Anthology*. Harmondsworth, U.K.: Penguin, 1981.

PART II

FOUNDATIONS

4. Rebirth and Karma

PREVIEW

Philosopher Karl Jaspers termed the period from approximately 800 to 200 B.C.E. the Axial Age, a pivotal point of change for the foundations of spiritual practices throughout the Eurasian continent. It was during the Axial Age that classical Hinduism emerged in India. As this period took hold on the subcontinent, the emphasis on ritual gave way to a theology more concerned with human nature and the final human destiny. As we consider this period in Indian religion, we will encounter new concepts, distinct from the Vedic tradition and key to classical Hinduism. Through the Upanishads, a Hindu scripture revered as *shruti*, we will explore in this chapter the ideas of reincarnation, samsara, and karma.

The middle of the first millennium B.C.E. was one of the most astonishing times in the history of humanity. Between 800 and 200 B.C.E., there appeared a cohort of brilliant individuals whose teachings left deep—perhaps indelible—impressions on the way human beings thought about themselves and the world around them. Today, we are still living out and living through the ideas and ideals introduced in this period.

Remarkably, this burst of creativity occurred almost simultaneously in four separate areas of the Eurasian continent. In West Asia, in Palestine, the prophets of Judah, including Jeremiah and Second Isaiah, helped shape the emerging religion of Judaism, which had just begun to assume its distinctive qualities. Also in West Asia, in Iran, Zoroaster had recently established Zoroastrianism, which later served as the state religion of three powerful empires

and contributed new ideas to Judaism and later to Christianity. In the northern Mediterranean region, in Greece, Thales, Pythagoras, Heraclitus, Socrates, Plato, and Aristotle essentially invented the Western philosophical tradition.[1] In East Asia, in China, Confucius and his followers established the religious, philosophical, and political foundations for over two thousand years of Chinese culture. At the same time, Daoist philosophers produced a compelling alternative to Confucianism, impacting Chinese culture in an equally powerful but very different way. Finally, in South Asia, on the Indian Subcontinent, profound religious and philosophical changes took place. During this era, under the sway of a widespread countercultural movement of ascetics and mystics, the classical Hindu traditions took shape. Near the same time and place, the Buddha and Mahāvīra attained new insights that inaugurated, respectively, Buddhism, the first major international religion, and Jainism, a small but highly influential Indian religion. Both of these spiritual traditions shaped the developing Hindu traditions and were influenced by them in turn.

Rarely in human history do we find such a dense concentration of creative individuals in such a short period of time, especially persons whose lives and teachings were to have such an extensive and long-lasting impact. Just as fascinating as the density of genius in this era is the similarity of ideas and modes of thinking developed by these individuals, despite their geographical distance from one another. Although they did not always come to the same conclusions or advocate the same practices and beliefs, these thinkers struggled with many of the same fundamental issues, such as the nature and destiny of the self, the basis and practices of morality, and the highest goods of human life.

The German philosopher Karl Jaspers (1883–1969) identified this extraordinary period as *die Achsenzeit*, or the **Axial Age** (box 4.1).[2] By this designation, Jaspers intended to signify the pivotal nature of this era of decisive change. During the Axial Age, as Jaspers eloquently observed, "the spiritual foundations of humanity were laid simultaneously and independently. . . . And these are the foundations upon which humanity still subsists today."[3]

The Axial Age in India

It was during the Axial Age that the characteristic features of what we may call the classical era came into view. The rise of the classical Hindu traditions did not mean that Vedic religion was no longer practiced or that it gradually faded into oblivion. On the contrary, the Vedic tradition was retained and incorporated into a larger framework. The older Vedic notions and practices were kept intact or reinterpreted. In addition, a set of new ideas and concerns was added to the solution, precipitating the amalgam many now call Hinduism. This development was not so different from the way Christianity emerged from Judaism, retaining many Jewish elements, reinterpreting others, and then adding novel features from other sources. The appearance of the classical Hindu traditions did not mean, therefore, the disappearance of Indo-Aryan religion.

But changes *did* occur, motivated by a number of factors, many of which seem to be characteristic of Axial Age changes throughout the world. One of the most important was the expansion of the Indo-Aryans into the Gangetic Plain of northeastern India, beginning around 1000 B.C.E. This extension of Aryan culture has been called the "second urbanization" of India. The Aryans began to give up the nomadic life, settle in villages and towns, and become farmers. This development eventually

---

Box 4.1 **THE AXIAL AGE, 800–200 B.C.E.**

The Axial Age saw a prodigious output of critical ideas and the appearances of some of the greatest individuals known to the world. Several factors seem to have converged to create the conditions that resulted in this remarkable epoch.

The Axial period occurred during times and in places of increasing urbanization. Previously nomadic peoples settled down to take up agriculture and enjoy the benefits of more sedentary existence. Those in

Box 4.1 continues on the following page

Box 4.1 (*continued*)

villages moved to larger towns and cities to take advantage of new economic opportunities there. One of urbanization's consequences is the disruption of conventional values and beliefs: customs and traditions are no longer taken for granted. This critical approach to received values seems to have been an essential ingredient of the Axial era.

The Axial centers were also characterized by political and social upheaval. In China, the Warring States Period (ca. 475–221 B.C.E.) was an extremely brutal era in which hundreds of thousands of Chinese lost their lives. India and West Asia also experienced rapid transformations or the constant threat of war and lawlessness. Such brisk changes generated great uncertainty and insecurity for many, but interestingly these times also saw innovations in religious and philosophical thought. Political and social instability often fosters conditions that evoke the best (as well as the worst) in human beings. Notably, during the Axial Age, attitudes toward death began to reflect a greater concern with the experience of dying and what occurs after it. Every conceivable possibility for the afterlife seems to have been entertained, from continued existence in a delightful place, to life in the most unpleasant realms of the underworld, to rebirth in this life, to the decomposition of body and soul and their return to the earth, to resurrection of the dead at the end of the age.

The Axial Age was also a time when people began to experience themselves as separate, autonomous individuals—as selves. With this new sense of selfhood came a greater consciousness of human beings as moral agents, accountable and responsible for their own actions. Selfhood also promotes a feeling of isolation, or at least differentiation, from the rest of the human community and the rest of reality, making it more difficult to accept dying as part of the natural process of living. The self does not wish to die, and it looks for ways to avoid death or to survive it.

The growing sense of selfhood and anxiety about life's transience stimulated further conjectures about the eternal. Axial sages developed a new way of thinking about the world and the place of humanity within it, what sociologist S. N. Eisenstadt calls "transcendental consciousness": the ability to stand back and to see the world comprehensively and reflectively, not merely accepting the world as it appeared or as tradition said it was.* Transcendental consciousness produced novel conceptions of the world's ultimate reality. Axial sages became progressively more interested in what we call epistemology—the meaning and limitations of knowledge. And the purpose of religion shifted from what theologian John Hick calls "cosmic maintenance" to "personal transformation."† As cosmic maintenance, religion functioned chiefly as a ritual means for human beings to collaborate with divine powers to keep the world in good working order. But in its new transformative role, religion provided the means for individuals to undergo whatever change was necessary to achieve immortality, happiness, or whatever that religion considered the highest good in life.

*S. N. Eisenstadt, *The Origins and Diversity of Axial Age Civilizations* (Albany: SUNY Press, 1986).
†John Hick, *An Interpretation of Religion* (New Haven, Conn.: Yale University Press, 1989).

led to a period of greater material progress and put the Indo-Aryans in greater contact with non-Aryan peoples.

These basic social changes were related to certain developments in Indo-Aryan religion. Late in the Vedic period, there seems to have been growing doubt about the value of ritual, associated in part with the middle castes' resentment of the power of the Brahmins and their monopoly on ritual performance. But perhaps even deeper than that was an emerging sense that what the rituals accomplished was not, in the final analysis, all that worthwhile.

We see these doubts arising in a story taken from a collection of writings from this time, near the end of the Vedic period and the start of the classical era. This collection, which we will discuss in more detail later, is known as the **Upanishads**. The story of particular interest is a dialogue between a young Brahmin and Yama, the king of death. Through an interesting set of circumstances, the young man, whose name is **Nachiketas**, finds himself sent to the underworld, where he is forced to wait for three days without food because the king of death is away, doing what the grim reaper does. When **Yama** returns home to the underworld, he realizes he has committed a great offense by neglecting his obligations of hospitality to a Brahmin. To atone for his mistake, Yama offers to grant Nachiketas three wishes.

For his third and most important boon, Nachiketas asks Yama to explain to him what happens when a person dies, a simple request to make of the god of death—or so one would think. Yama, however, is surprisingly reluctant to answer.

NACHIKETAS: When a man dies, this doubt arises: some say "he is" and some say "he is not." Teach me the truth.

DEATH: Even the gods had this doubt in times of old; for mysterious is the law of life and death. Ask for another boon. Release me from this.

NACHIKETAS: This doubt indeed arose even to the gods, and you say, O Death, that it is difficult to understand; but no greater teacher than you can explain it, and there is no other boon as great as this.

DEATH: Take horses and gold and cattle and elephants; choose sons and grandsons that shall live a hundred years. Have vast expanses of land, and live as many years as you desire. Or choose another gift that you think equal to this, and enjoy it with wealth and long life. Be a ruler of this vast earth. I will grant you all your desires. Ask for any wishes in the world of mortals, however hard to obtain. . . . I will give you fair maidens with chariots and musical instruments. But ask me not, Nachiketas, the secrets of death.

NACHIKETAS: All these pleasures pass away, O End of all! They weaken the power of life. And indeed how short is all life! Keep your horses and dancing and singing. Man cannot be satisfied with wealth. Shall we enjoy wealth with you in sight? Shall we live while you are in power? I can only ask for the boon I have asked. . . . Solve then the doubt as to the great beyond. Grant me the gift that unveils the mystery.[4]

This brief passage is important to our study for several reasons. Of great significance is what Yama offers Nachiketas as alternatives to an answer to his question. The king of death promises the young Brahmin cattle and horses; wealth, power, and land; and children and a long, comfortable life. What is crucial to observe is that all of these things are *precisely* what the Vedic rituals were intended to secure. In an earlier age, the Indo-Aryans considered these the highest goods of life. Wealth, children, long life—what more could one hope for?

Yet in this passage from the dawn of the Axial Age, those things count for very little. An important shift has occurred—or has begun to occur—among some practitioners of Indian religion. Things once seen as the most valuable in life were now regarded with significantly less favor and perhaps even a touch of contempt. As Nachiketas says, these things "weaken the power of life." The implicit criticism of the Vedic ritual system here should not be missed. The later Upanishadic sages were not suggesting that the old rituals did not work; rather, they were saying that what the rituals provided was ultimately not important.

A second point is also significant. For the first time in the early Indian literature, we hear overt expressions of anxiety about death. Nachiketas wants to know: after death, does the individual exist or not? There is an urgency and intensity in his question. He wants to know the answer, and he refuses to let the god of death off the hook. There is nothing quite like this in the earlier Vedic literature. Previously, when we considered some of the passages about death from the older *Rig-Veda*, we noted some speculation but the lack of any agreement about the ultimate human fate. If they gave it much thought at all, some of the Aryans believed that death conferred a pleasant existence in heaven with their ancestors; others imagined the dissolution of the self and body as they melted into their elemental forms; and some may have thought that the corpse was consumed by the gods. What seems to be lack-

ing in the Vedas was the sense that knowing what lay on the other side of death was a matter of crucial concern.

The stage was now set for change. In the next chapter of Indian religious history, questions that had appeared only here and there—questions about the ultimate destiny of human beings, about the nature of existence after death, and about the absolute reality of the entire cosmos—would take center stage. And a whole new cast of characters appeared to address them.

Death and Rebirth

As the Indian Axial Age came into full manifestation, death became a topic of greater interest and was contemplated with an unprecedented energy. As Nachiketas's dialogue with Yama intimates, the question of death and afterlife was a matter of much discussion and speculation among certain groups of Aryans acquainted with the Vedas and sufficiently leisured to ponder such matters. The evidence that remains suggests that their conjectures about death were very diverse and anything but consistent.

Among the many ideas tossed about among these philosophically minded individuals, one was of special import for subsequent Hindu thinking. We noted while looking at the *Rig-Veda* that some Aryans understood death as the transition of the body or the life-force to heaven, where the individual enjoyed a pleasant existence among the gods and ancestors. One of the Vedic hymns promoting this view encourages believers with the promise that "this pasture . . . shall not be taken away."[5] Although this was by no means a universal

Aryan view, a significant number of people apparently believed it and thought that performing the appropriate sacrifices and rituals was the way to secure it.

Still, at the end of the Vedic era and the start of the Axial Age, misgivings began to color this picture of the afterlife. Some of the later portions of the Vedas express suspicions about the permanence of existence in heaven once it has been attained. In these later texts, the fear arises that one might initially reach the heavenly goal only to lose it again through death. The word **redeath** entered the religious lexicon to describe the situation in which the individual dies and ascends to heaven, lives there for a time, and then dies again, this time dissolving into the elements of the natural world. This emerging notion of human destiny began to take on rather ominous qualities.

The idea of redeath was probably an intermediate step in the development of the concept of **reincarnation**, which is known more technically as the **transmigration of the self**. This idea—that the individual self endures a continual series of births, deaths, and rebirths—seems to have appeared for the first time in India at the start of the Axial Age, near the beginning of the first millennium B.C.E. Some have suggested that the idea of rebirth may have developed initially in the old Indus culture and then reappeared centuries later after a period of suppression by the Aryans, but there is little evidence to support that conjecture.

In any case, we are not altogether sure how the belief in reincarnation appeared and then became widely accepted throughout India. The concept of rebirth is certainly not unique to India. The notion also appeared among some Native Americans, among the Trobriand Islanders, and in West Africa. We even find the idea of rebirth in the thought of Pythago-ras, Socrates, and other Axial Age philosophers of ancient Greece, who like the Aryans were descendants of the Indo-Europeans. On the subcontinent, it is likely that the concept of rebirth began in Northern India among a small coterie of philosophers and holy persons, just as it did in Greece. These Indian thinkers taught the idea to growing numbers of ordinary folk, and eventually it was widely accepted. Interestingly, in ancient Greece the idea of rebirth remained the speculation of philosophers and was never accepted by the masses.

But in India, the idea of rebirth was so extensively accepted that it became the fundamental assumption of virtually all Indian religions and philosophies, including the Hindu traditions, Buddhism, Jainism, and Sikhism. Each of these traditions understands rebirth in different ways, but they share the basic idea that existence is characterized by an endless series of births, deaths, and rebirths. The term used by these traditions to denote this cycle is **samsara**, a word that literally means "wandering," suggesting a kind of aimlessness or pointlessness to the process.

The Upanishads

The first place in the ancient Indian texts where we get a clear sense of the idea of transmigration is the Upanishads. We mentioned this important collection of writings earlier in this chapter. It is now time to become better acquainted with it before we delve deeper into what it says about rebirth.

The most important Upanishads were probably composed between 800 and 400 B.C.E., placing them squarely in the Axial Age. We know almost nothing about the authors of these works beyond some of their names, but clearly they were individuals of a philosophical temper, seeking answers to the fundamental mysteries of life. There is no universal agreement about what works are included in this collection. According to some, there are as many as two or three hundred Upanishads. A more commonly given number is 108, which is a sacred number among Hindus and Buddhists. Most editions and English translations contain thirteen so-called principal Upanishads.

By tradition, the Upanishads are considered part of the Vedas. Like the earlier Vedas, the Upanishads are not systematic or internally consistent. But a careful reading of the Upanishads clearly reveals a worldview very different from earlier Vedic texts like the *Rig-Veda*. Whereas the earlier Vedas are centrally concerned with rituals and sacrifice, the Upanishads are much more contemplative and thoughtful in tone. They seem to reflect the outlook of the solitary ascetic or seeker rather than the world of the priest or religious official. Despite the apparent differences from the earlier Vedic texts, the Upanishads are still regarded as *shruti*, or revealed knowledge, which means they share the same sacred status as the earlier Vedas. The perspective of the Upanishads is often called **Vedanta**, which means "the end of the Vedas."

We might compare the relationship of the Upanishads to the earlier Vedas with the relationship between the Old and New Testaments as Christians typically understand them. The Old and New Testaments were written in different epochs, and a careful reader will discern obvious differences in the tenor and theology of the two texts. Traditionally, Christians explain this difference by asserting that both testaments are authentic revelations, but the New Testament reveals more clearly and completely what was less clearly indicated in the Old Testament. In a similar manner, the Upanishads were later regarded as the "completion" of the Vedas, both to assert continuity with the older Vedas and to recognize and explain the apparent inconsistencies and tensions between the two collections.

Transmigration in the Upanishads

One such tension between the older Vedas and the Upanishads is the issue of transmigration. It is evident that the earlier Vedas make no explicit mention of such an idea. But by the time the Upanishads began to appear, the concept of rebirth had started to enjoy widespread acceptance. Even so, the Upanishads do not express a fully coherent understanding of the nature of this process. The Upanishadic texts typically explain rebirth by means of metaphor and analogy. A well-known passage in "The Supreme Teaching," some of the oldest writings in the collection, describes rebirth in this fashion:

> It is like this. As a caterpillar, when it comes to the tip of a blade of grass, reaches out to a new foothold and draws itself onto it, so the self, after it has knocked down this body and rendered it unconscious, reaches out to a new foothold and draws itself onto it.

> It is like this. As a weaver, after she has removed the coloured yarn, weaves a different design that is newer and more attractive, so the self, after it has knocked down this body and rendered it unconscious, makes for himself a different figure that is newer and more attractive—the figure of a forefather, . . . or of a

god. . . . or else the figure of some other being.[6]

These excerpts imply that continued existence is driven by desire, that the self that is reincarnated *wills* to be reborn. And indeed, as we will see later in the development of Indian theology, desire for life is precisely what propels the process.

But this view of reincarnation was not universally accepted among the sages who composed the Upanishads. A passage from another early Upanishad offers a different perspective. Here the author hypothesizes that the cremation fires convert corpses into smoke, which carries them to heaven on the wind, and there, after other transformations, they become food for the gods.

> Then they return by the same path they went—first to space, and from space to the wind. And after the wind has formed, it turns into smoke; after the smoke has formed, it turns into a thunder-cloud; after the thunder-cloud has formed, it turns into a rain-cloud; and after a rain-cloud has formed, it rains down. On earth they spring up as rice and barley, plants and trees, sesame and beans. . . . when someone eats that food and deposits the semen, from him one comes into being again.[7]

This theory appears to be a further refinement of the older Vedic view that the corpse is cooked and consumed by the gods. It simply follows that process to its logical end, based on the ancient belief that the male semen actually contains the complete incipient human and the female womb serves as a kind of incubator but does not contribute materially to the embryo.

Together, these selections indicate that although the idea of rebirth gained wide acceptance during this period of Indian history, there was no consensus about how it worked or what it actually meant. It is not even clear *what* these sages believed was reincarnated or what determined the form of one's next life. One of the passages suggests one gets a newer and more attractive body—such as that of a god—but the later Hindu traditions will come to teach that rebirth does not always imply progress or improvement. In fact, rebirth might very well mean going from being human to being a dog or an insect (figure 4.1).

Fig. 4.1 Rebirth. This modern image depicts how rebirth is imagined by Hindus. The illustration suggests that transmigration comes to a halt with the sadhu, whose devotion to religious practice is able to end samsara. (© Himalayan Academy Publications, Kapaa, Kauai, Hawaii. All rights reserved. Licensed under Creative Commons Attribution-Share Alike 2.5 Generic.)

Karma and the Ethicization of Rebirth

As the Axial Age progressed, and as the Upanishads were further developed, many of the concepts integral to the idea of reincarnation were addressed and refined. One of the most important of these developments was the concept of **karma**. Karma added a unique dimension to the Indian view of rebirth. Whereas the idea of rebirth is not exclusive to India, the belief that one's future incarnation depends on how one behaves in this life *is* a distinctive Indian conception.

The **ethicization** of rebirth is what the doctrine of karma is all about. Like Zoroastrianism and the Western monotheisms, the Upanishads make moral behavior the decisive element in human destiny. Of course, the Upanishads imagine that destiny in a manner very different from the Western traditions, but the fundamental principle is the same. In the Upanishads, as in the Indian religions generally, karma determines the form and status of one's next birth.

Karma is a term with which most Westerners are familiar, but most who use the term are not completely sure about its meaning. Many people use *karma* as another word for luck. "Well, I guess that's just my bad karma" might be uttered to explain an unfortunate situation. Karma, however, is not luck, if luck means a random or chance occurrence, nor is it technically understood to be fate, if fate is a sequence of events preordained by a god or superhuman power. In fact, *karma* means the opposite of luck and fate in these senses. According to the theory of karma, the events in one's life—good or bad—are not chance occurrences, nor are they foreordained by powers outside of oneself.

Karma is actually quite simple to understand. It refers to one's actions and the consequences of those actions. Just as dropping a pebble into a pond causes ripples on the surface of the water, so our every action creates waves of consequences. There is no way to separate action and consequences; the effects of one's act can be considered part of the act itself, according to Indian thought. The doctrine of karma maintains that those effects will at some point return to the agent who performed the act in the first place. The waves created by a dropped pebble reach the edge of the pond and then reverberate back to the point where the pebble was dropped. The return of the action's consequences to the agent is called the **"fruiting" of karma**. The fruiting of karma is inevitable, and karma always returns to the agent who created it, no matter how long it takes. We sometimes experience the consequences of our actions soon after they are committed. An angry person might fairly quickly reap the fruit of his or her anger as other people act out of anger in return. Or it may take one or more lifetimes for karma to come to fruition. But return it will.

The concept of karma predates the Hindu classical age, but during that era it came to assume a new meaning. In the Vedic period, karma referred simply to ritual action; it was the work that the priests performed to make a sacrifice effective. But in the development of the classical traditions, it came to include the idea of *moral* action, which included not just deeds performed by the body but also thoughts and words. So with the idea of karma we see both the ethicization of ritual and a growing focus on the interiority of the spiritual life, two characteristics of Axial transformations throughout the world.

The addition of a moral dimension to karma suggests that karma could be of two kinds:

good and bad, or positive and negative. The philosophical literature on the various kinds of karma is quite complex, so we will here reduce the idea to its elemental forms. In essence, we can say that by performing good actions, one produces positive karma; wicked, immoral, or irresponsible actions create negative karma. At some point, whether in this life or another, the karma we have generated returns to us: to our benefit, if good; to our detriment, if evil.

In short, the concept of karma means that every person gets what he or she deserves. Karma is a principle of justice. The process occurs ineluctably and impersonally, like the law of gravity acting on physical bodies. In most of the Hindu traditions, there is no god or divine being meting out justice. The return of the consequence of action is just the way the world works. Even the gods are subject to the law of karma. What Hindus mean by karma is reflected in the Western expression, "What goes around comes around." For better or worse, we cannot escape the consequences of our actions.

Axial Age speculations in ancient India brought about an important new constellation of ideas connected by the belief that the individual is consigned to an endless series of births, deaths, and rebirths, governed by moral deeds. As this notion was worked out in greater detail, it gained wide acceptance throughout the Indian populace. But it also generated new problems for the way Indians thought about life. The older Vedic belief in maximizing the pleasures of earthly existence yielded to new concerns about how to face the world of samsara. Later, we will begin to explore the quests for answers to questions about living in this new world.

◆ KEY TERMS

Axial Age

ethicization

fruiting of karma

karma

Nachiketas

redeath

reincarnation

samsara

transmigration of the self

Upanishads

Vedanta

Yama

◆ QUESTIONS FOR REVIEW

1. What changes in Indo-Aryan society and culture contributed to the advent of the Axial Age in India?

2. Which aspects of Vedic ritual came under criticism during the Axial Age?

3. How does the story of Yama and Nachiketas reflect the changes in Indian thought taking place at this time?

4. What are the Upanishads, and what is their relationship to the older Vedas?

5. How did the concept of karma develop from the Vedic period to the Axial Age?

◆ QUESTIONS FOR FURTHER REFLECTION

1. In the tale of Yama and Nachiketas, the young Brahmin claims that wealth and prosperity "weaken the power of life." If material possessions are ultimately unimportant, what does this suggest the highest goods of life may be?

2. How does *shruti* compare and contrast with concepts of revealed knowledge in other religious traditions?
3. What are the consequences for humanity if existence is driven by desire?

◆ **FOR FURTHER STUDY**

Basham, A. L. *The Origins and Development of Classical Hinduism*. Edited by Kenneth G. Zysk. New York: Oxford University Press, 1991.

Easwaran, Eknath. *Dialogue with Death: A Journey through Consciousness*. Tomales, Calif.: Nilgiri Press, 2006.

Obeyesekere, Gananath. *Imagining Karma: Ethical Transformation in Amerindian, Buddhist, and Greek Rebirth*. Berkeley: University of California Press, 2002.

Roebuck, Valerie J., trans. and ed. *The Upaniṣads*. London: Penguin, 2003.

Sharma, Arvind. *Classical Hindu Thought: An Introduction*. New Delhi: Oxford University Press, 2000.

5. Dharma and Caste

PREVIEW

In addition to new ideas about the nature of life, the Hindu traditions were also defined by evolving social arrangements. This chapter discusses the social foundations of Hindu life, as does the next chapter on gender and the life cycle. We will observe how the relatively simple stratification of Aryan society transmuted into the exceedingly complex caste system. Spurred by the same dynamics that prompted speculation about the nature and destiny of human beings, what was once a division of labor became more deeply embedded into the Hindu social and religious fabric. Rules regulating appropriate behavior within and between castes were developed and joined to the emerging ideas about the self. These regulations had—and have—tremendous impact on Hindu social life, governing not only one's work but also matters such as marriage, diet, and hygiene.

During the Axial Age, the Indian traditions that focused principally on ritual and "cosmic maintenance" evolved into a more comprehensive and diverse collection of beliefs and practices. This transition involved preservation of the Vedas and its rituals as well as the development of new concepts to address an increasing curiosity and anxiety about the nature and destiny of the self and the fundamental powers of the universe. Among these new concepts was samsara, the view of life as an endless series of existences regulated by the principle of karma. In this chapter, we continue our inquiry into the foundations of the Hindu traditions by looking at two important and related elements, the concept of **dharma** and the **caste system**. Although the idea of dharma and the institution of caste were probably developed independently of the idea of samsara, they were soon integrated with it to shape a comprehensive and coherent view of life that was distinctively Hindu.

Dharma

In the classical period, as we have seen, the Vedic idea of karma assumed decidedly moral overtones. What was initially a neutral term that referred simply to the dynamics of ritual took on positive and negative connotations as a concept touching on all forms of human action. As karma acquired moral values, the meaning of dharma, another ancient concept, was broadened to provide the standard by which the quality of actions could be judged.

Like karma, *dharma* was a word from the early Vedas. In its Vedic sense, *dharma* meant something firm or established, a thing that supports or sustains. It was associated with ritual, which the Aryans understood as upholding the order of reality, and with *rita*, the cosmological principle of truth, harmony, and justice. By the classical Hindu period, however, the idea of dharma had begun to supplant the concept of *rita* and acquired the sense of setting the appropriate pattern for living. In other words, dharma came to mean the moral law, one's obligations and duties in life. Yet dharma also retained the cosmological connotations of *rita*. This ontological element conveyed the sense that the rules for appropriate living were rooted in reality itself and were not dependent on human beliefs or constructions.

As we noted in chapter 4, the Axial Age in which the classical Hindu traditions took root was a time of intense interest in the proper regulation of human behavior. Confucius in China, the prophets in Israel, and Plato and Aristotle in Greece were all deeply concerned with the ways human beings should treat one another. In India as well, new codes for human action were devised during this era. As a moral principle, dharma was rather abstract and required concretization to make it applicable to people's daily lives. Accordingly, numerous attempts to specify and codify the dharma were made and put forth. Over time there emerged a whole genre of literature, known as ***Dharma-Shastras***, to delineate dharma. It has since become the largest literary genre in India.

The most important and influential work in the *Dharma-Shastras* was the **Laws of Manu**, which were written down about the time of Jesus but almost certainly reflect earlier understandings of the structure of society. Manu, the purported source of these decrees, was the primal ancestor of all humanity according to some Hindu myths.

Manu's laws defined dharma according to one's place in society. Caste and sex, particularly, determined the specific nature of one's duty and moral obligations. A Brahmin woman, for example, was given different standards for proper behavior than a Vaishya man or even a Vaishya woman. In the rest of this chapter, we will explore the regulations of dharma as they pertain to caste, and in the next chapter we will examine dharma in relation to the duties of men and women.

The Caste System

Like the word *Hinduism*, the term *caste* is not an indigenous Indian word. *Caste* derives from the Portuguese word *casta*, which means "pure" or "chaste." Although *casta* does not fit the Indian social system precisely, it aptly calls attention to the fact that the basis of the system is purity. The problem with *caste* is that it is a single term used to indicate what is in reality two different systems of social organization. Where non-Hindus use the term *caste*, Hindus use two words: ***varna*** and ***jati***. We will first consider each of these systems separately and then discuss how they relate to one another. Because the *varna-jati* system is an extremely complex social, economic, political, and religious phenomenon, we must simplify it greatly for this discussion.

The *Varna* System

When non-Hindus think of the caste system, they usually think of what Hindus call *varna*, a Sanskrit word that means "color." The *varna* system is the traditional Hindu division of labor, comprising the four categories mentioned in our earlier discussion of Indo-Aryan society. At the top of the hierarchy are the Brahmins, the class of priests and intellectuals who today make up about 6 percent of the Hindu population. They are followed by the **Kshatriyas**, the *varna* of warriors and administrators; the **Vaishyas**, the class of merchants, farmers, and artisans; and finally the **Shudras**, the laborers or common folk, who currently comprise about one-third of the Hindu populace. The first three castes are known collectively as the **twice-born** (*dvija*), because as children their members undergo a ritual initiation, or second birth, which we will discuss later. The Shudras, however, have no such ritual initiation and so are known as the **once-born** (*advija*). An important group known as the **Dalits**, or outcastes, is a significant part of Hindu society,

but according to ancient tradition they are not part of the *varna* system (figure 5.1).

The *varna* system is based on a premise that stands at odds with the liberal democratic assumption that all people are created equal. From the traditional Hindu perspective, the idea of human equality is patently false. Rather, it is completely obvious that people are born with different intellectual and spiritual qualities and capabilities. These innate differences dispose different people to different sorts of occupations and responsibilities in society. It may have been the case, as some scholars have suggested, that in the Vedic and perhaps early classical periods, movement between the *varnas* was possible. An individual may have been able to join a specific *varna* based on an aptitude for its duties. But by the late classical period, when the *Dharma-Shastras* had begun to emerge, one's caste was fixed by birth. This social immobility was abetted by the understanding of karma developed in the classical period. Karma now meant that who and where we are in the present moment was determined by how we have been in the past, and how we act in this life will determine who we will become. Our place in life, whatever it may be, and the duties that are ours by virtue of that place are therefore wholly appropriate.

The Obligations of *Varna*

Because birth into a particular *varna* reflected an individual's character and talents, it was essential for each person to perform the duties of his or her caste without deviation. As the Laws of Manu state:

> It is better (to discharge) one's own (appointed) [dharma] incompletely than to perform completely that of another; for he

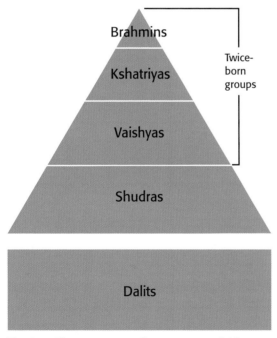

Fig. 5.1 **The *varna* system.** The *varna* system divides Hindu society into four major groups. According to an ancient tradition, the Dalits were not part of this system.

Box 5.1 PERSONAL EXPERIENCE WITH THE DYNAMICS OF CASTE

The mechanisms of caste were brought home to me dramatically one afternoon at tea in the home of a young man who was working for me while I was teaching in South India. The young man was a member of the high Kshatriya *varna*, but to earn money he performed domestic chores for others. Quite simply, he was able to earn a good deal more to support his struggling family with lower-caste work than he could earn performing the work of his caste. As I joined him and his family for tea that afternoon in their one-room mud hut, his mother-in-law—for no reason apparent to me—suddenly began to berate him mercilessly. Her anger was so intense I could not understand what she was saying. Later, I learned that the source of her outburst was the shame she felt at her son-in-law's willingness to do lower-caste work. My presence was the catalyst for the expression of her fury. Apparently, *her* friends had made disparaging remarks about her son-in-law, and she felt his choice brought embarrassment to the family.

This episode illustrated for me several important aspects of caste life. First, it demonstrated how caste strictures are ordinarily enforced, namely by family and intracaste pressure. It is usually not a matter of upper castes enforcing rules on lower castes, although that does happen. More frequently, enforcement comes from within one's own group. Most castes have caste councils in which the interests of the caste are discussed and advanced. Second, this episode revealed the very real tensions caste life may cause for an individual (an experience also explored in the Bhagavad Gita). My friend was torn between performing his caste's work and earning a better living to support his family. As we noted earlier, belonging to an upper caste does not necessarily mean greater wealth. Finally, I observed how the predictions in the Laws of Manu of the social chaos caused by caste mixture might seem empirically verified. Indeed, social and family harmony *is* disordered when caste rules are violated.

As the last statement indicates, the subservient qualities of the Shudra, like the specific qualities of each of the other *varnas*, were considered inborn and irremovable in this life. Thus, the dharma for Shudras encouraged their acceptance of a servile place in society. To act in a humble manner garnered good karma and boded well for one's rebirth, but to resent one's place and resist it had negative karmic effects.

In setting forth the various dharmas for each *varna*, the Laws of Manu made allowances for cases in which these duties could not be reasonably fulfilled by persons of the appropriate caste. For example, Manu allowed upper-caste members to do lower-caste work if necessary. Sometimes it was not possible for a Brahmin to find a job as a priest or teacher. It was not uncommon, then, for a Brahmin to take up work in a business or on a farm (box 5.1). Lower castes, on the other hand, were not permitted to perform the duties of upper castes. While this precept was generally enforced, it too was not without exception. To cite one example, throughout Indian history, the lowest castes often maintained their own shrines and temples because they were excluded from the temples frequented by the upper castes. At these low-caste temples, sacrifices and other rituals were enacted not by Brahmins, but rather by members of the lower castes who functioned in the priestly role.

Dalits

Outside of the *varna* system altogether are those who have no caste. These are the persons long known as **outcastes** and **untouchables**. Since the current Indian constitution has abolished untouchability, government documentation officially refers to this group as the "scheduled castes." That expression indicates that those without caste have now been assigned caste. Sometimes they are called **harijans**, or "children of God," an expression suggested by Mohandas K. Gandhi, but many members of this group have found this phrase patronizing and offensive. Today, the outcastes generally prefer to call themselves Dalits, a term meaning the "oppressed ones," or "those ground down." In this class are the handlers of leather and animal remains, the morticians and body-burners, the toilet cleaners, and the scavengers, in short, the persons who perform the dirtiest work of Indian society (figure 5.2a, b). Hindus regard the Dalits' work as highly polluting, so much so that members of that class cannot remove their ritual impurity by standard procedures of purification, such as bathing. A Hindu adage claims that untouchables are "so impure as to pollute the Ganges." Although devalued in this sense, the Dalits nonetheless perform the very essential function of absorbing the pollution of Hindu society. Because of their ambiguous status, Dalits often debate whether or not they are truly Hindus. In modern times, many have converted to other religions, particularly Christianity and Buddhism,

Fig. 5.2a,b **The Dalits.** These cobblers (a, top) and laundry-workers (b, bottom) are Dalits. Their occupations are essential to society, yet the tasks they perform are considered unclean. (Photos: Mark W. Muesse.)

because they have felt little benefit in identifying as Hindus.

Since the Laws of Manu do not recognize the Dalits as part of the caste system, the ancient text makes no mention of a dharma for the Dalit. The basic regulations for Dalit life derived both from the expectations of upper

Fig. 5.3   Twentieth-century Dalit leader. Dr. B. R. Ambedkar was a highly educated Dalit who spent his life opposing the Hindu *varna* system. In his later life, he and thousands of other Dalits embraced Buddhism. (Photo: MS Gopal, www.msgopal.com.)

castes and from the Dalits' internalization of their lowly status. They generally lived outside of villages and towns and could not use public facilities, like the well, or drink from the same vessels in a tea shop as upper caste members. In some places, they were required to prevent their shadows from falling upon a person of caste lest the shadow cause pollution. Until the twentieth century, Dalits were forbidden from entering most Hindu temples.

Despite their humble standing, Dalits in modern times have sometimes fared well in Indian society. Many have attained advanced educational degrees and have prospered economically and gained a measure of political power. One of these individuals, Dr. **B. R. Ambedkar** (1891–1956), was a principal author of the Indian constitution and the leader of a twentieth-century movement for Dalit liberation (figure 5.3). But in spite of the success of many individuals, and recent improvement for Dalits on the whole, traditional attitudes toward the Dalits still prevail. Untouchability remains a real part of daily Hindu life, particularly in the rural and less Westernized regions of the country.

The *Jati* System

Existing along with the *varna* system is a complex social structure made up of a vast number of *jatis*, or "birth groups." Although less well-known outside of India, *jatis* tend to be more important in the daily lives of Hindus than the broader *varna* categories. As the name implies, one's *jati* is determined by birth, and one does not leave it, except under very rare circumstances. Unlike the *varnas*, which are pan-Hindu, *jatis* are local groupings. A *jati* may exist in one region of India but nowhere else, or it may be found in many different locations throughout the country. Because they are local, the precise number of *jatis* has not been determined with certainty, but estimates suggest there may be more than three thousand discrete groups throughout the subcontinent.

Each *jati* is considered part of one of the *varnas*. Because of their categorization within what are often called castes, *jatis* are sometimes thought of as subcastes, particularly by outsiders. But in actual practice, Hindus often mean *jati* when they refer to caste. There are hundreds of *jatis* in each *varna*, and local ranking is not always the same. In one region of India a particular *jati* might be considered part of one *varna*, but in another locale it might be regarded as part of an altogether different *varna*. Finally, just as the *varna* system is hierarchical, so too is the *jati* system. Within a *varna*, the *jatis* are ranked, and there are specific regulations governing the way members of different *jatis* are expected to interact with one another.

While there is virtually no mobility for individuals in the caste system, whole *jatis* may improve their social status. Historically, members of some *jatis* gained a greater standing for their entire group by imitating the behavior of higher *jatis* or even higher *varnas*. Over time, by acting like members of a higher group, a whole community might attain acceptance into a superior *varna*. In the past, it has also been possible for individual social aspirants to buy a higher caste rank. There have even been lower-caste kings who had their genealogies reconstructed to "prove" they were of the warrior caste. These, however, are the rare exceptions to the rule. For the vast majority of Hindus, *jati* and *varna* are destiny.

In the absence of hard evidence, scholars have speculated about the historical development of the *varnas* and *jatis*. Many historians believe that *jatis* were endogamous birth groups native to the Indus Valley Civilization. When the Aryans migrated into India, they brought with them the *varna* system as a division of labor. According to this theory, the *varna* system then was imposed on the *jati* system.

Caste and Ritual Purity

While the *varnas* generally specify occupation, the *jatis* determine many other facets of everyday life. Like the ranking of the *varnas*, these basic rules are founded on the dynamics of purity and pollution. Virtually any activity that involves crossing bodily thresholds, such as having sex, eating, eliminating waste, menstruating, and giving birth, can be polluting. Furthermore, because ritual contamination is contagious—that is, it can be transmitted from one person to another, usually by touch—great care must be taken by the upper castes to avoid persons who might be polluted. This practice, obviously, is the origin of the term *untouchable*. Because many consider seeing to be tantamount to touching, some high-caste persons believe that even looking at an untouchable is ritually polluting.

Sexuality

Since sexual relations are a potential source of pollution, the *jati* system entails certain marital restrictions. Sexual activity with someone of another caste is inevitably polluting for the higher-caste person. Thus, individuals are expected to marry within their own caste. In the "matrimonials," the classified ads that many modern Hindus use for the purpose of arranging marriages, caste is always prominently featured. Even when couples have what are called love marriages—based on romance rather than family arrangement—they still overwhelmingly marry within their social groups, just as people throughout the world tend to do. There are, however, exceptions to the rule. In special cases, women are permitted to marry "up-caste" when, for example, an upper-caste male is unable to find a bride within his own caste. But according to caste strictures, men may not marry up-caste. Individuals who violate these restrictions risk excommunication by other members of their caste.[11]

Diet

Caste also establishes dietary guidelines. As with sexuality, eating and drinking are possible sources of ritual contamination. Thus, the kinds of food one may eat, the persons from whom one may receive food, and the people with whom one may dine are all determined by the principles of caste. High-caste Brahmins, for instance, maintain strict vegetarian diets, whereas eating meat may be acceptable among lower castes for whom ritual purity is of less concern. Animal flesh of any sort is regarded as unclean, and those who wish to maintain purity scrupulously avoid it (box 5.2). In much of South India, the region with the highest concentration of Hindus, most restaurants are

Box 5.2 COW PROTECTION

It is widely known that Hindus regard the cow as sacred and protect her from slaughter. Gandhi called cow protection "the gift of Hinduism to the world." This old Hindu tradition may be rooted in the influence of Jainism and Buddhism, two movements that opposed animal sacrifice and promoted the practice of non-harming (*ahimsa*).

There are many explanations for cow protection. Some say that the cow symbolizes the whole animal world, the realm of nonhuman creatures that deserve to live and be happy as much humans. After all, one may be reborn in the animal realm. The cow is also revered for all that she provides, especially milk, a major food source for Hindus. In this respect, the cow is symbolic of all mothers and what they provide for their children. The practice of cow protection reminds Hindus of their interdependence with all of life. Even the cow's dung and urine are highly regarded; both are used as purifying agents. Some Hindus have even claimed that cow urine contains potent medicinal properties, and they drink it for health reasons.

assumed to be vegetarian unless they explicitly advertise themselves as non-vegetarian.

Caste and Karma

The caste system in India has made for a highly stable society; it has not changed substantially in over two thousand years. While certainly there has been friction—and sometimes outright violence—between castes and subcastes, the *varna* and *jati* systems have remained constant. This fact may be surprising. How is it that a society based on a hierarchy of privilege and hereditary occupations has not been subject to a massive revolt of the lower classes? As Karl Marx once observed, in view of the great inequities in human societies, it is remarkable how *few* revolutions there have been in history.

To answer this question, we must return to the religious foundations of Hindu life. The concepts of transmigration and karma support the idea that one's station in life is the conse-

quence of one's own actions. One's social position is not accidental. Each person is responsible for where he or she happens to be, and where one happens to be is unquestionably fair and just. By this same token, these concepts encourage individuals not to resist the system but to fulfill the dharma of their castes, because doing so is sure to improve their positions in the next life. Failure to fulfill dharma, on the other hand, invites discord in this life and greater suffering in the next. This concern with one's next birth helps govern how an individual comports himself or herself in the present life.

But even beyond this concern is the general Hindu attitude that the world itself—with its caste structures and rebirths, its pains and misery—must be transcended. Ultimately, as we shall see in following chapters, the samsaric realm is of little value when compared with the reality that transcends it. The world of caste and rebirth can be more easily tolerated and endured when one knows that it is not of eternal significance.

◆ KEY TERMS

Ambedkar, B. R.

Brahmin

caste

Dalits

dharma

Dharma-Shastras

harijans

jati

Kshatriyas

Laws of Manu

once-born

outcaste

Shudras

twice-born

untouchable

Vaishyas

varna

◆ QUESTIONS FOR REVIEW

1. What are the social and cosmological consequences of failing to fulfill one's dharma?

2. How do the concepts of karma and dharma support the perpetuation of the caste system?

3. In what ways are dharma and *rita* similar? How are they different?

4. Could the caste system function without Hinduism? Could Hinduism exist without the caste system?

5. What aspects of Indian society are dictated by *varna*?

6. How do the duties of each *varna* help uphold the caste system?

◆ QUESTIONS FOR FURTHER REFLECTION

1. What are the advantages and disadvantages of basing social structure and hierarchy on religious practice or spiritual attainment? What are the advantages and disadvantages of basing social structure and hierarchy on wealth and fame?

2. Are there analogues to untouchables in other cultures?

3. The legal abolition of untouchability has failed to end discrimination against Dalits; what might put an end to this practice?

4. India's society has remained essentially unchanged for more than two millennia. What cultural and economic consequences might be the result of such a stable society?

◆ FOR FURTHER STUDY

Douglas, Mary. *Purity and Danger: An Analysis of the Concepts of Pollution and Taboo*. London: Routledge & Kegan Paul, 1966.

Dumont, Louis. *Homo Hierarchicus: The Caste System and Its Implications*. Rev. ed. Translated by Mark Sainsbury. Chicago: University of Chicago Press, 1980.

Olivelle, Patrick, trans. *Dharmasutras: The Law Codes of Ancient India*. New York: Oxford University Press, 2009.

———, trans. *The Law Code of Manu*. New York: Oxford University Press, 2009.

Radhakrishnan, Sarvepalli, and Charles Moore, eds. *A Sourcebook in Indian Philosophy*. Princeton, N.J.: Princeton University Press, 1957.

Zelliot, Eleanor. *From Untouchable to Dalit: Essays on the Ambedkar Movement*. 3rd ed. New Delhi: Manohar, 2001.

6. Men, Women, and the Stages of Life

PREVIEW

As with caste, specific patterns of behavior for men and women became a fact of daily life during the classical period. In this chapter, we will examine the traditional stages of life for men and women in Indian society. The Laws of Manu set out four orders, or *ashramas*, for males: student, householder, hermit, and renouncer. Although the Laws of Manu do not name specific stages for females, they do set forth rules governing the female life cycle in terms of a woman's dependence on her father, husband, and sons. Thus, the three stages of life for Hindu women—girlhood, marriage, and widowhood—are characterized by the men upon whom they are dependent.

The consolidation of the caste system during the classical period entailed assigning particular dharmas, or duties, for individuals according to their standing in society. At about the same time, the *Dharma-Shastras* articulated expectations—some old, some new—specifying different patterns of life for men and women. We turn now to examine the respective roles of men and women and the social mores governing relationships between them. As we shall see, the regulations formulated in the classical period prescribed particular stages of life to be followed by men and women of caste. We will explore each of these stages, giving special attention to the householder stage, the point at which the lives of men and women most significantly converge.

The same text that specified dharmas for each of the *varnas*—the Laws of Manu—also sets forth an ideal pattern of life for twice-born males. The Laws of Manu were written by and for these men. Concurrently, a parallel pattern began to emerge for high-caste females. Both ideals were based on the notion of life stages, a common cross-cultural way of thinking about an individual's passage from birth to death. It is important to bear in mind that these stages of life were regarded as ideals and as pertaining to the three upper castes. These patterns did not necessarily describe the life cycle of each and every Hindu; there were exceptions. But the stages did—and still do, to a large degree—depict how millions of Hindus thought life ought to unfold.

The Male Life Cycle

We begin by looking at the stages of life for a male, as elaborated in the Laws of Manu.

According to these laws, males should move through four **ashramas**, or orders, during the course of a lifetime.

Student

The orders began with **brahmacarya**, or the student stage, which commenced when a boy was initiated as a twice-born through an **upanayana** ceremony, a special ritual in which he received a sacred thread that he would wear for the rest of his life. This thread (*yajñopavītam*), which looped over the left shoulder and rested on the right hip, signified his standing as an upper caste member, although it did not indicate to which particular caste he belonged (figure 6.1). The Laws of Manu specified that the initiation should take place when a boy was seven if he was a Brahmin, ten if a Kshatriya, and eleven if a Vaishya. The initiation constituted his second birth.

In the classical, medieval, and much of the modern periods of India's history, the *upanayana* ritual marked the time when the initiate left home to live and study with his **guru**, or teacher. During this period, the young man lived a highly disciplined life. The Laws of Manu forbade the *brahmacaryin* from enjoying honey and meat, perfumes and garlands, spicy foods, dancing, singing, playing musical instruments, gambling, sexual intercourse, girlfriends, and even looking at women. All these things were believed to pollute or detract attention from studies. (Many students today would likely recoil in horror if they thought that studenthood meant giving up some of these things!) A boy's teacher taught him the Vedic scriptures, as well as the practices of personal purification, morning and evening devotions to the gods, and sacrificing. In return for his education, the *brahmacaryin* was expected to be completely devoted to his teacher, obeying his directives without question. Manu's laws also promised dire punishments for boys who showed any disrespect to their teachers. A student who criticized his teacher—even if the criticism was fair—was told he would become an ass in his next birth!

Fig. 6.1 The sacred thread. This young Brahmin has just undergone initiation as a twice-born and now wears the sacred thread representing his new status. (Photo courtesy of Creative Commons, Nagesh Rao.)

Householder

A young man remained a student until it was time for him to marry and become a productive member of society. Marriage was regarded as the natural state for adult men and women; to deviate from this pattern was considered unusual and often shameful. A man generally entered the **householder** stage (*grihastha*) in his early twenties, although marriage as a teen was not uncommon. As a householder, the young man raised a family, pursued an occupation appropriate to his caste, and established himself as financially independent and a responsible contributor to society. Because the householder was essential to the well-being of the social structure, the Laws of Manu proclaimed it "the most excellent order."[1]

It is at the householder stage that the lives of males and females were most closely intertwined. Indeed, this was the only stage of life shared by the two sexes in the traditional pattern. When we come to the life stages for females, we will return to study this *ashrama* with greater detail.

Hermit and Renouncer

The Laws of Manu go on to specify two other stages beyond the householder, although most men probably did not enter them. These final *ashramas* pertained to the pursuit of religious objectives. In the third stage, that of the **forest dweller** or **hermit** (*vanaprastha*), a man and possibly his wife moved to a modest dwelling, usually at the edge of the village near the forest. Here he, and perhaps she, began to withdraw from active social life to become more introspective and devoted to the life of the spirit. This stage began only after a man had raised a family, earned an income, and discharged his obligations to society. The *Dharma-Shastras* insist that a man could enter this *ashrama* only when his hair had begun to turn gray and his children were well established, with children of their own. The Laws of Manu and the other *Dharma-Shastras* were eager to keep men in their prime at the householder stage, in which they were industrious members of society. The articulation of this rule, in fact, was a response

to what had become something of a problem: young men setting off to seek spiritual transcendence and other religious experiences (see chapter 8). When such individuals renounced the world to live as ascetics, society was deprived of the members it saw as most useful. Thus, part of the purpose of the *ashramas* was to regulate religious experience by delaying its full pursuit until one's later years, when the energies of youth had begun to dissipate.

The fourth *ashrama* was so rigorous and austere that few men embarked upon it. This stage was known as **sannyasa**, or renunciation. When a man entered this stage, he renounced his former identity and everything associated with it: his name, his wife and family, and all material goods. Entrance into this *ashrama* was often marked by a mock cremation in which the **sannyasin's** effigy was burned. Following his "death," he lived out his remaining days as a wandering, solitary ascetic (figure 6.2). He

Fig. 6.2 **Sannyasin.** Individuals who have entered *sannyasa*, the fourth stage of a man's life, wear clothing of orange, the traditional color of renunciation. (Photo: Mark W. Muesse.)

performed no rituals or work and subsisted only on the generosity of others, who gained meritorious karma by contributing to his well-being. With no encumbrances, the *sannyasin* was free to devote his full energies to the search for god and salvation. Today, these holy persons are a familiar sight in India, easily recognized by their garb of orange, the color of renunciation.

The Female Life Cycle

Historically, the life cycle for Hindu females has been different from, but closely connected to, that for males. In the classical and medieval periods, and for most of the modern period, females have followed a three-stage pattern. Today, the roles of women in Hindu society are rapidly changing, as they are throughout the world, and increasingly the life pattern of females resembles that of males, especially in urban areas.

The basic principles governing the roles of girls and women throughout most of Hindu history were set forth in the Laws of Manu. The ancient code declared:

> Women must be honored and adorned by their fathers, brothers, husbands, and brothers-in-law who desire their own welfare. Where women are honored, there the gods are pleased; but where they are not honored, no sacred rite yields rewards.[2]

In the Vedic world, women's presence was required for rituals to function properly, even though they had no official role to play in them. Manu continued:

> Day and night women must be kept [dependent on] the males (of) their (families), and if they attach themselves to sensual enjoyments, they must be kept under one's control. Her father protects her in childhood, her husband protects her in youth, and her sons protect her in old age; a woman is never fit for independence.[3]

This brief and oft-quoted passage reveals the ancient Hindu belief that females are susceptible to "sensual enjoyments" such as jewelry, clothing, and material comforts. Because of this aspect of their nature, females were generally considered ill equipped for spiritual and intellectual development, which required great discipline of the mind and body. Because females were seen as pursuing pleasure rather than the disciplined spiritual life, it was essential for them to remain under the guard of the most important men in their lives. These men—father, husband, and sons—defined the three phases of the female life cycle: girl, householder, and widow.

Girlhood

As a girl, a female lived under the watchful protection of her parents, who were zealously concerned with protecting her virginity. At this stage, she was considered pure but "inauspicious" because she lacked life-giving power. When she married she became impure, due to menstruation and the practice of sexual intercourse, but also "auspicious" in the sense that she was now able to reproduce.

For most of Hindu history, girls were not allowed to have the same kind of education as their brothers. Boys left home to receive their education from a guru, but girls could not leave the safety of their fathers' watchful eyes. What education a girl got came from her parents. She spent most of her time learning domestic skills from her mother, as well as some rudimentary aspects of religion, particularly her role in the important domestic rituals. Women were generally considered incapable of studying the Vedas, although, as we shall see, there were some important exceptions to this belief.

Marriage

The onset of menstruation was a girl's rite of passage into adulthood, marking her change from "inauspicious" to "auspicious" status. Ideally, a wedding would take place shortly afterward on a date and time determined by a reputable astrologer. With marriage, young women entered the householder stage.

Until recently, marriages usually occurred early in a girl's life. Her family arranged her marriage just after she was born or sometime later in childhood, although she would not actually move to her husband's house until after the wedding. Often, a match was made with a boy who was relatively close to her in age. But it was not at all uncommon for a girl to be married to a much older man, perhaps twenty, thirty, or forty years her senior. Because of the anxiety about maintaining virginity, a girl's parents had a vested interest in arranging her marriage as early as possible. When a girl's marriage was arranged while she was young, her purity became the joint responsibility of her own family and the groom's family. Today, most Hindu women do not usually marry until their twenties, after their formal education, which they now usually receive in the same manner as their brothers.

Traditionally, marriage has meant something quite different in Hindu society than it does in the contemporary Western world. In India, marriages have been—and still are—principally regarded as alliances between families for the purposes of reproduction and economic stability and not so much as a means for personal enrichment, as they are often considered in the West. Hindu marriages have historically been arranged by the groom's and bride's older relatives, who sought the most advantageous match for the family as a whole as well as for the child. The couple usually did not meet until shortly before the wedding or at the wedding itself.

Arranging Marriages

In seeking a suitable spouse for one's son or daughter, family members took into account more than just personal compatibility between the bride and groom. The prospective family's wealth and social standing, caste and subcaste, health, the prospective spouse's occupation and salary, and the compatibility of the pair's astrological charts were issues of prominent concern (box 6.1). Marriage brokers were often consulted. Almost always, the groom's family received a **dowry** payment from the bride's family. The size or amount of the dowry was a matter of negotiation and had to be agreed upon before the engagement. Due to the need for a dowry and the great expense involved in weddings, girls were often seen as economic liabilities.

Hindu marriages, both past and present, rarely ended in divorce. Marital longevity was due in part to the culture's view of the purpose of marriage and in part to the social, economic, and legal pressures impinging on the marriage. Because the central point of marriage was to cement alliances between families and to provide a stable context for rearing children, getting a divorce was extremely difficult and socially stigmatized.

Box 6.1 **THE *KAMA SUTRA* ON CHOOSING A BRIDE**

The *Kama Sutra* is widely known as a manual for enhancing sensual pleasure. But its purview extends much further than simply offering techniques for sexual gratification, providing a wide range of advice for how to live, including these suggestions for arranging a marriage.

- For raising a family, the girl should be young; belong to the same caste; without previous sexual experience; observant of the sacred books as far as virtue and money are concerned; agreeable to the relationship; desirous of amorous relations and having children.

- One must seek a girl born of a noble family, with both father and mother alive, younger than the boy by three years at least, with a good character, rich, devoted to her family, fond of her kinsmen, having good relations with her neighbors, pubescent, obedient, pretty, well mannered, not banal, healthy in mind and body, without missing or too many teeth, nor decayed, her nails, ears, hair, eyes, and breasts without defect, without any constitutional disease.

- Consult the omens deriving from the position of the planets, their conjunctions, influence, and meaning for the boy's future.

- It is only after having established the concordance of the signs of destiny, the moments, omens, and the position of the stars, that the girl may be given in marriage.

- A girl who sleeps too much, weeps a lot, or goes out walking alone should be rejected.

- If she has a bad reputation, is secretive, breaks her word, is bald, has marks on her skin like a cow, has breasts that are too big, or yellowish hair; if she is round-shouldered, very thin, hairy, disobedient, immoral, has uterine hemorrhages, is agitated; if she has childhood friends or a very young brother, and if her hands are always damp, she should be rejected.

- In no case should one marry a girl who bears the name of a constellation, or a tree, or whose name ends with the letter "l" or "r."

- Having consulted the omens, the date of the meeting is decided on, then that of the marriage ceremony.

- According to local convention or one's own desire, the Brāhma [priestly], prājāpati [royal], ārsha [ancestral], daiva [astral], or other kinds of marriage should be performed according to the rites laid down by the sacred books. Here ends the subject of marriage.

Adapted from *The Complete Kama Sutra*, trans. Alain Daniélou (Rochester, VT: Park Street Press, 1994), 217–24.

Weddings

Specific wedding rituals varied from region to region but were always conducted by a priest and usually involved circumambulating a sacred fire, a practice dating back to the Vedic period. We will discuss these rituals in more detail in chapter 7. It was at the wedding that the bride typically received the ornamentation that marked her

Fig. 6.3 Marriage ornamentation. These women wear a *sindura*, or red powder at the part of their hair. The *bindi* was once a marking identifying married women, but now both married and unmarried females wear it as a cosmetic adornment. (Photo courtesy of Creative Commons, Sigismund von Dobschütz.)

Fig. 6.4 Bride and groom. Hindu weddings are typically elaborate occasions, as suggested by the ornate dress of this bride and groom. (Photo courtesy of http://commons.wikimedia.org/wiki/File:Vinay_neha.jpg.)

change in status, including a wedding necklace, bangles, and a ***sindura***, a streak of red powder in the part of her hair (figure 6.3). The application of the *sindura* appears to be another ancient practice. Some of the female figurines found in the ruins of the Indus Valley Civilization had red color added to the hair part. Once married, a woman was also entitled to wear a ***bindi***, a red dot or jewel on the forehead indicating her auspicious, life-giving powers. Whereas the *bindi* was once the prerogative of married women, today it is often worn by girls and unmarried women as simple adornment (figure 6.4).

The Life of a New Bride

Following the wedding, the new bride went to live with her husband and his family. In the ideal pattern, sons were expected to live with their parents. Thus, in traditional Hindu homes,

grandparents, parents, and brothers, with their wives and children, all lived together under the same roof. Upon entering her husband's home, the new bride became subject to her mother-in-law, the mistress of the house. The young wife was expected to defer to and obey her mother-in-law and contribute to the well-being of the family. The mother-in-law/daughter-in-law relationship was—and frequently still is—a notoriously painful one in India. Reports suggest that a mother-in-law made jealous by her daughter-in-law's presence would make the new bride's life especially difficult. Thus, the transition to married life could be terribly traumatic for a young woman. One day she was in the affectionate, protective atmosphere of her parents' home, and the next she found herself in the home of strangers where often she was treated as little more than a servant.

The Dharma of Wife and Husband

As a wife, the Hindu woman was expected to live up to the ideals of **stridharma**, the duties of women. According to the mandates of *stridharma*, a wife was to regard her husband as a god. She was to serve him, eat after him, follow him (figuratively and literally), and pray for his well-being. Because she shared his karma, she fasted and went on pilgrimage to ensure his long life and success. If he died prematurely, it was often regarded as her responsibility, the fruiting of her negative karma.

For his part, the husband was expected to provide for his wife's material needs, security, protection, and social status. The husband was encouraged to revere his wife as if she were a goddess incarnate. The Laws of Manu tell husbands that the happiness of the wife is the key to the stability of the family. "Where women are honored, there the gods are pleased."[4] Today, in many places throughout India, women are still accorded certain privileges. For example, in some municipalities there are special public buses for women only, and women are allowed to avoid waiting in lines by going to the head of long queues for such things as purchasing train tickets.

Motherhood

Although the early part of marriage was often distressing for a bride, there were opportunities for a young wife's status to improve. Giving birth to a son, for example, could vastly improve her standing with her mother-in-law and the rest of her husband's family. A proverbial Hindu blessing for women is "May you be the mother of a hundred sons." Popular Hinduism has rituals to help a couple ensure the conception of a son, but there are no corresponding ceremonies for a daughter.

Indeed, as in many cultures, including pre-Islamic Arabia, it was once acceptable in Hindu culture for unwanted female infants to be abandoned and left to die of exposure. Even today, recent studies have shown that virtually all abortions in India were performed on female fetuses. The perceived economic liability of daughters is cited as the rationale: "Spend 50 rupees today," claims a saying, "and you'll save 50,000 rupees tomorrow." Even though it is clear that most Hindu couples today want boys more than girls, once a child arrives it is ideally loved for its own sake, whether male or female. Hindus have great affection for babies, and popular culture resounds with songs and lullabies proclaiming all infants to be gifts from god.

Exceptions

Before we turn to the final stage of life for women, let us also mention some notable exceptions to the expected roles of wives and mothers. Although marriage is by far the most common pattern for both men and women, the Hindu traditions maintain respect for some remarkable women who deviated from this path. One excellent example is **Lalla**. Lalla, also known as Lalleshwari or Lal Ded, lived in Kashmir during the fourteenth century c.e. According to legend, she left an unhappy marriage and mistreatment by her mother-in-law in order to study spiritual disciplines. She became a wandering teacher and poet in the Kashmir Valley. Her poetry displays a knowledge of Sanskrit and the Hindu scriptures and is still recited today, especially in her native Kashmir. Lalla is representative of a class of women who were revered for their love of god, even when that meant forsaking marriage. Today, she is venerated by Hindus as well as Muslims and Sikhs (box 6.2).

Box 6.2 **THE POETRY OF LALLA**

Lalla's poetry is intensely personal. In these representative verses, she alludes to the experiences that prompted her to seek the spiritual life and to the lessons she gained in that pursuit.

In this poem, Lalla indicates that it was the spiritual quest that allowed her to transcend the taunts of others:

> I endured verbal abuse and slander.
> Scandals broke out
> about my past and present.
> I am Lallā
> and my yearning never stopped.
> When I achieved my goal,
> nothing affected me.*

Like most renouncers in the Hindu traditions, Lalla sought the guidance of a guru, who advised her to develop her introspective capacities. In these verses, she gives credit to that directive for her adoption of the practice of wandering naked. While many Hindu holy persons renounce the wearing of clothing, it is not certain that Lalla actually engaged in that practice herself or simply used the image of nudity as a trope to suggest her lack of concern with the material world. Many legends suggest that wandering naked (or mostly naked) was indeed her habit.

> My guru gave me only one advice –
> from outside transfer the attention within.
> That became Lallā's initiation –
> that is why I began to wander naked. (p. 87)

Here Lalla reveals part of her spiritual path, indicating a practice avoiding the extremes of both extravagance and harsh asceticism:

> Indulging in eating
> will lead you nowhere.
> By refraining from eating,
> you will become egotistical.
> By eating moderately,
> you will achieve equanimity.
> By practicing moderation,
> the closed doors will be unbolted. (p. 116)

The following two poems are addressed directly to god in a manner that indicates Lalla's affinity for mysticism.

> When I was attached to the self,
> you remained hidden from me.
> Time passed as I searched for you.
> When I saw you within –
> you and I were united
> in ecstasy. (p. 65)

> You are the sky,
> and you are the earth.
> You are the day,
> the night and the wind.
> You are grain,
> sandalwood, flowers and water.
> You are everything –
> what should I offer you? (p. 71)

*Jaishree Kak, trans., *Mystical Verses of Lallā: A Journey of Self-Realization* (Delhi: Motilal Banarisdass Publishers, 2007), 50. Pages numbers listed for subsequent citations.

Widowhood

The death of a husband was a crisis for every Hindu wife, marking her entrance into the third stage of life: widowhood. As a result of the sometimes great disparity in the ages of husband and wife, men almost always predeceased their wives. Up until the nineteenth century, this crisis often meant a choice between two undesirable alternatives: **sati** or widowhood.

Sati

Sati, or *suttee*, is the ritual in which a wife burns alive on her husband's funeral pyre. Sometimes the ritual is called the "going with." According to the traditional beliefs of many Hindus, a woman who immolated herself at her husband's cremation was guaranteed great rewards for their family and an immediate opportunity to be with him in the next life. The place where a *sati* occurred was consecrated and often became an auspicious pilgrimage site (figure 6.5).

The term *sati* is taken from a mythic tale of Sati, one name for the wife of the great god Shiva. In the myth, Sati's own father snubs Shiva, and Sati responds with rage; in her anger, she bursts into flames and dies. When Shiva returns home, he finds her charred corpse and, in his grief, picks it up and carries it aimlessly all over India. As he wanders, parts of the goddess's remains fall to earth. At the locations where they fell, temples were later built to honor those sacred body parts. Today, one may find temples dedicated to Sati's remains throughout India. But for the "going forth" ritual, the theological import of Sati's story is most significant: her loyalty to her husband was so great that she was willing to die by fire rather than endure an insult to his dignity (figure 6.6).

This story was often told to suggest that a "good" wife would eagerly follow her husband in death. Yet there is great debate about the extent to which women actually chose this fate

Fig. 6.5 "A Hindoo Widow Burning Herself with the Corpse of Her Husband." This engraving by Frederic Shoberl depicts *sati*, a practice outlawed in the nineteenth century by the British. (Photo courtesy of http://commons.wikimedia.org/wiki/File:A_Hindoo_Widow_Burning_Herself_with_the_Corpse_of_her_Husband.jpg.)

Fig. 6.6 Shiva carrying Sati's corpse. Widow burning was often justified by appeal to the myth of Sati, the wife of Shiva. (Photo courtesy of http://en.wikipedia.org/wiki/File:Dakshayani.jpg.)

Widows

Perhaps some of the women who freely chose *sati* did so when they considered the alternative: the life of the widow. Because widowhood has been historically very difficult, some have suggested that even a grisly death might seem preferable to it. In general, Hindu widows did not remarry, although that practice was more a matter of custom than legislation. This observance has prevailed even into modern times, although in India's urban areas it is becoming more acceptable for widows to remarry. Often a widow was required to wear a white sari for the rest of her life; white is the color of mourning in South Asia. She was also sometimes expected to shave her head to make herself unattractive to men. At home, she was frequently given the hardest household tasks to perform and forbidden to eat with the rest of the family. She was viewed as dangerous, inauspicious, and unlucky, the embodiment of all negative qualities in women. She could not attend weddings or be around pregnant women and was subject to her sons, as Manu's laws prescribed. Some families reportedly took widows on "pilgrimage" to the holy city of Vrindavan, a city known for its large population of widows, and abandoned them there (figure 6.7). An estimate made in the year

for themselves. Strong evidence suggests that in many cases women were thrown onto the pyre against their will by their sons, other family members, or villagers. In other instances, women were drugged or intoxicated when they performed *sati*. The British outlawed *sati* during the nineteenth century, and since that time the ritual has become extremely rare. The most recent cases were reported in 1987 and in 2002.

Fig. 6.7 The "City of Widows." Many Hindu widows live together in small communities such as this one in Vrindavan, a town famous for its large number of widows. (Photo courtesy of the Women's United Nations Report Network.)

2000 indicated that there were 25 to 35 million widows in the Republic of India.

The life of the widow in general has not been a happy one. Numerous Hindu movements have arisen seeking to improve widows' lives, and these programs are apparently having positive effects. In fact, there are growing movements throughout India seeking to improve all areas of women's lives.

Lasting changes, however, cannot be made simply by decree. The vast majority of Hindus live in villages, and laws made in New Delhi and the provincial capitals can be hard to enforce. Changes in the established patterns of life for women and men, therefore, must be enacted at the local level. One popular manner of encour-aging the improvement of women's treatment in rural areas has been the performance of plays by traveling troupes. In brief skits, men and women act out domestic situations with the aim of improving the treatment of brides and widows.

Women's access to political power has also had a positive effect on the general treatment of women. Individuals such as Indira Gandhi, the late prime minister of India, and her daughter-in-law, Sonia Gandhi, stand as examples of suc-cessful women working in what has traditionally been a male realm (figure 6.8a,b). It is impor-tant to note that powerful women in politics are common throughout the subcontinent. Paki-stan, Bangladesh, and Sri Lanka have also had female prime ministers.

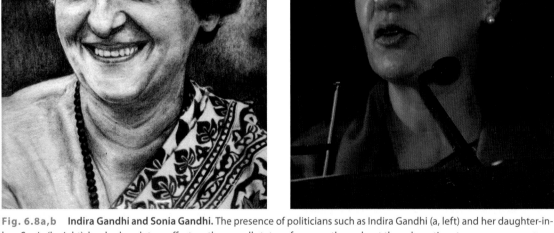

Fig. 6.8a,b **Indira Gandhi and Sonia Gandhi.** The presence of politicians such as Indira Gandhi (a, left) and her daughter-in-law, Sonia (b, right), has had a salutary effect on the overall status of women throughout the subcontinent. (A: Image courtesy of http://commons.wikimedia.org/wiki/File: Indira-Sapta.jpg. B: Photo courtesy of Creative Commons, copyright World Economic Forum/photo by Prabhas Roy.)

As these movements indicate, the roles of Hindu men and women are changing, more today than ever before in India's history. But social changes evolve slowly, and patterns of behavior are etched deeply in the soul of Hindu India. It will be important to see how these roles develop with the support and resistance they receive from traditional Hinduism.

◆ **KEY TERMS**

ashrama

bindi

brahmacarya

dowry

forest dweller/hermit

guru

householder

Lalla

sannyasa

sannyasin

sati

sindura

stridharma

upanayana

◆ **QUESTIONS FOR REVIEW**

1. Like caste, specific patterns of behavior for men and for women became a daily fact of life during the emergence of classical Hinduism. How do caste responsibilities and gender roles intersect to determine the expected stages of life for Hindus?

2. According to the Laws of Manu, what are the four *asramas*, or orders, that males ideally undergo? What are the three stages of life for women?

3. What roles do ritual and ceremony play in the transitions from one life stage to another?

4. How do the Indian and Western perspectives on marriage differ? How are they similar?

5. What is the Hindu household dynamic like throughout the various life stages for men and women?

◆ **QUESTIONS FOR FURTHER REFLECTION**

1. What are the social and personal benefits to envisioning the final stage of life as one of renunciation?

2. Are there advantages to making marriage a family decision rather than simply an individual one?

3. What are the possible benefits of a learning environment in which students cannot criticize their teachers? What are the benefits of a learning environment in which students are encouraged to be critical of their teacher's lessons?

4. How does the Hindu concept of feminine purity and "auspiciousness" compare to Western religious and cultural views on female sexuality?

5. Many religious traditions encourage a life of renunciation. What are the possible spiritual benefits of living outside of normal society, regardless of faith?

◆ **FOR FURTHER STUDY**

Bumiller, Elisabeth. *May You Be the Mother of a Hundred Sons: A Journey among the Women of India*. New York: Random House, 1990.

Daniélou, Alain, trans. *The Complete Kama Sutra*. Rochester, Vt.: Park Street Press, 1994.

Desai, Neera, and Maithreyi Krishnaraj. *Women and Society in India*. Delhi: Ajanta, 1990.

Hawley, John Stratton, ed. *Sati, the Blessing and the Curse*. New York: Oxford University Press, 1994.

Leslie, Julia, ed. *Roles and Rituals for Hindu Women*. Rutherford, N.J.: Fairleigh Dickinson University Press, 1991.

Narasimhan, Sakuntala. *Sati: Widow Burning in India*. New York: Anchor, 1990.

Water. DVD. Directed by Deepa Mehta. Toronto: Mongrel Media, 2006.

PART III

PATHS
TO LIBERATION

7. The Way of Action

PREVIEW

In the classical era, Hindus defined the fundamental problem of existence as samsara, the cycle of continual transmigrations of the self. As Hindu history unfolded, three traditions emerged as ways to reckon with this problem. This chapter focuses on the first of the three ways, the path of action; subsequent chapters will cover the other two. The path of action may be the most important religious discipline for the majority of Hindus. The principal feature of this form of spirituality is the performance of meritorious religious deeds, including rituals, festivals, and pilgrimage, with the central aim of improving future births.

In previous chapters, we discussed some of the principal developments of the classical period. We examined the elements of caste and gender and their impact on the order of Hindu life. Prior to that, we discussed the ideas of samsara, or transmigration of the self, and karma, the law of cause and effect. It is time now to return to the problem of samsara and begin our examination of how Hindus seek to address it. It was essential for us first to develop a clearer understanding of caste and gender, because they impinge on the ways individual Hindus live the spiritual life and seek liberation from the samsaric world.

Samsara as Problem

According to Hindu understanding, transmigration and the law of karma do not simply describe the way things are. Together, they also constitute the central problem of life, the existential situation that must ultimately be addressed. It is crucial to understand that Hindus regard reincarnation as undesirable in the final analysis. Many outside the Indian religious world think of reincarnation in a positive light, perhaps because they think rebirth constitutes a form of immortality. A Western perfume company, Guerlain, even markets a fragrance called Samsara, which it advertises as "a timeless fulfillment." It is not clear whether that slogan reflects mere ignorance or an actual optimistic understanding of the idea of reincarnation, but Hindus would in no wise think of samsara in such terms. Samsara is the realm of suffering, sorrow, and ennui. The idea that one might continue wandering in the samsaric world for an eternity is absolutely horrifying. Imagine having to repeat junior high school over and over again! This ominous view was intimated, as we noted previously, in earlier philosophers' uneasy contemplations of the possibility of redeath. Far from being a form of immortality, Hindus consider reincarnation as the perpetual experience of mortality.

The idea of rebirth might be appealing if we imagine that we return to this existence with the privileged status that many of us currently enjoy. Constant transmigration might then be viewed as a wonderful opportunity to experience and learn everything the world has to offer. Samsara, however, involves the possibility of returning to life in unpleasant or unwanted forms. Many living things—both human and animal—experience great suffering; their lives are "poore, nasty, brutish, and short," to quote the philosopher Thomas Hobbes.[1] Yet even if we were to come back continually to a life of privilege and pleasure, we would eventually find that routine tedious and distasteful. Forever is a long, long time.

The *Trimarga*

The ultimate goal of Hinduism is to gain one's freedom from samsara. The Hindus call this achievement **moksha**, which means "release" or "liberation." Attaining *moksha* is what each of us must do in this lifetime or the next—or a hundred thousand lifetimes from now. Over time, we will all tire of samsara and muster the discipline it takes to break free from it.

Although *moksha* is the ultimate aim of all Hindus, many Hindus are not primarily concerned with attaining it in *this* life. *Moksha* is often a distant objective, something that is best pursued in another birth. The concerns of this life are demanding enough; there are many needs that require attention in this world.

For most Indians, just getting their daily rice consumes the greater part of the day. Even those who do not struggle with mere subsistence have good reason to let final liberation be the concern of a future life. According to the dynamics of dharma and karma, properly attending to one's obligations in this life puts one in a better position in the next. A better rebirth makes the pursuit of *moksha* much easier. Although it is the ultimate objective, one need not devote this life exclusively to seeking *moksha*.

The Hindu traditions speak of **four goods of life**: the good of dharma, or duty; the good of *artha*, or wealth; the good of *kama*, or pleasure; and *moksha*. Each of these constitutes a valuable, worthwhile aim. It is good to do one's duty, to live in material abundance, and to enjoy the many pleasures life has to offer. All of these things can be pursued while generating meritorious karma and avoiding evil karma. As long as the pursuit of pleasure and wealth occur within one's moral obligations and dharma, these aspects of life are karmically positive.

Moksha, however, is a different matter. It is not just one of the four goods of Hindu life; it is also the summum bonum, the highest good. Consequently, to gain liberation from samsara, one must be willing to forsake the other three goods. The reason for this is simple. Even though doing one's duty and pursuing wealth and pleasure are viewed positively, they nonetheless keep one bound to the wheel of rebirth. Generating good karma will most certainly improve one's station in future lives, but karma—even good karma—binds a person to samsara. For those who are not yet prepared to abandon a life of duty, material acquisition, and enjoyments—as most householders are not—the religious life means doing one's best to improve this life and the next.

Beginning with this chapter, we will undertake an exploration of the ways in which Hindus seek ultimate liberation. Given the Hindu appreciation of plurality, it is not surprising that there is not one prescribed path to ultimate freedom, but many. Three traditions have emerged as ways to live the spiritual life. Collectively, these spiritualities are known as the **Trimarga,** which literally means "the three paths." (The term *marga* is a common word in India, often used to designate streets or avenues [box 7.1].) In the final analysis, however, the paths to *moksha* are many more than three. Because there are endless permutations of these basic pathways and much overlap among them, liberation comes in an astonishing variety of ways.

The *Trimarga* is really a typology that categorizes certain emphases within the Hindu traditions. The three paths are the **karma-marga**, or the way of action; the **jñana-marga**, or the way of knowledge; and the **bhakti-marga**, the way of devotion. Because Hindus understand that different people have different characteristics and are at different stages in their spiritual journeys, these three paths are considered to provide suitable spiritualities for different kinds of persons. Sri Ramakrishna

(1836–1886), the nineteenth-century mystic from Bengal, explains this attitude in a domestic image:

> You must know that there are different tastes. There are also different powers of digestion. God has made different religions and creeds to suit different aspirants. . . . The mother brings home a fish for her children. She curries part of the fish, part she fries, and with another part she makes pilau. By no means can all digest the pilau. So she makes fish soup for those who have weak stomachs. Further, some want pickled or fried fish. There are different temperaments. There are differences in the capacity to comprehend.[2]

Those whose personalities are oriented toward the will or volition may find the way of action most appealing. Those who are disposed toward a life of the mind and contemplation may gravitate to the way of knowledge. Those whose lives are characterized by strong emotion and passions may be attracted to the way of devotion. But since most people do not fit squarely within a single type, an ordinary Hindu will often incorporate elements of each pathway in his or her daily life or at different times during the course of his or her life.

Box 7.1 *MARGA* **AND YOGA**

The word *yoga* is often used interchangeably with *marga* to describe the spiritual pathways. The term *yoga*, which many in the West identify with a specialized form of physical yoga known as hatha or asana yoga, means "discipline" or "regimen" and derives from the Sanskrit root that means "yoke." The meaning of *yoga* is much broader than simply the discipline of practicing postures; it involves all manner of practices relating to one's spiritual well-being, including meditation, fasting, ascetic practices, ethical behavior, and study. All these things might be suggested by the word *yoga* as Hindus understand it. (See also box 12.6 on page 186.)

Rituals

We have already discussed how individuals might improve their rebirths by following dharma, the moral law prescribed for one's caste and gender. Diligently doing one's duty is thus one component of the path of action. Let us now explore another component: meritorious religious activity. Our examination of this dimension of the karmic way will include consideration of ritual, festivals, and pilgrimage, all very prominent aspects of Hindu life. Sincere participation in these activities generates the merit that yields favorable future lives conducive to the attainment of *moksha*.

When we discussed the Vedic and Indus Valley traditions, we noted that some ritual practices of these cultures were forerunners of later Hindu rituals. As we study Hindu ritual, the influences of earlier Indian culture will become apparent. But now we observe how these rituals serve a different purpose. Prior to the classical period, rituals were used to obtain the goods that made this life more prosperous (*artha*) and enjoyable (*kama*). But after the transformations wrought by the Axial Age, rituals were understood also to assist in the fulfillment of one's obligations (dharma) and ultimately to enable final liberation from samsaric existence (*moksha*). Our study of ritual practices in this chapter will focus on two types: the personal rituals performed by individuals as part of their daily routine and the rites of passage associated with important moments as one proceeds from birth to death.

The Daily Round

Although most of the formal rules that govern the daily life of Hindus pertain mainly to upper-caste males, almost all Hindus practice daily personal rituals of some sort, depending on caste, family custom, and geographical region. A typical householder will follow a basic routine similar to this: he will rise before the sun and utter the name of his personal god, or ***ishta-devata***, before speaking to anyone. Then he touches the earth and bows to the images of the deities in his room. Virtually every Hindu home contains sacred images of gods and goddesses, particularly those to whom the inhabitants are most devoted (box 7.2).

The guidelines for daily ritual prescribe a morning bath, a precept that is widely observed. Besides serving the purposes of good hygiene, the bath removes the pollution that accumulates during the ordinary course of a day and puts one in proper condition for interacting with the divine. If a person bathes in the

Fig. 7.1 *Tarpana.* Offering libations of water is rooted in ancient rituals for honoring *devas* and ancestors. (Photo courtesy of Creative Commons, Steve Evans.)

Box 7.2 CHOOSING ONE'S GOD

Although the Hindu pantheon is theoretically infinite, in practice individual Hindus worship a very limited number of divinities. The deities selected for personal devotion ordinarily divide into three basic types.

First, there are spirits worshiped by all members of the community, which are called *grama-devatas*. These village goddesses (and occasionally gods) function as the guardians of particular communities. Although the *grama-devata* is manifested throughout her or his community, she or he is worshiped in a particular location in the community. In villages, these *devasthanas*, or sacred shrines, are usually located at a tree or a clump of trees, but other natural features such as earthen mounds, rocks, or bodies of water may also be the locus of worship. Generations of villagers may have worshiped at the same spot for hundreds or even thousands of years. Brahmin priests may preside over these village shrines, but usually lower-caste devotees themselves serve as the *pujaris*, the ones who conduct the *puja*. At the village level, non-Brahmin *pujaris* are often women.

Second are the deities associated with the family and ancestral home, known as the *kula-devatas*, which are thought to inhabit the family home and provide assistance to the clan. Rituals for revering the *kula-devatas* are passed down to children to maintain continuity of the family's connection to a deity.

Finally, and most important to the individual's spiritual practice, is the *ishta-devata*, one's personal favorite god. Children grow up worshiping the same gods or goddesses as their parents, but in their adolescence they frequently choose a divine figure they consider personally meaningful. The selection of a specific god to worship may be based on an affinity one feels for a *deva* or *devi* or on one's horoscope. A worshiper may find the powers or characteristics of a particular divine figure to be especially relevant to his or her needs. Students, for example, may turn to Sarasvati, the patron of education and the arts. Individuals may find aspects of the mythology surrounding a deity to be compelling or intriguing. Or they may simply choose to continue in the worship of the divine manifestation with which they are most familiar. Gender is usually not a consideration in the choice of one's personal deity. Generally, men are as likely to worship goddesses as they are to worship gods, and women are as likely to worship gods as goddesses. Additionally, decisions about one's *ishta-devata* are not necessarily lifelong. As a person ages or matures spiritually, he or she may find another god or goddess more relevant to his or her life.

river, as many do, she or he scoops up water in folded hands and releases it back into the river while reciting mantras to please the deities and ancestors, a practice called **tarpana** (figure 7.1). Afterward, the worshiper applies colored paste in a forehead marking (*tilak*) indicating devotion to a particular god or religious community.

These markings are important; without them, rituals are considered ineffective.

Following the bath, the householder recites a morning prayer, usually an ancient poem from the *Rig-Veda* known as the **gayatri-mantra**. This prayer is repeated daily by millions of Hindus. The invocation is followed by hymns, readings from sacred texts, and the worship of one's chosen deities. Worship might involve burning incense, lying prostrate, and waving flames of burning camphor before images of the gods. Collectively, these activities of worship are known as **puja**. The specific forms of *puja* are prescribed by each religious community. These rituals are extremely significant, and we will study them in more detail when we discuss Hindu theism in theory and practice (chapter 9). The morning rituals are followed by similar but less elaborate rites at noon and in the evening, thus completing the daily round (box 7.3).

The Rites of Passage

The various communities of the Hindu traditions, like all cultures, celebrate and ritualize

---

Box 7.3   **THE *GAYATRI-MANTRA***

The *gayatri-mantra* comes from the *Rig-Veda* (3.62.10) and was often used during *shrauta* rituals. It was also shared with boys as part of their initiation into the twice-born. Originally part of the daily religious practice for Brahmin males, it is now widely recited by Hindus of both sexes and all castes and traditions. The mantra is chanted in the original Sanskrit, transliterated as:

> *tat savitur varenyam*
>
> *bhargo devasya dhimahi*
>
> *dhiyo yo nah pracodayat*

A rather literal translation of the recitation was made by Ralph T. H. Griffith in 1896*:

> May we attain that excellent glory of Savitar the god:
>
> So may he stimulate our prayers.*

A less literal rendering is:

> Let us contemplate the radiance of the sun,
>
> the glory of the divine,
>
> and may it inspire our thoughts.

The mantra is usually preceded by the *Prāvnava aum* and a Sanskrit formula that literally means "earth, air, heaven" (the components of the Vedic *triloka*).

This ancient and well-known mantra is addressed to Savitar (or Savitr), a Vedic deity associated with the sun at sunrise and sunset. (At other times the sun is usually known as Surya.) Other *gayatri-mantras* may be addressed to other divine beings, such as Shiva or Devi. The deeper meaning of the mantra is the subject of many commentaries.

*Ralph T. H. Griffith, trans., *The Rig Veda* 3.62.10 (available at http://www.sacred-texts.com/hin/rigveda/rv03062.htm).

the moments of transition in an individual's life. These events, however, are more than just personal celebrations. They also allow the entire community to recognize and facilitate the significant life changes that each of its members undergoes. Rites of passage help individuals negotiate the transition from one state of being to another and provide an opportunity for the community to express and celebrate its solidarity.

Hindus mark life's stages with a series of ceremonies known as *samskaras*, or sacraments. Some Hindu communities observe as many as sixteen different *samskaras*, but others observe considerably fewer. Virtually all Hindus, however, ritually mark what are considered the most significant turning points in life: birth, initiation, marriage, and death.

Birth and Childhood

The rituals of birth include *samskaras* that are celebrated before and after the child arrives. Birth, like death, is an event that is highly polluting and susceptible to the influence of malevolent forces. To mitigate the impact of evil influences, some Hindus conduct a "parting of the hair" ritual to ensure a safe and healthy pregnancy. In this rite, the husband parts his wife's hair and applies red powder (*kum-kum*) to protect her and the child from wicked spirits. After the child is born, he or she is given a ritual bath and *aum*, the sacred syllable, is inscribed on his or her tongue with honey.

Ten days after the child is born, a naming ceremony (**namkaran**) is conducted by a Brahmin priest. The ten days after birth is a period of impurity. The naming ritual marks the end of this time of uncleanness. During the ceremony there is a great deal of singing and chanting. The child's astrological horoscope is also prepared for this event. The horoscope will be

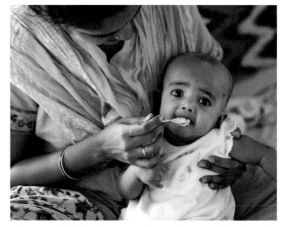

Fig. 7.2   First rice. The first taking of solid food is a rite of passage in many Hindu communities. (Photo courtesy of Creative Commons, Srinayan Puppala.)

consulted many times throughout the child's life, especially as he or she approaches marriage. When the child is about six months old, another *samskara* is often observed to celebrate the first taking of solid food, usually a mixture of rice, honey, and ghee (figure 7.2). Even the first haircut, when the child is about three, is frequently the occasion for a ritual.

Initiation

Initiation usually occurs before a child reaches the teen years. We have already discussed the initiation of upper-caste boys, marking their second birth and entrance into studenthood (chapter 6). In this ceremony, the boy receives the sacred thread (*yajñopavītam*) comprised of three cotton strands representing god, parents, and guru. He will wear a sacred thread for the rest of his life, exchanging it for a new one each year. While the orthodox traditions of the Brahmins do not prescribe an initiation for girls, many Hindu communities do in fact celebrate a girl's passage to womanhood with a menstruation rite, often consisting of a period of seclusion, a ritual bath, and a feast. Some

Hindus are now making the sacred thread, traditionally reserved for male initiations, a component of girls' rites of passage as well.

Marriage Rituals

Betrothal and wedding rituals signify what many Hindus consider the most important rite of passage in life. In our examination of the life cycles of men and women, we introduced these ceremonies. Wedding rites are always grand (and usually expensive) events and are celebrated in diverse ways throughout India, with each region contributing its own distinctive elements. Most ceremonies, though, are conducted by a priest and involve the exchange of flower garlands followed by the *saptapadi* (figure 7.3), the circumambulation of a sacred fire, an ancient ritual dating back to the Vedic period (box 7.4).

Although the actual marriage ritual, known as *vivah*, lasts only a few hours, the entire wedding celebration may last for several days both before and after the *vivah* ceremony. During

Fig. 7.3 **Saptapadi.** Most Hindu weddings involve the circumambulation of an altar of fire, a tradition that dates back to the Vedic era. (Photo courtesy of Lorena Mena, http://www .flickr.com/photos/22721465@N02/. Used by permission.)

Box 7.4 **THE *SAPTAPADI***

It is customary for a bride and groom to seal their marriage by walking together around an altar of fire as they invoke seven wishes for the well-being of themselves, their families, and the entire world. This practice, known as the *saptapadi*—literally, the "seven steps"—is a ritual that has been practiced in India for thousands of years, dating back to the Vedic period. By taking these steps, the couple participates in a procession of generations that stretches back to humanity's earliest recollections. The *saptapadi* is considered by most Hindus to be the most important element of the wedding ritual.

The rite is conducted in different ways in different parts of South Asia. In some locations, the couple walks around the altar seven times; in other places, they take seven steps to complete a single circumambulation. At each step or circuit, they make specific prayers or take specific vows. The content of the prayers or vows also varies from tradition to tradition. In general, they include wishes for an abundance of food and material comforts; peaceful and healthy lives; the development of their spiritual qualities; the welfare of their children; a relationship of mutual love, respect, and trust; the longevity of the marriage; and blessings for all beings throughout the universe.

this time, there is much singing, dancing, and feasting.

Funerals

The final *samskara* in any Hindu's life is the funeral. Because death carries high potential for pollution, extreme care must be taken by those closest to the deceased. The surviving family members usually fast until after the funeral, and the household gods are often removed from the home.

Cremation is by far the most common way of disposing of bodily remains. Only the bodies of very young children and members of small, atypical sects are buried in the earth rather than burned. The remains of *sannyasins*—the wandering ascetics—are usually committed to the river.

Ordinarily, funeral rites begin almost immediately after a person dies. After the body is washed, anointed with sandalwood oil, and wrapped in cloth, it is taken by a procession to the cremation grounds. Funeral processions are a common sight throughout India. The body is conveyed on a bier or bullock cart and surrounded with flower garlands. There is usually no coffin, so the body is not hidden from view.

At the burning grounds, usually located near a river or other body of water, Dalits take charge of the cremation. If near a sacred river, such as the Ganges, the corpse is immersed for purification and then placed on a pyre of wood with the feet pointing southward, the direction of Yama, the king of death (figure 7.4). The cremation fire is usually lit by the eldest son, who prays to the fire god Agni to transport

Fig. 7.4 Cremations. Open-air cremation is by far the most common form of funeral among Hindus. At this cremation site in Nepal, the rituals of death are fully integrated into daily life. Mourners, at the far left, have shaven their heads and dressed in white. (Photo: Mark W. Muesse.)

the deceased to heaven, the place of the ancestors. The ceremony must be conducted in the proper fashion to ensure that the spirit makes the transition safely. That the cremation ritual emphasizes sending the self to the ancestors rather than to its rebirth reflects the Vedic origins of these funeral customs. When the corpse has been reduced to its elemental forms, the ashes and unburned portions of the body are committed to the river. Since wood is scarce in India, funerals can be expensive. In some localities, the unburned body of a poor person may be simply cast into the river to decompose.

After the cremation, the family members turn and, without looking back at the pyre, go to take a purifying bath and return home. They often shave their heads as part of the purification process. The home is then thoroughly cleaned, and the images of the gods are returned to their customary place in the house. The last rites, however, continue even after the cremation. Additional rituals take place for many days, weeks, and months after the cremation. These ceremonies, known as *shraddha* rites, often involve offerings of rice cakes and water and the recitation of mantras for the soul's safe journey. They also serve the purpose of allowing the survivors to remember the deceased, express their gratitude to him or her, and grieve.

Festivals

Virtually every day of the year, a major festival is being celebrated somewhere in India, and Hindus celebrate their festivals exuberantly (box 7.5). Keeping track of the innumerable Hindu feasts is an impossible task. The multitude of Hindu festivals is largely due to the multitude of Hindu gods. If every god and

goddess were honored with a feast, the Hindus would do nothing but celebrate holidays! It does not happen that way, of course, since Hindus usually observe only the occasions associated with their personal and family deities, the deities connected to the place they live, and the deities who govern areas of particular concern to the devotee, such as business, education, or health. But even when limited to these gods and goddesses, there are a considerable number of festivals to celebrate. The abundance of holidays is also related to the fact that the great majority of Hindus still reside in small villages. Approximately 80 percent of all Indians live in half a million villages throughout India. Festivals are important events that integrate the local community and define the social practices of its residents. These occasions also help express and establish the bond between villagers and their gods and goddesses.

Given the great number and variety of Hindu festivals, there is simply no way to say anything meaningful that applies to them all. Let us, therefore, consider two especially popular holidays rather than generalizing about all of them. Since most festivals are regional rather than pan-Hindu, we will examine celebrations from different areas of the subcontinent: **Holi** and **Thai Pongal**.

Holi

Holi may be the most important Hindu celebration in North and Central India; it is certainly the most colorful. In fact, it is often called the Festival of Colors. South Indians generally do not observe Holi.

According to one explanation, the festival of Holi celebrates the god Vishnu's triumph over a demon named Holika. There are, how-

Box 7.5 **A SELECT LIST OF HINDU FESTIVALS**

The following list represents only a sampling of the many Hindu celebrations occurring on a periodic basis. Some festivals, such as Divali, are celebrated for several different reasons.

Festival	Time (Gregorian calendar)	Occasion
Thai Pongal	January 14–15	Harvest
Holi (Festival of Colors)	February–March	Spring renewal
Mahashivaratri	February–March	Shiva's favorite night
Sri Rama Navami	April	Birthday of Rama
Mahalakshmi Vrata	July–August	Married women's celebration of Laksmi
Raksabandhana	July–August	Renewing bonds between brothers and sisters
Sri Krishna Jayanti	August–September	Birthday of Krishna
Kumbha Mela	July–August, every four years	Pilgrimage to one of four cities on the Ganges River (Allahabad, Haridwar, Ujjain, Nashik)
Ganesha-Chaturthi	August–September	Honoring Ganesha
Durga Puja/Navaratri/Dassara	September–October	Honoring Shakti
Divali/Deepavali (Festival of Lights)	October–November	Harvest, Laksmi, and the triumph of good over evil

ever, other beliefs about the holiday's origin. Some Hindus think the festival honors the youthful pranks of the roguish god Krishna. Another account explains the festival as a spring celebration marking the coming of the new year and the return of life after the dead of winter. That a single holiday has many different stories about its origin typifies the Hindu embrace of diversity.

During Holi, conventional rules of caste, social standing, and gender are relaxed. The day's activities include playfully throwing colored water and powder at passersby, scream-ing obscenities, and drinking bhang-water, a concoction of cannabis extract and sweetened milk. During this festival, Brahmins might find themselves jokingly attacked by members of lower castes, men might find themselves dressed in saris and wearing makeup, and a poor woman might berate her landlord. Humiliation is heaped on those who rule the roost during the rest of the year. Even strict vegetarians might eat a piece of meat on this day. To a culture with many social restrictions, Holi offers an opportunity to forget them momentarily (figure 7.5).

Fig. 7.5 **The Festival of Colors.** During Holi, revelers throw colored powders and water at one another. (Photo: FaceMePLS/Flickr. [Creative Commons Attribution 2.0 License]. Used by permission.)

The revelry of Holi follows a pattern found throughout the world's religions. Mircea Eliade, the great twentieth-century scholar of comparative religion, observed that New Year's celebrations are often understood to be cosmic re-creations. As Eliade put it, the creation of a new year is tantamount to the creation of a new world.[3] Consequently, the festivities associated with the advent of a new year frequently follow the pattern of cosmogenesis: the old world is dissolved, reduced to its basic components before it can be re-created and given new structure. This same pattern is reflected in the traditional Hindu belief that Shiva dissolves the universe when it has become decrepit and is no longer sustainable. Then the creator god Brahma shapes a new world out of the elements of the old, reestablishing order amid chaos. In a similar fashion, Holi—and similar holidays throughout the world—enacts and celebrates the moment of chaos, the dissolution of structures prior to the new year, when order is reinstituted. Throughout the parts of India where Holi is celebrated, great bonfires burn, symbolizing for some the consumption of the old year and old world before the arrival of the new. At the same time, others interpret the fire as representing the cremation of the demon Holika.

Thai Pongal

The festival of **Thai Pongal** is a harvest celebration observed chiefly in South India and Sri Lanka by Tamils. Coming in the month of Thai, this holiday coincides with *Makar Sankranti*, an astrologically significant event recognized and honored throughout India. *Makar Sankranti* marks the winter solstice, according to an ancient Hindu reckoning. Thai Pongal is the only major Hindu festival based on the movements of the sun rather than the moon. It is celebrated on a fixed date, January 14 or 15, according to the Gregorian calendar.

Thai Pongal, like the American Thanksgiving holiday, celebrates the traditional end of the farming season. Worshipers express gratitude to Surya, the sun god, whose ministrations have been responsible for the year's bounty. Before the celebration, homes are given a scrupulous cleaning and old, useless items are gathered up to be burned in evening bonfires. The homes are then painted and decorated with colorful **kolams**, the freehand geometrical designs drawn by South Indian women using rice flour and other powders (figure 7.6). These designs are believed to invite prosperity into the home.

On the day of the celebration, the central ritual of the holiday is enacted at sunrise. In homes and temples throughout the region, sweetened mixtures of newly harvested rice and milk are boiled in new clay or brass pots and allowed to bubble up and spill over. (The word *Pongal* derives from the Tamil word *pongu*, which means "boiling over.") At the moment the hot liquid bubbles over, a conch shell is blown. Watching the mixture brim over the pot is considered especially auspicious and lucky. The overflow symbolizes the wish for an abundance of food and material comforts during the coming year. The milk rice is then offered to Surya in thanksgiving for his generosity and then consumed by members of the family as **prashad**, or sacred food. Other foods that were prepared in advance are also served and eaten. During the rest of the day, celebrants usually visit one another's homes, exchanging good wishes for a prosperous year, and gifts are often given to children.

During the two days immediately after Pongal Day, the festivities continue with a variety of activities. In the rural parts of the state of Tamil Nadu, cattle are bathed; decorated with flower garlands, bells, and colorful powders such as turmeric and *kum-kum*; and given Pongal rice to eat. These rituals honor the cattle that help cultivate the fields and provide sustenance throughout the year. It is also customary for girls and young women to prepare meals of rice and vegetables on banana leaves and offer them as a feast for the crows. The girls offer prayers for the well-being of their brothers and ask that their relationships as siblings remain strong, just as the crows maintain strong familial ties. These days are also times for family reunions, outings to parks, and other forms of relaxation.

Fig. 7.6　*Kolam.* Temporary designs such as this are made daily by women and girls to attract prosperity and good fortune to the home. (Photo courtesy of Creative Commons, Ranveig Thattai.)

Pilgrimage

As a final topic in this exploration of the *karma-marga*, we turn to the practice of pilgrimage (**yatra**). Just as there are many and varied festivals throughout India, so too are there many and varied pilgrimage sites. On any given day, millions of Indians are making their way to them.

Pilgrimage is an important and widely practiced aspect of the Hindu traditions, not only because pilgrimage is religiously meritorious but because India itself is holy. It is difficult to overestimate the importance of India itself for Hindus. India is the Holy Land, as sacred to Hindus as Israel is to Jews or Makkah and Madinah are to Muslims. For this reason, Hindus often refer to Bharat Mata, Mother India. Pilgrimage to the sacred places in India brings one closer to the divine and purifies the soul.

While the whole of India is sacred, certain sites are especially holy. At these locations the presence of the divine is more apparent than other places. The town of Mathura, for instance, is the birthplace of the god Krishna. The River Ganges is not only a sacred body of water but also the physical manifestation of a goddess. Bathing in the Ganges is one of the most auspicious acts a Hindu can perform. The city of Varanasi, or Banaras, on the Ganges is especially holy; many dying persons travel to this most sacred of cities, hoping to expire there (figure 7.7). Mount Kailash in the Himalayas is the heavenly home of the deities Shiva and Parvati (figure 7.8). Intrepid pilgrims make the 15,000-foot ascent to its base. No one attempts to climb the peak, out of deference to its religious significance, but circumambulating it is considered meritorious by Hindus as well as Buddhists, Jains, and practitioners of Bön, the indigenous religion of Tibet. Like Mt. Kailash, Kataragama in southeastern Sri Lanka is a pilgrimage site for the faithful of many religious traditions, not just Hindus. Hindus and Buddhists journey to this city to worship at the

Fig. 7.7 **Varanasi.** Varanasi on the Ganges River is considered the most sacred of cities. Pilgrims flock here, many with the hope of dying in this auspicious place. (Photo: Mark W. Muesse.)

Fig. 7.8 **Mt. Kailash.** Situated in the Himalayas, Mt. Kailash is sacred to Hindus, Buddhists, Jains, and the practitioners of Bön. Shiva is believed to reside here when he practices austerities. Although it is considered too holy to climb, many devotees circumambulate it as part of their pilgrimage. (Photo courtesy of Creative Commons, Ondřej Žváček.)

shrine of Murugan, a son of Shiva and Parvati. For Hindus, Murugan is a favorite deity of common folk and a god who never fails to come to the aid of his devotees. For Buddhists, he is known as Kataragama Deviyo, the divine patron of Buddhism. Interestingly, Kataragama is also a sacred site for Muslims, who take pilgrimage to worship at the mosque located within the confines of Murugan's temple complex.

Making the arduous journey to view these sacred sites is an activity that brings great spiritual benefit. Pilgrims often shave their heads and wear special clothing to mark their passage to a sacred place. They frequently travel in groups to the pilgrimage site, where they take *darshan*—a viewing—of the sacred place.

In this chapter, we have discussed *karma-marga*, the way of action, a fundamental mode of spiritual life for most Hindus. The way of action is an avenue for generating positive karma by following dharma and fulfilling religious obligations and opportunities. The *karma-marga* is a way steadily to improve one's place in life, over the course of many lifetimes, until one is in a position that is especially favorable for realizing *moksha*. In the next chapters, we turn to the ways the Hindu traditions offer for those who are ready to achieve final liberation from samsara.

◆ KEY TERMS

bhakti-marga

darshan

four goods of life

gayatri-mantra

Holi

ishta-devata

jñana-marga

karma-marga

kolam

moksha

namkaran

prashad

puja

samskara

saptapadi

shraddha

tarpana

Thai Pongal

Trimarga

yatra

◆ QUESTIONS FOR REVIEW

1. Why is samsara the "central problem of life" for Hindus?

2. What are the three paths of the *Trimarga*?

3. Why do most Hindus choose the path of action, even though following the *karma-marga* will keep one bound to the cycle of reincarnation?

4. What are the four goods of Hindu tradition? What are the consequences of pursuing each of these goods?

5. How can attending religious festivals and making pilgrimages garner positive karma?

◆ QUESTIONS FOR FURTHER REFLECTION

1. What is the value of continuing to observe rituals associated with the life of a deceased individual well after his or her funeral?

2. Why might the Western perspective on reincarnation be much more idealistic than the Hindu belief in samsara?

3. What social and cultural functions are served by marking life transitions with ceremony?

4. Do worldly obligations and pleasures inherently hinder spirituality?

◆ FOR FURTHER STUDY

Daniélou, Alain. *Virtue, Success, Pleasure, Liberation: The Four Aims of Life in the Tradition of Ancient India.* Rochester, Vt.: Inner Traditions International, 1993.

Eck, Diana L. *Banaras: City of Light.* New York: Columbia University Press, 1998.

Huyler, Stephen P. *Meeting God: Elements of Hindu Devotion.* New Haven, Conn.: Yale University Press, 1999.

8. The Way of Knowledge

PREVIEW

The way of knowledge is rooted in the philosophical speculation and ascetic experimentation of the early classical period in Hindu history. This spirituality came to focus on discovering the true essence of the human being and the fundamental principle of the whole of reality. The Upanishads, the collection of texts in which this path was first recorded, declare that to know the human essence is to know absolute reality. On this basic vision was founded not only a discipline for liberation, but also a powerful philosophical perspective that deeply influenced many of the Hindu traditions.

The way of knowledge, the second component of the *Trimarga*, is an austere and demanding discipline. It is not the path to liberation that most Hindus choose to follow. Yet it encompasses a vision of reality that has profoundly influenced the religious outlook of almost all Hindus and provides the metaphysical foundation for many Hindu traditions. In this chapter, we will examine the historical dynamics that contributed to the development of this spirituality and the seminal text in which its philosophical and theological elements are set forth. We will discover how a special understanding of the self and world is believed to confer freedom from the incessant turnings of the wheel of samsara. We will also explore some ways this knowledge has been interpreted philosophically and some of the practices that have been employed to realize it.

The Quest for Liberating Knowledge

The path of knowledge was first articulated in northern India during the classical period, particularly the years 800 to 400 B.C.E. This was an era of rapid material and spiritual transformation, especially in the area surrounding the Ganges River. New cities and towns were established throughout the numerous small republics and kingdoms of the region. Farming and commerce flourished, and many people came to enjoy greater prosperity. Modern historians consider this period the "most decisive phase for the development of Indian culture."[1] It was certainly decisive for Indian religion.

As we discussed in chapter 4, this was a time when traditional religious practices and beliefs were reassessed. The Brahmins and the rituals they performed no longer enjoyed the same prestige they had in the Vedic period. For some Indians, even the Vedas were no longer sacrosanct. The concepts of transmigration and karma had been introduced and accepted throughout the subcontinent. With traditional religious doctrines in question and conventional social structures in flux, conditions were conducive to the sort of spiritual experimentation that came to characterize the age.

The Renouncer Movement

In response to this ferment, many individuals abandoned their homes, families, and jobs to seek solutions to the new religious and philosophical questions that now seemed so urgent. This extensive movement of renouncers, who were called **shramanas**, or "strivers," included men and women of all ages and castes, but it especially attracted male Brahmins and Kshatriyas in the later stages of life. Owning no more than a change of clothes and a bowl for begging food—and often less—they typically wandered from place to place, living the "life gone forth," from the home to homelessness. Occasionally, they might settle for a while to live alone in a cave or to join an **ashram**, or ascetic community. The *shramanas* believed that they could not find final liberation from samsara while attending to their familial and social obligations. One individual who left his home to join this movement of *moksha*-seekers described his decision this way, many years after the fact:

> Household life is crowded and dusty; [but] life gone forth is wide open. It is not easy, while living in a home, to lead the holy life utterly perfect and pure as a polished shell.

[So I said to myself:] Suppose I shave off my hair and beard, put on the [orange] robe, and go forth from the home life into homelessness.[2]

We hear in these words a note of discontent with domestic existence and perhaps with the burgeoning new culture. But we also detect a yearning for high adventure, the desire for a complete life that very few persons ever dare to try. Those who joined the strivers did so not merely to escape a world they found abhorrent, but because they saw in renunciation their only hope for a life of freedom and fulfillment. Although the ordinary world as we know it is a vale of tears, they thought that by perfecting the spiritual life, they might conquer the samsaric realm and enjoy greater bliss. That was the conclusion of the individual who left his home because it was cramped and dirty—the man who was later known as the Buddha.

Without the encumbrances of domestic and social life, the *shramanas* were free to dedicate their energies to finding life's summum bonum. As they wandered the forests and solitary places of northern India, they often sought out gurus to teach them new doctrines and practices. The Buddha himself followed this pattern before striking out to seek liberation on his own. It was during this period that many of the spiritual disciplines commonly associated with Indian religion were refined: meditation (box 8.1), hatha yoga, and the countless varieties of self-denial and self-mortification, from fasting and celibacy to standing for extended periods on one leg and lying on beds of nails. Teachers of these disciplines and doctrines frequently competed with one another for the allegiance of students and lay followers. Debates were held; conversations became heated and rivalries were common. Often, this competitiveness seemed anything but spiritual or enlightened. But the intensity and spirited energy of these times also underscored the profound importance and urgency of the quest.

Shramanas and Householders

The householders who retained their places in society were very much aware of these homeless ascetics and sages. They were a common sight in the villages and towns. Often householders sought them out for advice and lessons for living. So large and familiar was this countercultural movement that the *shrama-* *nas* were practically regarded as a caste unto themselves.

The relationship between the *shramanas* and the ordinary householders became quite symbiotic. The holy men and women relied on the support of ordinary folk to make their quests for liberation possible. And providing food, clothing, and shelter to the renouncers allowed laypeople to gain merit for a better rebirth. The common householder might help the *shramanas* in this life, knowing that in a future lifetime others would help her in her effort to attain *moksha*. This mutually beneficial

---

Box 8.1 **HOW TO MEDITATE**

In the Bhagavad Gita, the god Krishna instructs the warrior Arjuna on the practice of yogic concentration, or meditation:

The yogi should absorb
the self constantly in yoga,
remaining in secrecy,
Alone, with thought
and self subdued,
without cravings and
free from all possessiveness.

There, having the mind actively
focused upon a single point,
with thought and
sense activity controlled,
Sitting on a seat,
one should practice yoga
for purification of the self.

without looking about
in any direction;
With the self quieted,
with fear dissipated,
established in
a vow of chastity;
Controlling the mind
with thought

In a clean place,
one should establish
for oneself a firm seat.
Neither too high nor too low,
made of kusha grass, then
covered with deerskin and cloth.

With an aligned body,
head, and neck—
keeping these steady,
without movement;
Focusing the vision toward
the tip of one's nose

focused upon me—
one should be seated
while absorbed in yoga,
holding me as the highest.*

In this teaching, Lord Krishna directs his student to concentrate attention on god. Other forms of meditation offer nearly identical instructions but alter the concentrative focus. The breath, a mandala or *yantra* (abstract sacred images), a mantra, or the *pravnava aum* might also serve as the center of awareness.

*Graham M. Schweig, trans., *Bhagavad Gītā: The Beloved Lord's Secret Love Song*, 6.10–14 (San Francisco: HarperSanFrancisco, 2007), 94–95.

relationship consolidated an important difference in the respective religious orientations of the *shramanas* and the householders. The *shramanas* sought *moksha* in this very lifetime. But the householders could not afford to devote their energies to the pursuit of final liberation and chose to postpone that endeavor until a later lifetime, when circumstances would favor it. In the meantime, the householder's religious goal was to improve future rebirths by accumulating positive karma.

Liberating Knowledge

The practices and beliefs of the *shramanas* varied widely, but they were united in their conviction that relief from samsara was to be gained by means of special knowledge. Knowledge had of course played an important role in earlier forms of Indian religion. For rituals to succeed, it was essential that the priests knew precisely what needed to be done and said. Brahmins had to study for at least a dozen years to gain the understanding necessary to function as priests.

But in the classical age, the quest for knowledge took a different turn, now in pursuit of the new goal of liberation from samsara. The *shramanas* were not interested in the mere knowledge of ritual performance and mantra recitation. Such knowledge, they believed, could only be useful in acquiring worldly goods or a temporary respite in heaven, not the bliss of ultimate freedom. Rather, they wanted to grasp the deep reality that was the basis of ritual practice, and, by implication, the deep reality that was the foundation of existence. They thus sought a knowledge that was comprehensive and fundamental (box 8.2). One student asked his master, "What is that which, being known, illuminates everything else?"[3]

This knowledge, the *shramanas* believed, would be a special kind, gained by rigorous methods of **asceticism** and introspection and not merely transmitted by lectures or conversations. The Sanskrit word for this form of knowledge is **jñana**, a term closely related to *gnōsis*, the Greek word that describes an esoteric, mystically apprehended mode of understanding that confers salvation. Like those of the ancient Greco-Roman world who sought *gnōsis*, the Indian *shramanas* pursued a supermundane knowledge, one to be gained only by those willing to make the sacrifices required

---

Box 8.2   A THEORY OF EVERYTHING

The sages' desire to grasp reality's elemental nature might be fruitfully compared to modern physicists' quest to construct a unified field theory, sometimes called the Theory of Everything. For decades, physicists have worked to reconcile the four basic forces in the cosmos (electromagnetism, strong interaction, weak interaction, and gravitation) and understand them by a single mathematical formula, in essence reducing them to a single principle. The unified field theory has been the Holy Grail for the physicists who believe that finding it will unlock some of the deepest mysteries of the universe. In their own ways, the sages of ancient India were trying to develop their own Theory of Everything. They wanted to understand it all, not because they valued knowledge for knowledge's sake, but because knowledge of the fundamental basis of existence, they believed, could bring genuine freedom and fulfillment. This was a knowledge that conferred liberation.

to get it. And many of these ascetics claimed to have found what they were looking for: the path to *moksha* and the secrets of the universe itself.

The Vedantic Solution

Although we have no record of the teachings of many of the *shramanas*, we know a considerable amount about a few of them. Among the *shramana* traditions that remain, the perspectives of three schools of thought have been especially important in Indian religious history. Each of these systems purported to solve the existential challenges posed by samsara. The first was Vedanta, the view first offered in the Upanishads and later developed into an extensive, systematic philosophical school. The other perspectives were Buddhism and Jainism. Because all three emerged out of the same cultural context, they shared common features and addressed similar issues. Nonetheless, the three traditions offered different visions of the nature of reality and hence distinctive solutions to the problem of samsara. Today, Hindus consider only Vedanta to be orthodox because of its acceptance of the authority of the Vedas. Since Buddhism and Jainism deny Vedic authority, they are regarded as heterodox. Although all three traditions have been significant in Indian religious history, Vedanta has been the most crucial to the development of the Hindu traditions (box 8.3).

For our study of the Vedantic approach, we return to the Upanishads, which we first encountered in chapter 4. These texts—at least, most of them—were probably composed by *shramanas* and other thinkers of like mind. This collection clearly reflects a more intense philosophical interest than the earlier Vedas. The sages who composed the Upanishads sought to unlock the deepest mysteries of existence. Their pursuit of these secrets followed two apparently opposite trajectories. On the one hand, they wanted to comprehend the universe in its greatest possible sense by knowing the fundamental power or principle underlying the totality of the world. On the other hand, they sought to discover the essential nature that lies deep within each individual. Apprehending these, they believed, would yield the knowledge that would halt the samsaric cycle and bring about a state of utter bliss.

The *Atman*

Human beings have long wondered what lies at the core of who we are. We are aware of many dimensions of our existence—our bodies, our mental capacities, our affective and emotional nature, our ability to form purposes and intentions. But which of these aspects—if any—constitutes who we *really* are? In what dimension does our sense of identity reside? When we use the word *I*, to what exactly are we referring? Is there anything that underlies and supports everything else that we call *me*? Intuitively, we suspect there is a "true self" lurking somewhere within our multifaceted personalities, but finding and specifying that essence is not easy.

The composers of the Upanishads regarded that task as vital to their quest for *moksha*. Their speculation about the true self was guided by a concept from the Vedas. These ancient documents referred to the **atman**, a Sanskrit word originally used as a reflexive pronoun, as in "myself." *Atman* eventually came to indicate the animating force of life and, even more specifically, the essential core of personhood. In some of the Vedas, the *atman* seems to have been associated with the breath. (The German verb

Box 8.3 THE ORTHODOX SCHOOLS OF HINDU PHILOSOPHY

Historically, Hindu philosophy was divided into orthodox (*astika*) and heterodox (*nastika*) schools. Orthodox philosophies were those that accepted the authority of the Vedas, including the Upanishads. Heterodox schools denied Vedic authority. Tradition names six orthodox schools—Samkhya, Yoga, Nyaya, Vaisheshika, Mimamsa, and Vedanta—and three heterodox—Buddhism, Jainism, and the long-defunct Carvaka, a materialist and atheistic philosophy.

Samkhya was probably the oldest orthodox school. It had a highly dualistic worldview that regarded all reality as composed of two fundamental substances, *purusha* and *prakriti*. *Purusha*, which takes its name from the primordial being sacrificed by the gods in the Vedas, was the name for soul or consciousness. *Prakriti* was matter and energy, the basic substance comprising the material world. In its earliest articulation, Samkhya was a nontheistic school.

Samkhya was long associated with Yoga. Most Hindu philosophers have regarded Samkhya as the theoretical foundation for Yoga. Samkhya provided the concepts and analysis for comprehending the world, while Yoga provided the practical means for the self's liberation. The classical expression of the Yoga school is *Yoga Sutras of Patanjali*, which describes eight specific disciplines for attaining *moksha*: ethical conduct and self-restraint; religious study and devotion; physical exercises; control of breathing; withdrawal of the senses; concentration; meditation; and *samadhi*, or bliss.

The school of Nyaya was concerned mainly with matters of epistemology, the branch of philosophy dealing with knowledge. Nyaya developed principles of logic and criteria for establishing the validity of truth claims. Its methodology was subsequently adopted by most of the other philosophical schools. Knowing the validity of claims, Nyaya philosophers argued, was essential to finding the end to suffering and release from samsara.

Vaisheshika arose independently of Nyaya, but because of their affinities with one another, the two were often considered part of a single system. Vaisheshika adopted the view that the physical reality comprised a finite number of indivisible atoms. In this philosophy, Brahman was understood to be the force that causes consciousness to arise in the physical universe.

The early Mimamsa school sought to establish the authority of the Vedic texts by means of logic and argumentation. It posited that absolute faith in the Vedas and the regular performance of the fire sacrifices were essential to valid knowledge. The Mimamsa philosophy argued that because knowledge is self-certifying, the revelation on which the Vedas are based can be rationally accepted as true.

Vedanta, like Mimamsa, endeavored to establish Vedic authority, but Vedanta (as the name implies) focused on the revelation contained in the Upanishads and consequently did not emphasize the importance of sacrifice. Rather than ritual, Vedanta stressed the realization of liberating knowledge, working out with philosophical rigor the basic insight of the Upanishads that identified *atman* and Brahman. Ultimately, Vedanta became the most prominent of the six schools, building the foundation for the path of knowledge and many varieties of Hindu mysticism.

meaning "to breathe" is *atmen*.) The Vedic notion that the breath might be the human essence was based on the rather commonsensical view that without breath, the human being is just a corpse.

The sages of the Upanishads proposed a variety of ideas about the nature of the *atman*, but on one point they were in accord. The *atman* was not the body or subject to the body's infirmities. In one of the Upanishads, the god Indra is even depicted as worried about this association. In response to a *shramana* who claims that the body and the true self are identical, Indra reasons:

> If our self, our Atman, is the body, and is dressed in clothes of beauty when the body is, and is covered with ornaments when the body is, then when the body is blind, the self is blind, and when the body is lame, the self is lame; and when the body dies, our self dies. I cannot find any joy in this doctrine.[4]

The *shramanas* and sages of the early classical period believed the *atman* must be a more permanent and substantial reality than the breath or the body. By now, the idea of transmigration had begun to influence speculation about the *atman*. Since it survived the death of the body and was reborn in another, the sages concluded that the true self must be immortal. Thus, the *Katha Upanishad* declared:

> The wise one [the essential self] is not
>> born, nor does it die.
> It is not from anywhere, nor was it anyone.
> Unborn, everlasting, eternal, primeval,
> It is not slain when the body is slain.
>
> If the slayer thinks it slays;
> If the one who is slain thinks *it* is slain:
> Neither of them understands.
> It does not slay, nor is it slain.[5]

The *atman*—whatever it might be—cannot be subject to the passage of time. It cannot die. But if it cannot die, it is also not subject to birth. Thus, it does not come into being at a specifiable moment. Uncreated, it simply always has been (box 8.4).

Since it made little sense to identify the *atman* with the body, some contributors to the Upanishads suggested it might be the mind or consciousness. After all, the mind seems for most of us to be the center of our experience of the world, the seat of our personality.

Box 8.4　**WESTERN RELIGIONS ON ENSOULMENT**

We might contrast the Upanishadic view of the eternity of the *atman* with the recent positions of some Western religious traditions on the question of the soul's creation while struggling with the ethics of abortion. Roman Catholicism contends that the soul is created at conception; some Protestant groups have said it starts fourteen days after conception; a Jewish tradition says forty days after conception for boys and ninety days after for girls; and Islam maintains that an angel breathes the life-force into the fetus 120 days into pregnancy.* Though they disagree on the exact moment of "ensoulment," the Western traditions are united in saying the soul comes into being at a particular moment in time.

Science and Theology News, May 2006, 19.

It would make sense to regard this faculty as the true self. But the Upanishadic sages were reluctant to make this identification. How can anything as capricious and as unsettled as the mind be our immortal self? they asked. One of them writes: "It is not the mind that we should want to know; we should know the thinker."[6] What was of greatest interest was not the content or the activity of the mind, but rather that which existed beneath or beyond it. Believing the *atman* to be an agent or substance deeper than mental function, many philosophers came to regard the mind as an organ of sense, similar in function to the other five senses. Some of the sages reasoned further that if the *atman* is beyond or beneath the senses and the mind, then it could not be sensed or thought about. From this insight, the Upanishads ultimately conclude that the true self is imperceptible, beyond the categories of thinking, and beyond comprehension. Although it dwells within the body, the *atman* is different from the body and all its parts and functions.

Although the Upanishadic thinkers were not of one mind concerning what exactly constitutes the true human self, they all subscribed to the general understanding that the higher or true self should be distinguished from the lower self, or phenomenal self, which comprises the body, the senses, and the mind. These aspects are all transitory and mortal. The higher self, or *atman*, is distinguished from these other elements by virtue of its eternal and spiritual nature. Confusing the higher with the lower self brings great anguish to the human condition. But knowing the higher self, in the way made possible by intense effort, brings freedom from sorrow, death, and rebirth. The path to liberation through knowledge thus entails learning to discriminate between the higher and lower selves (box 8.5).

Brahman

As Indian thinkers sought to understand the essential nature of the self, they likewise wanted to comprehend the ultimate reality, the fundamental power or principle supporting and accounting for all that is. Like their quest for the *atman*, the sages' pursuit of absolute reality was inspired by an idea from the Vedas. The Vedas used a technical term to refer to a mysterious power that lay hidden within the ritual. The Brahmins called this power **Brahman**, and they believed it was this reality that made their sacrifices effective.

During the classical period, the quest for liberating knowledge came to focus on discovering the true nature of Brahman. The search for Brahman was a logical development in the course of Indo-Aryan religion. The ritual and its sacred words had always been understood to correspond to greater cosmological and moral realities beyond the ceremony. The account of the sacrifice of the Purusha discussed in chapter 3 suggested that society, the various elements of the world, ritual practices, and the Sanskrit language itself were all intrinsically and mystically connected to one another. Seeking the deeper meaning of existence by understanding Brahman was merely a natural outcome of this pattern of thought. Brahman had come to mean more than simply the power of ritual. It now referred to ultimate reality itself.

The authors of the Upanishads did not agree about the exact nature of Brahman, but there was consensus that it was a singular, undifferentiated unity sustaining all reality. In fact, Brahman was sometimes simply called "the One." There could be no parts or divisions to Brahman. It was sometimes called the thread that strings together all creatures. Brahman was said to permeate all things, yet it could not be perceived. It embraced good and evil and yet

Box 8.5 JAINISM AND BUDDHISM ON THE SELF

Because they denied the authority of the Vedas, Buddhism and Jainism were branded as heterodox schools by orthodox practitioners. But despite that label, the Buddhist and Jain perspectives shared a good deal with the traditions that were later called Hindu, including belief in rebirth and karma. Indeed, many Hindus would still regard Buddhists and Jains as coreligionists. Yet the Jain and Buddhist views of the soul or self were significantly different from the way the *atman* was conceived in the Upanishads.

Mahāvīra (599–527 B.C.E.), a contemporary of the Buddha and the twenty-fourth Tirthankara of Jainism, conceived of the soul as unchanging in essence, although its attributes were subject to alternation. He also thought there were an infinite number of souls, each an actual, separate individual. Thus, Mahāvīra would not have accepted the Vedantic idea that the soul and ultimate reality are consubstantial, since that view denies individuality.

In contradistinction to Jainism and Vedanta, the Buddha simply denied the existence of the *atman*. This denial, known as "no self" (*anatman*), is perhaps Buddhism's most distinctive contribution to the world's religious thought. According to the Buddha's teaching, a permanent, immortal, substantial soul is nowhere to be found. Furthermore, he maintained, believing in the *atman* is precisely what leads to suffering and rebirth. An old Buddhist quip captures the idea exactly: "There is thought but no thinker; there is feeling but no feeler." Thinking is real, feeling is real, but there is no subject or self who experiences them.

---

transcended both. In short, Brahman encompassed and supported the whole of reality and also surpassed it. There was nothing beyond the scope of Brahman, not even the gods themselves. It was the ground of all being.

This excerpt from the *Isha Upanishad* captures the sense of the magnificence and elusiveness of Brahman:

One, unmoving, swifter than mind,
The gods cannot catch it, as it goes before:
Standing still, it outruns others that are
    running.
. . . .
It moves, it does not move;
It is far and near likewise,
It is inside all this:
It is outside all this.

. . . .

It is different, they say, from becoming;
It is different, they say, from non-
    becoming:
So we have heard from those wise ones
Who have revealed it to us.[7]

By means of paradox and negation, this passage asserts that Brahman transcends human categories and images. Claiming that it moves and does not move, for instance, the author demonstrates that Brahman exhausts and depletes our categories for understanding it. How can it both move and not move? What kind of sense does that make? It makes no sense—according to conventional forms of logic. The very point of such a phrase is to confound our thinking. Many Hindu theologians later came to say of Brahman that it was **nirguna**, or "without qualities." To try to describe it in anything other than a paradoxical or negative way makes it into something that can be comprehended, which by definition it cannot be.

Eventually, the Upanishadic sages came to believe that Brahman was ultimately unknowable; at least, it could not be grasped in the way we understand other elements of our experience. At this level, Brahman eludes conception and perception, and so these faculties are ineffective in discovering the absolute reality. What the sages sought was the deepest kind of knowing, an apprehension of reality that we can best call mystical or ineffable. This kind of knowledge is based, paradoxically, on "unknowing," the recognition of the mind's inadequacy in the face of life's great mystery. An excerpt from the *Kena Upanishad*, one of the shortest of the principal Upanishads, describes the mystical features of this knowledge:

> The eye does not go there,
> Speech does not go, nor mind.
> We do not know, we do not understand,
> How anyone could teach it.

> It is different from the known;
> It is different too from the unknown:
> So we have heard from those of old
> Who have revealed it to us.

> What is not expressed by speech—
> By which speech is expressed—
> Know that as *brahman*,
> Not what they worship as such.

> What one does not think of by the
>   mind—
> By which, they say, the mind is thought
>   of—
> Know that as *brahman*,
> Not what they worship as such.

> What one does not see by the eye—
> By which one sees eyes—
> Know that as *brahman*,
> Not what they worship as such.

> What one does not hear by the ear—
> By which the ear is heard—
> Know that as *brahman*,
> Not what they worship as such.

> What one does not breathe by the
>   breath—
> By which the breath is breathed—
> Know that as *brahman*,
> Not what they worship as such.[8]

This approach to ultimate reality is known as **apophatic** or **negative theology**. It is often used to describe elliptically a mystical knowing that cannot be described directly. Thomas Aquinas, the medieval Christian theologian, explained the apophatic method this way: "By its immensity, the divine substance surpasses every form that our intellect reaches. Thus we are unable to apprehend it by knowing what it is. Yet we are able to have some knowledge of it by knowing what it is *not*."[9] The *Kena Upanishad* states: "It is not understood by the understanders; It is understood by those who do not understand."[10]

The Identity of *Atman* and Brahman

As the composers of the Upanishads pondered the essential nature of the self and ultimate reality, a new insight began to break into awareness, an epiphany that came to full expression in the later Upanishads. As the sages increasingly appreciated the incomprehensible and unutterable nature of both the *atman* and Brahman, these two conceptions converged. The sages concluded that what they sought as the true self was nothing other than ultimate reality. *Atman* and Brahman were different names for the self-same reality.

The Upanishads express this insight in a variety of ways. The *Chandogya Upanishad* rhapsodizes:

> This self of mine within the heart is smaller than a rice-grain or a barleycorn or a mustard-seed or a millet-grain or the kernel of a millet-grain. This self of mine within the heart is greater than the earth, greater than middle-air, greater than the sky, greater than these worlds.[11]

Another celebrated passage describes how a Brahmin named Uddalaka taught this revelation to his son Svetekatu, a young man who had just completed his formal schooling in the Vedas but who also apparently missed the most important lesson of all. Uddalaka creates an object lesson by asking Svetekatu to take a fruit from the great banyan tree, break it open, and dissect one of the seeds. Svetekatu does as he is told. When he tells his father he finds nothing within, Uddalaka makes his point:

> My son, from the very essence in the seed which you cannot see comes in truth this vast banyan tree. Believe me, my son, an invisible and subtle essence is the Spirit of the whole universe. That is Reality. That is *Atman*. THOU ART THAT.[12]

To know one's true self is to know the absolute.

According to the **Advaita Vedanta** tradition in Hindu philosophy, these statements do not merely claim that the essential self is a *part* of god or carries a divine spark or is created in the *image* of god. Rather, the identity of *atman* and Brahman means they are consubstantial, two names for the same reality. The true self *is* ultimate reality. Brahman/*atman* is the only reality there is (box 8.6).

It is hard to imagine a more exalted view of humanity. This assessment of the self seems almost diametrically opposite that of the central thrust of Western monotheism, in which there is an "infinite qualitative difference" between god and humanity, to quote the Christian theologian Søren Kierkegaard. Even the Bible emphasizes this difference between the divine and human. One of the psalms rhetorically asks: "When I look at thy heavens, the work of thy fingers, the moon and the stars which thou hast established; what is man that thou art mindful of him, and the son of man that thou dost care for him?"[13]

The Path to Liberating Knowledge

Despite the Upanishads' lofty view, the *atman* finds itself on an apparently endless cycle of birth, death, and rebirth. Like many religious traditions of the West and East, the classical Hindu view understands that the embodied self is not at rest, is not in its true home. It continues in this restless state, seeking ever-new manifestations until it finds, as Augustine would say, its rest in god. Why then does the true self—at one with ultimate reality—nevertheless suffer the rounds of incessant rebirth?

According to the Upanishads, samsara is a consequence of ignorance—our misapprehension of reality. We fail to realize our true divine nature, mistaking our lower selves for our higher selves. Our lower selves, because they are transitory and inconstant, are ultimately not real. Until we fully recognize the truth about Brahman and

Box 8.6 VEDANTA

The school known as Vedanta includes two of the greatest Hindu philosophers, Shankara and Ramanuja. Both thinkers base their systems on the Upanishads, but they each develop the Upanishadic insights in different ways. Shankara's philosophy, known as Advaita Vedanta, offers a nontheistic interpretation of the Upanishadic tradition. Ramanuja, on the other hand, reads that same tradition in a theistic way. His school is called Vishishtadvaita Vedanta.

Shankara (788–820 C.E.) is considered by many to be the greatest Hindu thinker of all time. Yet he is perhaps best remembered in India not as a philosopher but as a religious adept who invigorated and reformed the Hindu traditions at a time when Buddhism was the dominant religion of the subcontinent. Like most Hindu thinkers, Shankara claimed that his philosophy was not novel. He considered it simply a precise interpretation of *shruti*, the revelation contained in the Vedas and the Upanishads.

Shankara's perspective can be characterized as a thoroughgoing monism, the view that reality is one, or more precisely, nondual. Only Brahman is real. All else—the phenomenal world—is *maya*, a "veil" over Brahman. *Maya* is the intricate power of Brahman that creates the appearance of multiplicity. Thus, although Brahman is one, reality seems to comprise a great many separate things. The belief that the individual's *atman* and ultimate reality are in any way distinguishable is pure *maya*. The power of *maya* is so great, however, that ignorant beings fail to recognize the world for what it truly is. The path to liberation is thus a matter of penetrating the illusory veil of *maya* to realize Brahman itself. This discernment is possible because *maya*, like a veil, both conceals and reveals Brahman. For Shankara, the way of knowledge entails recognizing that the *atman* is consubstantial with Brahman; they are absolutely the same in all respects.

Like Shankara, Ramanuja (1017–1137 C.E.) was a religious reformer as well as a theologian. The philosophies of these two thinkers converged at many important points, yet Ramanuja found he could not completely accept the Advaitan perspective of Shankara. The school he represented was thus known as Vishishtadvaita, or "qualified" Advaita.

Rightly or wrongly, Ramanuja, like many other Hindu thinkers, believed that Shankara had relegated the phenomenal realm to pure illusion. Ramanuja argued the world is indeed real, even to the extent that it could be considered the manifestation of the divine. Identifying Brahman with Vishnu, Ramanuja declared that the world and the individual *atman* are actually attributes of god, constituting his very body. On this view, human beings can be regarded as parts of the sacred reality.

By interpreting Brahman in personal terms, Ramanuja resisted Shankara's insistence that Brahman is *nirguna*, without qualities, claiming that an ultimate reality absolutely devoid of attributes is not founded on scripture. To Ramanuja, Brahman is *ishvara*, the supreme controller, who is endowed with an infinite number of superlative qualities. Because this ultimate cosmic spirit directs all events, liberation from samsara depends on divine grace.

atman, we continue to suffer on the wheel of samsara because we continue to generate karma, which binds us to the phenomenal world. Believing ourselves to be discrete individuals, we tend to think and act in self-centered ways, creating the desires and deeds that perpetuate the illusion of our separateness from Brahman. This sense of separateness engenders fear and hatred of others, the greed for material goods and power, and ultimately the fear of death. The *Maitri Upanishad* says, "Whenever the [*atman*] has thoughts of 'I' and 'mine,' it binds itself with its lower self, as a bird with the net of a snare."[14] To see ourselves as anything other than Brahman is the source of our misery. But to realize our oneness with the absolute frees us of the burdens of fear and self-centered desire.

The realization of the unity of Brahman and *atman* is the theoretical foundation and the practical goal of the path of knowledge. Taking this path means living in a way that embodies the truth of this principle. It is not enough that the identity of *atman* and Brahman be grasped intellectually. Conceptual knowledge must become a deep knowing that pervades the whole of one's being.

To realize this kind of knowledge, the Upanishads advise the aspirant to find a guru who himself has traversed the path to *moksha*. Under his tutelage, the student learns the various yogic practices of the ascetic. Many of these disciplines provide exercises for learning renunciation. The aspirant must give up all attachment to anything that encourages a sense of separateness or individuality. Living the homeless life reduces attachment to the material world to the bare minimum. More extreme practices of self-mortification—fasting, celibacy, self-flagellation, nudity, silence, piercings—further encourage nonattachment to the body and individuality (figure 8.1).

Fig. 8.1   The Buddha as *shramana*. The man who became the Buddha renounced his worldly life to practice the demanding disciplines of the path of knowledge. He later renounced extreme asceticism in favor of what he called the "Middle Way." (Photo: World Imaging [Wiki Commons GNU Free Documentation License].)

The path of knowledge also entails a different orientation to discovering truth. Whereas some forms of religion may encourage practitioners to look for truth in a book or another external source, the Upanishads declare that the truth is found within one's deepest self. To discover oneself is to discover God. A person "must find his own [*atman*]. He who has found and knows his [*atman*] has found all the worlds, has achieved all his desires."[15] Meditation and hatha yoga are techniques for delving deeper within to discriminate between the lower and higher selves.

It is important to recognize that taking the path of knowledge is not what brings about the unity of soul and absolute reality, although the language of some Upanishadic passages may suggest it. Rather, the higher self and Brahman *are* one and always have been. The way of knowledge only confers the *awareness* of this unity; it does not create it. The result of this deep awareness is the serenity that comes from knowing there is nothing to fear. There is no rebirth, because there is no clinging to life: "The Spirit of man has crossed the lands of good and evil, and has passed beyond the sorrows of the heart."[16]

◆ KEY TERMS

Advaita Vedanta

apophatic theology

asceticism

ashram

atman

Brahman

jñana

negative theology

nirguna

Ramanuja

Shankara

shramanas

Vishishtadvaita Vedanta

◆ QUESTIONS FOR REVIEW

1. How did the concepts of *atman* and Brahman change from the early Vedic period to the emergence of the classical era?

2. What is *atman*? How is it similar to the concepts of mind, spirit, and consciousness? How is it different?

3. What is *maya*? How does it help perpetuate the cycle of reincarnation?

4. When trying to understanding ultimate reality, why might an apophatic, or negative, approach work better than positive theology?

5. How does renunciation help followers of the *jñana-marga* understand the truth?

◆ QUESTIONS FOR FURTHER REFLECTION

1. What are the theological advantages and disadvantages of conceiving ultimate reality as devoid of all qualities and characteristics?

2. From whence does thought arise?

3. Is it possible that there is no human essence?

4. What are the consequences of conceiving the ultimate and the self as the same, rather than distinct from one another?

◆ FOR FURTHER STUDY

Brereton, Joel. "The Upanishads." In *Approaches to the Asian Classics*, edited by Wm. Theodore de Bary and Irene Bloom. New York: Columbia University Press, 1990.

Deutsch, Eliot. *Advaita Vedanta: A Philosophical Reconstruction*. Honolulu: University of Hawaii Press, 1969.

Koller, John M. *Asian Philosophies*. 4th ed. Upper Saddle River, N.J.: Prentice Hall, 2002.

Mascaró, Juan, trans. *The Upanishads*. Harmondsworth, U.K.: Penguin, 1965.

Roebuck, Valerie J., trans. and ed. *The Upaniṣads*. London: Penguin, 2003.

9. Seeing God

PREVIEW

Because of its many gods and the prominence of images in its worship, early Western interpreters often regarded "Hinduism" as a crude and hopelessly idolatrous religion. This view still lingers in the Western imagination, due in no small measure to basic misunderstandings of the nature of Hindu theism and iconography. In this chapter, we will explore the dynamics of Hindu theism in theory and practice. We shall see how the immense pantheon of the Hindu traditions and devotion to images actually militate against idolatry, the confusion of the absolute with the relative. We will also explore some of the various rituals associated with worship. The god Shiva, one of the most widely revered Hindu deities, will be the focus for our investigations.

As *nirguna* Brahman, absolute reality is so far beyond our human capacity to conceive it that all efforts to do so are, in the final analysis, futile. Brahman simply cannot be fully conceptualized, described, or represented in any way. According to the path of knowledge, it can only be realized by a personal experience of transcendent consciousness in which the primordial unity of self and Brahman is made manifest. The aspirants who seek this realization must penetrate *maya*, the veil of illusion that cloaks the phenomenal world and gives rise to false apprehensions about the nature of the self and cosmos. To see through *maya*, one must give up everything that hinders the full awareness of deepest reality. This renunciation includes, especially, the markers of individual identity, since the separate individual self is an illusion, as well as all concepts and images of the divine, because they ultimately lead us astray.

But anyone who knows about the Hindu traditions knows that the overwhelming majority of Hindus have hardly given up concepts and images of the divine. India, in fact, is a land of an astounding array of divine images. There are pictures and statues of members of the Hindu pantheon everywhere you go. In public buildings, on buses, in taxis and rickshaws, at the tea stalls and shops, and on the sides of roads, the gods and goddesses cast a watchful eye over everything. And this doesn't even mention the images in the temples and in homes, where the gods are usually worshiped. In India, the divine is inescapable (figure 9.1).

We have just described two different approaches to the ultimate mystery of our world, both of them familiar in world religious

Fig. 9.1 **Omnipresence of the divine.** Images of the gods and goddesses are on prominent display throughout the subcontinent. This depiction of Bhairab, a fearsome manifestation of Shiva, appears in a public square in Kathmandu. (Photo: Mark W. Muesse.)

history. One approach is to say nothing at all, to think nothing, to imagine nothing. That is a mystical approach, the approach embodied in the path of knowledge. The ultimate is ineffable. Say *anything* about it, and it has been distorted. In words, the infinite becomes finite. By simply uttering a truth, one lies. This is the anxiety that some religious persons have about discussing or depicting god or ultimate reality in any fashion (box 9.1). A Zen saying puts it very succinctly: "Open mouth, already a mistake."

But there is another and far more prominent approach in the mainstream of the world's religions. If we are to relate to the ultimate reality at all, we *must* think about the unthinkable and we *must* imagine the unimaginable, even if those efforts are ultimately to no avail. This impulse is based on the conviction that we are not at liberty to discard language and images of the divine. Even the Western monotheisms, which generally consider themselves iconoclastic, still employ images and theological language. One of the Ten Commandments forbids the making of *graven* images of god, yet *linguistic* images and metaphors are used in abundance throughout the Bible and the Qur'an. To call the divine being "father," "lord," and "king" is to ascribe such images to ultimate reality. Perhaps it is true, as Aristotle once wrote, that "the soul never thinks without an image."[1] Unquestionably, depicting the divine in images and concepts—whether linguistic or material—is the more common approach among the religions of the world. The mystical tradition of imageless silence may appeal to some, but most religious persons need symbols to guide their spirits. And on this point, most of the Hindu traditions are in accord with the rest of the world.

Indeed, not only do the Hindu theistic traditions accept this fundamental principle; they implement it with far greater energy and inventiveness than most other religious traditions. The sheer exuberance of Hindu theism, in fact, may be the greatest stumbling block for those outside the traditions. They often ask, Why do Hindus worship so many gods? Why do they make physical images of their gods, especially images that seem at times rather strange and even unpleasant? Are not polytheism and material representations of god crass **idolatry**? In this chapter, we begin to answer these questions. Careful study of Hindu theism will reveal that, far from the crude worship of "false gods," most Hindus practice within a highly sophis-

Box 9.1 THE INEFFABILITY OF THE DIVINE

As in the *nirguna* tradition, many religions and philosophies throughout the world affirm the absolute transcendence of ultimate reality. One of the most eloquent theologians to assert this position was Denys, also known as Dionysius the Areopagite and Pseudo-Dionysius. Denys was a Christian monk living in Syria around the fifth century. He was convinced that unknowability was inherent in the nature of the absolute. In this classic instance of negative theology, Denys systematically denies all attributes of ultimate reality to bring this fact to consciousness.

It [ultimate reality] is not soul or mind, nor does it possess imagination, conviction, speech, or understanding. Nor is it speech per se, understanding per se. It cannot be spoken of and it cannot be grasped by understanding. It is not number or order, greatness or smallness, equality or inequality, similarity or dissimilarity. It is not immovable, moving, or at rest. It has no power, it is not power, nor is it light. It does not live nor is it life. It is not a substance, nor is it eternity or time. It cannot be grasped by the understanding since it is neither knowledge nor truth. It is not kingship. It is not wisdom. It is neither one nor oneness, divinity nor goodness. Nor is it a spirit, in the sense in which we understand that term. It is not sonship or fatherhood and it is not known to us or to any other being. It falls neither within the predicate of nonbeing nor a being. Existing beings do not know it as it actually is and it does not know them as they are. There is no speaking of it, or name or knowledge of it.*

Note how Denys' position compares in substance and style with some of the Upanisadic passages we examined in chapter 8.

*Paul Rorem, trans., *Pseudo Dionysius: The Complete Works* (Mahwah, N.J.: Paulist, 1987), 141.

ticated theological structure that provides a refined understanding of ultimate reality that militates against idolatry.

The One and the Many

Let us begin with the question of polytheism: How many gods and goddesses are there, and do Hindus worship them all? A famous story from the Upanishads helps to settle these questions.

In the tale, the great sage Yājñavalkya was questioned about the number of *devas* in the world. Yājñavalkya gave a traditional answer: 3,306. The interlocutor, however, was not sat-

isfied and pressed for another answer: "Yes, of course," he said, "but really, Yājñavalkya, how many gods are there?" Seeing that his first answer did not satisfy, the sage offered another number: thirty-three, the purported number of Vedic gods. Once again the questioner responded, "Yes, of course, but really now, Yājñavalkya, how many gods are there?" Yājñavalkya next offered the number six, and once more he heard, "Yes, of course, but really, Yājñavalkya, how many gods are there?" Yājñavalkya then said three, and again the interlocutor pressed him. Yājñavalkya went on to give the number two, then one and a half, and finally one. And with that answer, the questioning ceased.[2]

So how many *devas* and *devis* are there, according to the Hindu traditions? Although one tradition puts the figure at 330 million, perhaps a better answer is, simply, as many as you like. Although in the story of Yājñavalkya the questioning stops with the number one, the passage does not say the other answers are *wrong*. Indeed, Yājñavalkya gives a rational explanation for each of his answers. By his account, they are all true. In a characteristically Hindu fashion, the story of Yājñavalkya affirms both the oneness and manyness of ultimate reality (box 9.2).

Saguna Brahman

Theologically, this affirmation is made possible by distinguishing *nirguna* Brahman from **saguna Brahman**. Whereas *nirguna* Brahman is the absolute without qualities and beyond concept, *saguna* Brahman is ultimate reality as it is known or revealed, the supreme reality with characteristics and attributes. The concepts of *nirguna* and *saguna* Brahman represent two ways of considering the same reality. The many *devas* and *devis* of the Hindu pantheon, according to this distinction, are just so many different expressions of the one Brahman in its sagunic aspect. By virtue of the distinction between *nirguna* and *saguna* Brahman, it is possible to classify the Hindu traditions as *both* monotheistic and polytheistic.

The many gods and goddesses furnish an astounding number of ways to enrich the understanding of the divine. To Hindu ways of thinking, the ultimate reality is so far beyond our imagining, so complex, so utterly rich in potential, that a single image or even a mere handful of images will not do. If the absolute must be portrayed, then many, many images

---

Box 9.2 THE ONE AND THE MANY

This brief poem by the Shaivite poet Basavanna (1134–1196) succinctly captures the Hindu understanding of the divine as both one and many.

The pot is a god.

The winnowing fan is a god.

The stone in the street is a god.

The comb is a god.

The bowstring is also a god.

The bushel is a god and the spouted cup is a god.

Gods, gods, there are so many
There's no place for a foot.

There's only one god—
He is our Lord of the Meeting Rivers.*

As a devotee of Shiva, Basavanna regards all particular manifestations of the sacred as expressions of his *ishta-devata*, whom he here calls "our Lord of the Meeting Rivers." A Vaishnavite might regard Vishnu, rather than Shiva, as the supreme one, and both might acknowledge Shiva and Vishnu as names for the unnamable Absolute sometimes called Brahman.

*A. K. Ramanujan, trans., *Speaking of Shiva* (Harmondsworth, U.K.: Penguin Classics, 1973), 84.

and symbols will be more successful than just one or a few. The very number of gods and their complex manifestations, so outrageous in their extravagance, astonishes and overwhelms the human mind—a response that reminds us of the unspeakable nature of the ultimate reality. Presented with just a few images, the human mind would be more likely to reify them, believing them to be not merely symbols but rather the reality the symbols were intended to represent.

Even though the Hindu pantheon is immense, individual Hindus do not worship all the gods equally or even attempt to do so. Those who wish to worship god through symbols, as we have seen, have an *ishta-devata*, a personal deity of choice. Often one's personal *deva* is the same god worshiped by one's family (*kula-devata*) or village (*grama-devata*), but it is not uncommon for family members to be devoted to different gods. Devotees worship their particular deity as the supreme god but do not feel compelled to deny the reality of other gods or their supremacy for their followers. Because people are different—with different proclivities, different ways of understanding, different aesthetic tastes—they require different ways of conceiving of and relating to the divine. The recognition that individuals have different spiritual needs helps sustain the spirit of tolerance that has been the hallmark of the Hindu mainstream. In this manner, both the one and the many are preserved.

Iconography and Idolatry

We turn now to iconography, the representation of the divine by means of physical forms. The practice of creating images of god has long been considered scandalous in the dominant religious traditions of the Western world. A nineteenth-century Christian hymn still sung in many churches laments the custom of creating material images to represent the divine: "The heathen in his blindness bows down to wood and stone."[3] Many Westerners continue to refer to physical representations of the divine not as *images*, but by the disparaging term *idol*. In the strict theological sense, the word *idol* generally refers to a false god, an object of devotion that is unworthy of absolute faith and allegiance. Hindus, like the faithful of all theistic traditions, would deplore the practice of idolatry in this sense.

The simplistic identification of divine images with idolatry actually betrays a superficial understanding of the nature and function of religious iconography. As we shall see shortly, rather than promoting idolatry, the production and use of visible symbols of devotion in Hinduism actually works to *diminish* the risks of idolatry. Those who deplore "idols" of wood and stone usually fail to recognize how their own understanding of god is laden with images venerated just as much as some Hindus revere physical representations of the divine. As we noted earlier, metaphors such as "father," "lord," and "king" are in fact images meant to assist with grasping ultimate reality. The only real difference is that one group limits its images to the mind, and the other finds no compelling reason for that restriction. Indeed, the latter group finds that confining images to the mind unnecessarily impoverishes the spirit, which can be nourished through all the senses, especially sight. For many Hindus who cannot read, the avenues to the divine opened up through the senses are especially important; divine images are a principal source of their theology. But even for those who can read, images of the divine greatly augment what mere words can say.

Symbols of the Divine

In the view of most Hindus, Brahman pervades everything, and nothing is beyond its scope. Accordingly, there is nothing that cannot, in principle, manifest divine reality and yield access to the sacred for those who have eyes to see. Every object of the phenomenal world and every experience has the potential to symbolize and reveal Brahman. Some of these symbols are naturally occurring; others are made by human hands. All are regarded as legitimate conduits to or receptacles for the ultimate. The Hindus refer to these forms as **murtis**. *Murti* literally means "embodiment" or "manifestation."

The Manifestation of the Sacred in Nature

Among natural phenomena, many Hindus hold special regard for things such as stones, earthen mounds, trees, rivers, and celestial bodies. They consider these to be particularly potent sites where sacred energy can be encountered in an extraordinary way. Temples and shrines are frequently erected near such places, especially trees and bodies of water. Such locales are often understood to be abodes for *devas* and *devis*. For Vaishnavites, the *tulsi* plant is actually a manifestation of the goddess Lakshmi, and millions of Hindus grow the plant in a special container at the front of their home and partake of its leaves (figure 9.2). Vaishnavites also revere the *saligram*, a black stone found only in the Gandaki River in Nepal, as a material form of the great god Vishnu (figure 9.3). Sometimes the sacred nature of these objects is not associated with any particular god or goddess but is simply deemed auspicious. By the same token, natural objects can also be infused with

Fig. 9.2   *Tulsi.* Many Hindus cultivate *tulsi*, or Holy Basil, at their homes. The plant is considered a manifestation of the goddess Lakshmi. (Photo courtesy of Creative Commons.)

Fig. 9.3   *Saligram.* According to many, this sacred stone manifests the god Vishnu. (Photo: © Miroslava Holasová / istockphoto.)

diabolical force, and great care must be taken to avoid the ire of any malevolent spirits who might inhabit them.

Human-Made Images

Just as significant as sacred objects in the natural world, and in some respects even more so, are human-made symbols. Images made by human hands appear in a vast array of forms, but for analytical purposes we may categorize them as iconic and aniconic. **Iconic** images are simply those whose subject is anthropomorphic, or humanlike. The word *icon* derives from the Greek *eikōn*, which means "likeness." **Aniconic** images, on the other hand, are nonanthropomorphic. Both types of images play key roles in the dynamics of Hindu practice.

Anthropomorphic Images

Depicting divine reality as anthropomorphic is an extremely common practice in the world's religions. Ludwig Feuerbach explained this frequency by suggesting that humanity "can conceive no form more beautiful, more sublime than the human."[4] Perhaps Feuerbach is correct. To imagine ultimate reality as in some measure like us—with intelligence, will, emotions, desires, and perhaps even a body—provides a great measure of solace in knowing that the fundamental powers of the universe may be appealed to, reckoned with, and, if only partially, understood.

The danger in personalizing the divine realm in this fashion, however, is to bring it too close to the human sphere, making it so much like ourselves that it seems finite. Hindus avert this danger by subtly reminding devotees that although the gods may share some elements of our humanity, they are decidedly *not* like us

and cannot be reduced to human status. Thus, images of the Hindu gods juxtapose features that are human with features that are nonhuman. The immensely popular god **Ganesha**, the remover of obstacles, has a very human body but the head of an elephant (figure 9.4). Lord Rama, a manifestation of the god Vishnu, appears to be completely human, but his blue skin suggests his divinity (figure 9.5). Durga looks like a human woman, but her eight arms indicate that she is not (figure 9.6). The nonanthropomorphic aspects of the divine image militate against idolatry by thwarting the tendency to reduce divinity to a form that can be fully understood. In addition, nonhuman elements often convey essential information about the nature of the divine. Durga's many arms, for

Fig. 9.4 Ganesha. Jovial Ganesha, the remover of obstacles, is one of the most popular gods. (Photo courtesy GNU Free Documentation License [WikiCommons].)

Fig. 9.5 **Rama.** Rama is one of the most widely worshiped avatars of Vishnu and is ordinarily depicted with blue skin. (Public domain image [Wikicommons].)

Fig. 9.6 **Durga.** Durga's many arms suggest her formidable powers. (Photo courtesy of Creative Commons, Sujit Kumar.)

example, indicate her great power, just as Brahma's many heads suggest his superior knowledge (figure 9.7).

Aniconic Images

Providing further safeguards against reducing the divine to the level of the human are the innumerable forms of aniconic images. If imagining ultimate reality as anthropomorphic threatens to make it seem comprehensible—thereby denying its status as genuine mystery—then nonanthropomorphic symbols serve to lessen the danger. Regarded as no less powerful

Fig. 9.7 (left) **Brahma.** Considered by many Hindus to be the creator god, Brahma is often depicted with four heads or faces to indicate his omniscience. In this figure, the fourth face is hidden from view. (Photo courtesy of Creative Commons.)

than anthropomorphic depictions of the divine, aniconic representations subtly suggest that the deepest reality cannot be limited to the human or humanlike form. We have already encountered two examples of the aniconic image in the ancient swastika and the *Prāvnava*, the written representation of *aum*, the primordial syllable. Two other prominent aniconic images are the **lingam** (figure 9.8), which symbolizes the presence of Shiva, and the **yantra** (figure 9.9), colorful geometric designs frequently associated with the goddess. We will consider the *lingam* and *yantra* in later discussions.

Fig. 9.9 *Yantra.* Geometric designs known as *yantras* are believed to manifest divine power. (Photo courtesy of Creative Commons.)

Fig. 9.8 *Lingam.* The *lingam* is an aniconic, or non-anthropomorphic, representation of Lord Shiva. (Photo courtesy of Creative Commons, Yosarian.)

The Iconography of Shiva

To provide concrete illustration of the role of images in the Hindu traditions, we will now explore in greater detail the iconography of one of the great gods, Shiva. In our study of the Indus Civilization, we encountered the figure of Pashupati, the meditating horned man, whom many scholars identify as an early form of Shiva. Some historians also suggest that Shiva may have associations with the Vedic god known as Rudra, the Howler. Neither of these suggestions has been universally accepted as conclusive. But virtually all scholars believe that Shiva as he is known today is the result of a process of amalgamation, in which ideas and stories from regional and local traditions were gradually assimilated under his name. The fact that Shiva is still known by many different names in various parts of India attests to this coalescence. Today, Shiva, whose name means "the auspicious one," is at the center of Shaivism, one of the three most prominent religions in the Hindu family. His devotees are known as Shaivites. The other two major religions focus on Vishnu and the goddess respectively, and we will discuss them later.

The iconography and mythology of Shiva depict him as an extremely paradoxical and immensely complex deity. He is both the creator and destroyer of the universe. He is movement and tranquility, light and darkness, male and female, celibate and promiscuous. One scholar calls him the "erotic ascetic."[5] He afflicts with fevers and illness, yet he is the physician who possesses a thousand medicines. He is wild but compassionate. These paradoxes symbolize the limitlessness and freedom of the divine. They also suggest that the kinds of things we might ordinarily consider oppositions are in fact closer than we think. Destruction must precede creation. Birth comes before death, which leads again to birth. That which afflicts can also heal. Erotic impulses may be transmuted into spiritual power.

Four prominent images of Shiva illustrate this theology—or, better expressed, *are* this theology: Shiva as the Great Yogi (**Mahayogi**), as the Lord of the Dance (**Nataraja**), as the Lord Who Is Half-Woman (**Ardhanarishvara**), and the aniconic *lingam*.

The Great Yogi image accents Shiva's tranquil, ascetic aspect. It provides a model for Shaivites who practice asceticism as part of their spiritual discipline. Shiva is depicted here in a meditative posture. His eyes are half-shut to the world, suggesting that he is in the world but not of it. He wears wild animal skins emblematic of his primal energy and his closeness to the natural world. His home is in the Himalayas, the abode of the gods and ascetics. He carries a trident that represents his control over

body, mind, and intellect. Around his neck is a tamed cobra, symbolizing his triumph over ego, because the ego, like the serpent, harasses us with its desires. In the topknot of his hair lives the goddess **Ganga**; from here the river Ganges flows softly to earth, suggesting Shiva's compassionate nature (see figure 1.8 on page 25).

The Nataraja is one of the best-known images of any Hindu deity. It depicts Shiva's cosmic dance during the auspicious occasion of the *Mahashivaratri*, the great night of Shiva (figure 9.10). He dances the night away, dispelling the ignorance of the dark. His dance is wild and free, as indicated by his flying hair, but his face is tranquil and composed, unperturbed by the motion. His four arms indicate his great power, and each of them expresses a meaningful gesture. In one hand he holds a *damaru*, a two-headed hand drum; in the other he holds a

Fig. 9.10   Dancing Shiva. The Nataraja, or the dancing Shiva, is one of the best-known Hindu images. The icon is one of the clearest representations of the paradoxes of divinity.
(Photo courtesy of Creative Commons: http://commons.wikimedia.org/wiki/File:Khairatabad_Ganesh.jpg.)

flame. With the drum he sounds the world into existence; with the flame he destroys it in order to create another. One hand is raised in a gesture that tells the devotee to fear not. The other hand points down to the uplifted foot, where the devotee may find refuge; it is an invitation for the person of faith to approach. The lifted foot symbolizes his freedom from the world and the ecstasy of divine consciousness. With the planted foot he crushes the demon of ignorance and sin. Surrounding the entire image is a ring of fire; this is samsara, the phenomenal world.

The Ardhanarishvara image illustrates Shiva's androgynous nature. As we shall discuss in greater detail in chapter 11, all the great gods of Hinduism have their female counterparts, their **shakti**. The female aspect of the divine is depicted in a variety of ways, most frequently as a goddess who is married to the god. One of the more interesting depictions, however, is the image of Shiva as the Lord Who Is Half-Woman. In this representation, Shiva's androgyny is portrayed as a single individual with male and female halves (figure 9.11). Such an image suggests the all-encompassing nature of the divine and reminds the devotee of the limitations of anything in human experience to capture it.

The *lingam* is the principal aniconic image of Lord Shiva (see figure 9.8 on page 137). It is the *murti* of Shiva that is most commonly found in temples. Like the Ardhanarishvara image, the *lingam* comprises a male and a female component. The male element is a short pillar that many consider phallic, although most Hindus would not think of it that way. The female element, called the *yoni*, is the base on top of which the male part sits. Some scholars believe this image derives from the cultic practices of the Indus Valley Civilization. Many phallic-shaped stones were found in the

Harappan ruins, but none quite the same as the *lingam* as it now appears. Other scholars believe the image comes from Indo-Aryan culture and associate it with the worship of Rudra. Most Shaivites, however, contend the image is eternal, without beginning or end. Interpretations of the meaning of the *lingam* have been diverse, but most center on the image as symbolic of

Fig. 9.11 **Ardhanarishvara.** This depiction of Shiva, entitled "The Lord Who Is Half-Woman," illustrates the Hindu conviction that masculine and feminine energies must be balanced. (Photo courtesy of Creative Commons, Sailko.)

divine power and the creative union of male and female energies. The *Puranas*, the medieval mythological texts, support this view by declaring the *lingam* to be the source from which the universe was created and the form into which it will dissolve at its destruction. In this sense, the *lingam* recalls the *murti* of the Nataraja, in which the cosmic functions of creation and dissolution are represented by a drum and fire.

As these images of Shiva demonstrate, Hindu depictions of the divine can be exceedingly rich with significance. They convey to the devotee whole worlds of meaning that are inaccessible in other ways. The all-embracing, paradoxical nature of Shiva, so aptly portrayed in these images, cautions the faithful never to assume that one can pin down the divine with an image or a concept. Ultimate reality cannot in any way be limited by the human mind. Ironically, Shiva's *murtis* use the mind's limitations to make this very point.

Image as Incarnation

The Hindu images of the divine, both iconic and aniconic, function symbolically to point beyond themselves to the ultimate, infinite reality. As symbols, no one would confuse the images with that to which they refer. Shiva's *murtis* are not Shiva. Yet there is a special sense in which the images *are* understood to manifest or embody the divine reality, making the images actual incarnations of the god. Paul Tillich argues that what distinguishes a symbol from a mere sign is that a symbol "participates" in the reality to which it points.[6] Tillich's description of the symbol helps to illuminate the Hindu understanding of divine images. While the *murti* signifies a sacred reality beyond itself, that reality is also regarded as dwelling within the image in a special way, as if the image were participating in its sacred quality.

When an image is completed by a Hindu craftsperson, the god or goddess it represents may be invited to inhabit it through elaborate rituals of consecration. Ordinarily, the incarnation lasts for a specific period of time, perhaps for a weeklong festival in honor of a particular *deva* or *devi*. When the designated term is up, the divine being is invited to return home and the physical image is usually destroyed, often by burning or immersion in water, in what amounts to a funeral. This practice reminds devotees that although the god may indeed be incarnate in the image, the image is not the god. It is still the product of human creation.

Puja

The incarnation of god in Hindu images has important implications for ritual and worship practices (*puja*) (box 9.3). In a temple, during the period of incarnation, the image is treated as if it were god in living form. In the morning, it is gently wakened from sleep, bathed and clothed, decorated with flower garlands and vermillion paste, and offered food. In every respect, the image is given the hospitality accorded a royal guest.

During the day, the image is offered gifts such as flowers, water, betel nuts, and coconuts. Especially pleasing to the deity is *arati*, the waving of a camphor flame before the image (figure 9.12 on page 142). At specific times during the day, the temple image is made available to worshipers for *darshan*, a special viewing of the divine image. Seeing the god and being seen by the god is a transaction of great importance for Hindus. At night, the image is lovingly put to bed. According hospitality to the image of the god is a manifestation of

Box 9.3 **TEMPLE *PUJA***

Although temple worship is not required in most Hindus traditions, participating in a temple *puja* is an important practice in the spiritual lives of most Hindus. Temple *pujas* honor and please the divine embodied in a *murti*, usually daily or several times per day. In every respect, the god or goddess is treated as a royal guest and given lavish hospitality and entertainment to foster intimacy between deity and devotee.

Prior to the ritual, the officiating priest prays to Ganesha, the remover of obstacles, and prepares the sacred space by purifying the various ritual implements with sacred chants and substances. As the time for the *puja* draws near, crowds gather to see and be seen by the deity, who is often hidden from view by a curtain or door as preparations are made.

In larger temples, the *puja* may begin with music—often very loud and dissonant music—from drums, bells, and horns, while *pujas* in smaller temples and shrines may be performed without music and in a simpler style. As the music begins, a chanter starts to intone Sanskrit mantras to invite the presence of the deity.

Once the deity has been "installed" in his or her *murti*, the image may be bathed during elaborate rites called *abhishekas*, where sesame oil, honey, yogurt, milk, coconut water, orange juice, and a sweet mixture called the "five nectars" may be poured over the sculpture. Ordinary *pujas* do not usually involve such complex bathing procedures—a mere sprinkling with sacred water suffices. After the bath, the image is then dressed and decorated with fine, colorful clothing, sprinkled with perfume, trimmed with flowers and jewels, and adorned with cosmetics, particularly *tilaks*, just like those worn by devotees.

Once adorned, the image is revealed to the crowd for *darshan*, a sacred viewing. The deity is then given food, usually cooked rice, fresh fruits, coconuts, and sweets, and other pleasing things to enjoy. Fragrant incense is offered as well as light from special lamps that may burn oil, ghee, or camphor. The priest waves these lamps in circles before the image with his right hand while ringing a bell with his left. Ordinarily, he circles the space in front of the feet, body, and head of the image separately with the lamp. At this point, the drumming often becomes very loud, signaling the high point of the *puja*, and worshipers shout words of praise to the deity. The lamp is passed among the assembly, and individuals place their cupped hands over the flame and then touch their eyelids or cover their eyes with their fingertips, thus partaking in a divine blessing and symbolic purification. Food that was initially offered to the image, now considered to be sacred and imbued with spiritual energy, is then taken and distributed to the crowd. The priest may also offer a plate or bowl containing white ash (*vibhuti*) or colored powder (*kum-kum*) to allow participants a chance to mark their foreheads with a *tilak*. With the distribution of *prashad*, the sacred food, and the ritual powders, devotees now take their leave of the god, perhaps departing with a final prayer on their lips.

bhakti, the tradition of devotion and faith. In the next chapter, we will return to this important path in the Hindu world. Then we will talk about how the many images, rituals, and practices are affirmed in the most beloved of Hindu scriptures, the Bhagavad Gita.

Fig. 9.12 *Arati*. A devotee offers fire-light to the goddess manifested as the river Ganges in a ritual practice known as *arati*. The practice recalls the use of fire in the Vedic period. (Photo: orvalrochefort / Flickr [Creative Commons Attribution 2.0 License].)

◆ KEY TERMS

aniconic

arati

Ardhanarishvara

bhakti

Ganesha

Ganga

iconic

idolatry

lingam

Mahayogi

murti

Nataraja

puja

saguna Brahman

shakti

yantra

◆ QUESTIONS FOR REVIEW

1. What are iconic and aniconic images? What are the advantages and disadvantages of each kind of depiction?

2. Why do anthropomorphic images of the *devas* often include distinctly nonhuman features?

3. How can Hinduism be both monotheistic and polytheistic?

4. What is the difference between *nirguna* and *saguna* Brahman?

5. How can venerating divine images actually prevent idolatry?

6. What might be the consequences of venerating only mental images of God, such as anthropomorphic metaphors?

◆ QUESTIONS FOR FURTHER REFLECTION

1. Is it ultimately important to try to understand the divine—that which is beyond human conception?

2. What spiritual needs are met through worship that engages all of the senses?

3. How could conceptualizing god as gendered affect the relationship between deity and devotee?

4. What are the advantages and disadvantages of worshiping a god with humanlike characteristics?

◆ FOR FURTHER STUDY

Eck, Diana L. *Darśan: Seeing the Divine Image in India.* 3rd ed. New York: Columbia University Press, 1998.

O'Flaherty, Wendy Doniger. *Śiva: The Erotic Ascetic.* New York: Oxford University Press, 1973.

Sarma, Deepak. *Hinduism: A Reader.* Malden, Mass.: Wiley-Blackwell, 2008.

Sharma, Arvind. *Classical Hindu Thought: An Introduction.* New Delhi: Oxford University Press, 2000.

Tillich, Paul. *Dynamics of Faith.* New York: HarperOne, 2001.

10. The Way of Devotion

PREVIEW

The Hindu traditions offer multiple paths for reaching divine reality because different people require different spiritualities. Previously, we have explored two such paths, the ways of action and knowledge. In this chapter we will look at a third, the path of *bhakti*, or devotion. Oriented toward faith in a personal deity of choice, the path of devotion is a road to god heavily traversed by Hindus. Our introduction to *bhakti* practice will be through one of the most important and beloved of Hindu texts, the Bhagavad Gita. This wonderful story of a warrior's dilemma and the counsel of the god Krishna has been a treasure trove of spiritual enrichment for centuries.

As we have seen, the Hindu traditions affirm innumerable ways of conceptualizing the divine and a variety of spiritual disciplines for achieving the ultimate goal of release from the samsaric world. We have already explored the way of action, which allows the great majority of Hindus to improve future rebirths to attain a suitable life in which *moksha* can be realized. But a life based solely on action—even the noblest of actions—is insufficient to win release from samsara, since karma keeps one bound to the cycle of rebirth. We have also studied the way of knowledge, which provides a path to enlightened freedom in this life for those inclined toward asceticism and the life of the mind. But the way of knowledge is arduous and does not appeal to everyone. Its goal—the effacement of the individual self to realize union with the absolute—leaves many cold. As the Hindu mystic Ramakrishna is credited with saying, "I want to eat sugar. I don't want to be sugar."[1]

Bhakti Is Loving Devotion

Because they find the path of knowledge unsuited to their temperaments, many Hindus turn to the way of devotion as the principal discipline of their spiritual lives. The devotional path focuses one's passionate nature on the love of a personal deity. The way of **bhakti**, the term for "devotion," is founded on the conviction that the love of god is paramount. From a complete, wholehearted love for god come all good things, including release from samsara. Those who follow this path are called *bhaktas*.

The way of devotion became very important during the late classical and early medieval periods of Hindu history, and its prominence continued unabated into the modern era. In the early period of the *bhakti* movement, new texts were added to the canon of sacred Hindu writings. These writings include the **Mahabharata** and **Ramayana**, the two great epics of

India, which function much as the *Iliad* and *Odyssey* did in ancient Greece. Also composed and accepted as *smriti* is a collection known as the **Puranas**. Assembled between 300 and 1700 C.E., this compilation related much of the mythic lore about the gods and goddesses. These texts were crucial in shaping Hindu piety in the *bhakti* movement and continue to inform the faith of millions to the present day. As we mentioned earlier, the *smriti* works are much more widely read than the *shruti* texts, which are considered to be the most sacred and authoritative.

Our study of *bhakti* will be by means of the **Bhagavad Gita**, one of the most popular religious texts among Hindus and the first to use the term *bhakti*. Although not the most sacred or most authoritative Hindu writing, the Gita is widely read and extremely well known. Many Hindus have it completely memorized. Studying the Gita not only provides us with an exposition of the path of devotion; it also enriches our understanding of the paths of action and knowledge. Although the Gita primarily endorses the spirituality of *bhakti*, it does not do so at the expense of the other ways of the *Trimarga* or other Hindu practices. Indeed, part of the popularity of the Bhagavad Gita is its embrace of virtually all Hindu traditions. For grasping the wide expanse of these traditions, there is probably no better text.

Vishnu and Vaishnavism

Before we venture into the Gita itself, let us first get better acquainted with the god Vishnu, who, in his manifestation as Krishna, is one of the story's two central characters. Hindus who read or hear the Gita, of course, would be aware of this background.

Vishnu

Vishnu was a *deva* in the Vedic period, but he was not especially prominent. The Vedas refer to him as the younger brother of Indra and call him the "three-stepper." Other sources relate how Vishnu acquired this epithet: Bali, a demon-king, invited the gods to a great sacrifice in their honor. To impress his divine guests with his magnanimity, Bali offered to fulfill any wish each might have. Vishnu, who attended the banquet in the guise of a dwarf, asked only to be given as much land as he could cross in three steps. Bali agreed to the request, thinking it would be a simple boon to grant. Then Vishnu suddenly grew to immense proportions. His first step covered the earth; the second reached the sun; and there was no space left for a third step. Bali lowered his head in acknowledgment of Vishnu's superiority.

In later Hindu history, Vishnu's prominence increased immensely. Eventually, he became a member of the **Trimurti**, the cosmic triad of gods responsible for creating, maintaining, and destroying the universe. The Trimurti tradition maintains that the cosmic creator is Brahma, and the cosmic destroyer is Shiva. The god who sustains the cosmos between the times of generation and destruction is Vishnu. This schema, however, is a bit too tidy and does not always reflect the actual roles of these gods in their respective mythologies and cults. The stories of Shiva, as we noted earlier, depict him as creator as well as destroyer of the world. Likewise, other myths attribute all three roles to Vishnu.

In iconography, Vishnu is identified by the symbols he carries in each of his four hands. In one hand, he has a club symbolizing knowledge; in another, a ball signifying the earth; in a third, he has a *chakra*, or disc, symbolizing

Fig. 10.1   Vishnu. Vishnu is at the center of one of the three major Hindu religions. (Photo courtesy of Creative Commons, Nyoe.)

power; and in the fourth, a conch shell to suggest water and the origins of existence (figure 10.1).

The Avatars of Vishnu

What is most distinctive about Vishnu, however, is his **avatars,** or incarnations. The Sanskrit word *avatāra* literally means "to descend into." According to Vaishnavite belief, god descends to earth and assumes an earthly manifestation at critical junctures to rescue its imperiled inhabitants and restore dharma. The dominant tradition maintains that Vishnu has done this nine times in the current world era and will do so once again before its conclusion. Vishnu's previous avatars include a boar that raised the earth above the primordial waters that threatened to engulf it; a fish that saved

the first human, Manu, from a terrestrial flood; a tortoise; a dwarf; an ax-wielding sage, and a man-lion. According to this tradition, Vishnu also appeared as the Buddha. Thus, in a classic instance of Hindu inclusivity, the Buddha, the teacher of another great Indian tradition, has been incorporated into the Hindu pantheon.[2] In his final avatar, Vishnu will return at the end of the age as Kalki, an apocalyptic judge riding a white horse (figure 10.2).

From the standpoint of religious practice, Vishnu's most important avatars have been **Rama** and **Krishna.** Both figures are widely revered among Hindus. As Rama, Vishnu appeared on earth as the royal figure who defeats his wife's abductor in the great epic the *Ramayana.* Rama is regarded as a great example of moral conduct, and his marriage to Sita is upheld as the Hindu ideal. Today, *Ram* is one of the most common terms for god among Hindus.

Krishna, however, is a name that many Westerners would also recognize. In the last half of the twentieth century, many in the West have become familiar with the name *Krishna* through a movement known as the **International Society for Krishna Consciousness (ISKCON).** ISKCON, known colloquially as the Hare Krishnas, was founded in 1966 by Swami A. C. Bhaktivedanta. It belongs to the Gaudiya Vaishnavite tradition, a devotional sect based on the teachings of fifteenth-century saint and religious reformer Sri Caitanya Mahaprabhu. This tradition focuses on abstinence from karmically negative activities such as eating meat, illicit sex, and intoxication, and on the frequent chanting of the name of god. It is from their chanting of the mantra "Hare Krishna," among others, that these Vaishnavites acquired their nickname (box 10.1).

Fig. 10.2 **Vishnu's avatars.** According to myth, Vishnu assumes earthly forms called avatars during times of great crisis.
(Photo courtesy of Creative Commons, Steve Jurvetson.)

Box 10.1 **THE HARE KRISHNA MANTRA**

Members of the International Society for Krishna Consciousness (ISKCON) have popularized the sixteen-word mantra that has been one of the centerpieces of the Gaudiya Vaishnavite tradition.

> Hare Krishna Hare Krishna
>
> Krishna Krishna Hare Hare
>
> Hare Rama Hare Rama
>
> Rama Rama Hare Hare

The mantra is addressed to god and comprises the repetition of three divine names. Krishna and Rama are two of Vishnu's avatars. *Hare* refers to "Hari," a name for Vishnu that means "the one who dispels illusion."

Since the 1960s, this chant has found its way into popular American culture in a variety of forms. One of the most notable is George Harrison's song "My Sweet Lord," in which the refrain "Hallelujah" almost imperceptibly becomes "Hare Krishna."

Krishna

Krishna's popularity in India derives primarily from two sources. One is his image as a playful and adventurous boy and young man. This Krishna is remembered as a child who steals butter and as a youth who has amorous escapades with village girls (figure 10.3). One of the most delightful pieces of Vaishnavite literature is the **Gita Govinda**, or the *Song of Govinda (the Protector of Cows)*, composed by the twelfth-century poet Jayadeva. This poem tells the story of Krishna's consort **Radha**; her passionate love for him informs what is easily some of the most erotic literature in world religion. The *Gita Govinda* illustrates how, on the path of devotion, one might long for god as a lover longs for her beloved (box 10.2).

Fig. 10.3 **Youthful Krishna.** Krishna, widely revered as a child and youth, is celebrated in this eighteenth-century painting for his roguish exploits as the "thief of butter." (Photo courtesy of http://commons.wikimedia.org/wiki/File:Indischer_Maler_um_1750_(I)_001.jpg.)

Box 10.2 **RADHA'S LONGING FOR KRISHNA**

Because of her passionate yearning for Krishna, Radha is regarded as the ideal devotee in Vaishnavism. In the *Gita Govinda*, Radha is one of many *gopis*, or female cowherds, with whom Krishna cavorts in the forest outside the village of Vrindavan. When she is separated from her god, Radha pines for him, imagining her great delight when he returns. Her obsession with the lord is presented as the proper attitude of the true worshiper of god, who longs for the divine with the intensity of someone who has fallen in love.

Lord Hari,
Radha suffers in her retreat.

Her body bristling with longing,
Her breath sucking in words of confusion,
Her voice cracking in deep, cold fear—
Obsessed by intense thoughts of passion,
Radha sinks in a sea of erotic mood,
Clinging to you in her meditation, cheat!

She ornaments her limbs
When a leaf quivers or a feather falls,
Suspecting your coming,
She spreads out the bed
And waits long in meditation.
Making her bed of ornaments and fantasies,
She evokes a hundred details of you
In her own graceful play.
But the frail girl will not survive
Tonight without you.*

*Barbara Stoler Miller, trans., *Gita Govinda of Jayadeva: Love Song of the Dark Lord* (New York: Columbia University Press, 1997), 96.

The Bhagavad Gita

The other source of Krishna's popularity is the Bhagavad Gita. This work, the title of which is usually translated as the "Song of the Lord," was probably composed between 400 B.C.E. and 100 C.E. Its author, or authors, is unknown. Although it is usually read as a self-contained story, the Bhagavad Gita is part of the *Mahabharata*, the world's longest epic poem, with more than one hundred thousand verses. The Gita, as it is commonly known, has influenced Indian thinkers and ordinary folk throughout its two-thousand-year history. Many of India's great philosophers and theologians have penned commentaries illuminating its meaning. Gandhi called it his "eternal mother" and, despite its messages urging the protagonist to war, he found in it support for his disciplined practice of nonviolent resistance to tyranny. The Gita has also impressed many Western intellectuals, including Ralph Waldo Emerson, Henry David Thoreau, and T. S. Eliot. It is probably the work of Indian literature most familiar to Westerners.

The Gita is essentially a dialogue between Vishnu, in his avatar as Krishna, and a warrior by the name of **Arjuna**. Their conversation takes place on the battlefield just as two grand armies are about to go to war. The combatants are the Kauravas and the Pandavas, who are fighting for the right to rule a northern Indian kingdom. The Kauravas and the Pandavas are members of the same clan, making this a family feud. Arjuna is a member of the Pandava family, and it is precisely because he must fight his uncles, cousins, and teachers that he is so aggrieved.

As the battle lines are drawn, Krishna steers Arjuna's chariot between the two armies. Suddenly, all action is suspended, as though a moment of eternity has opened in the midst of time. Arjuna surveys the scene and becomes melancholic and philosophical. When he sees his family members across enemy lines, he drops his bow, having lost his will to fight (figure 10.4).

Fig. 10.4 Krishna and Arjuna on the Field of Dharma. The mature Krishna is guru to Arjuna, a tormented warrior, depicted in the chariot on the left, in the Bhagavad Gita, one of the best-loved Hindu texts. (Photo courtesy of http://commons.wikimedia.org/wiki/File:Arjuna_and_His_Charioteer_Krishna_Confront_Karna.jpg.)

Arjuna sadly tells Lord Krishna that he cannot go to war: he has no desire to fight the revered members of his clan. Arjuna concludes that such a battle can only lead to chaos. The term he uses is **adharma**, which means the opposite of dharma. He can see no value in gaining wealth (*artha*) and earthly pleasure (*kama*) if having these traditional goods of life entails destroying his own family. Informed by this moving story, the fear of ruining the family exerts tremendous influence on individual behavior in India. Even today, in South India, bottles of beer often carry a warning label that frankly tells the purchaser "DRINKING LIQUOR WILL RUIN THE FAMILY."

Rather surprisingly, Krishna's first response to Arjuna's qualms is to shame him. He taunts Arjuna, questions his masculinity, and then commands him to get up and fight. Krishna tells Arjuna that fighting is his dharma. As a Kshatriya, he will find no greater honor or responsibility than to do battle. We recall the Laws of Manu:

> A king who, while he protects his people, is defied by (foes), be they equal in strength, or stronger, or weaker, must not shrink from battle. . . . Not to turn back in battle, to protect the people . . . is the best means for a king to secure happiness.[3]

When Arjuna still refuses to fight, Krishna tries another tactic. He tells Arjuna to think of his reputation: "People will tell of your undying shame, and for a man of honor shame is worse than death."[4]

Arjuna does not respond to these appeals. He has become much too thoughtful, too philosophical to be bullied or shamed into war. Arjuna's conflict is deep and genuine, and he is paralyzed until he can see his way

clear. His inner turmoil is a familiar one: it is the dissonance one feels when competing values clash. The most poignant human dilemmas are not those between good and evil, which are relatively easy to solve. The most difficult problems in life arise when we must choose between the lesser of two evils or the greater of two goods. Arjuna must negotiate between two moral alternatives: to refuse to fight, thus disobeying his dharma as a warrior, or to go to war and thereby invite the negative consequences of karma, including family ruin, social chaos, and continued rebirth into samsara.

Arjuna's intellectual dissonance becomes a teaching moment. In the story, he wisely asks Krishna to be his guru. When such a moment arrives, a superior teacher knows it to be a great opportunity for breakthrough. The student is prepared for insight. Krishna accepts the challenge.

Krishna's first lesson to the warrior recalls the teachings of the Upanishads. Indeed, Krishna essentially quotes a famous Upanishadic passage about the nature of the *atman*:

> He who thinks this self a killer
> And he who thinks it killed,
> Both fail to understand;
> It does not kill, nor is it killed.
> It is not born,
> It does not die;
> Having been,
> It will never not be;
> Unborn, enduring,
> Constant and primordial, it is not killed
> When the body is killed.[5]

Krishna's point is a logical conclusion in a philosophy based on the immortality of the *atman*. Life and death are ultimately meaningless.

But Arjuna presses further. He is concerned with another matter now, the problem of karma. Perhaps it is true that one cannot kill the immortal self, but killing the body is action, and all action generates karma. How does one avoid the negative karmic consequences of killing—or the consequences of any action? Arjuna is well schooled in the idea that karma keeps one bound to the wheel of samsara.

Krishna now responds with another lesson: learning to act without attachment or aversion. In propounding this idea, the Gita deepens our understanding of the way of action. Krishna tells Arjuna that it is impossible *not* to act, but it is possible to act *without creating karma*. The secret lies in acting with equanimity, without desire or hatred.

> Be intent on action,
> Not on the fruits of action;
> Avoid attraction to the fruits
> And attachment to inaction!
>
> Perform actions firm in discipline,
> Relinquishing attachment;
> Be impartial to failure and success—
> This equanimity is called discipline.
>
> Arjuna, action is far inferior
> To the discipline of understanding;
> So seek refuge in understanding—pitiful
> Are men drawn by fruits of action.[6]

Krishna maintains that the true effects of karma come from the heart and the will, not the action itself. Thus, an equanimous disposition frees one from bondage to karma and consequently from samsara itself.

> Action imprisons the world
> Unless it is done as sacrifice;

> Freed from attachment, Arjuna,
> Perform action as sacrifice![7]

Using the metaphor of sacrifice, Krishna encourages Arjuna to relinquish all actions just as one relinquishes a sacrificial victim to the gods. Thus, according to the Gita, it is not action that perpetuates rebirth, but rather attachment and aversion. Without attachment or aversion, mere action cannot bind the self to the world of samsara.

When Arjuna asks how one might learn to perform "karmaless" action, Krishna tells him it takes discipline; he then proceeds to discuss, over the span of many chapters, the entire panorama of Hindu practices. The divine charioteer discusses the value of asceticism, renunciation, study of the sacred Vedas, the sacrifices of the Brahmins, fasting, prayer, and meditation. One can get a comprehensive view of virtually all the Hindu worldviews and practices just by reading the Gita.

As the discussion continues, Arjuna raises objections and Krishna responds. At one point, Arjuna becomes terribly frustrated. He complains to Krishna, "You confuse my understanding with a maze of words; speak one certain truth so I may achieve what is good."[8] Like all of us, Arjuna longs for clarity and simplicity. He merely wants to know the right thing to do. Such a simple answer, however, is not forthcoming. Krishna continues to spin a swirl of words as rich and complex as the Hindu traditions themselves.

This richness and lack of clarity is one of the reasons for the Gita's vast appeal. Every Hindu finds something of value here, some wisdom that pertains to his or her place in life. The Brahmins find their sacrifices honored; the *sannyasins* and *shramanas* see their renunciation and asceticism valued; the warriors have their dharma affirmed. All ways of genuine spirituality are embraced and accepted.

As the dialogue proceeds, Krishna's lessons gradually focus more and more on himself. Late in the text, the teachings become increasingly characteristic of the path of *bhakti*. Krishna encourages Arjuna to focus his mind, will, and heart on god and to let all else go.

> Men who worship me,
> Thinking solely of me,
> Always disciplined,
> win the reward I secure.[9]

> The leaf or flower or fruit or water
> That he offers with devotion,
> I take from the man of self-restraint
> In response to his devotion.

> Whatever you do—whatever you take,
> Whatever you offer, what you give,
> What penances you perform—
> Do as an offering to me, Arjuna!

> You will be freed from the bonds of action,
> From the fruit of fortune and misfortune;
> Armed with the discipline of renunciation,
> Your self liberated, you will join me.[10]

For *bhakti* practice, *what* is done is not as important as *the spirit* in which it is done. All that matters is to do all things with faith and devotion to god. It does not even matter whether or not one is devoted to Krishna by name. One can worship other gods in *bhakti* practice, as long as it is done with fidelity.

> When devoted men sacrifice
> To other deities with faith,
> They sacrifice to me, Arjuna,
> However aberrant the rites.[11]

All paths performed in the right spirit lead to Krishna. The tradition has come a long way from Vedic times, when priests insisted that the mantras of the sacrifice had to be pronounced at just the right pitch and inflection to please the gods and ensure the effectiveness of the rites.

As Krishna's teachings center more and more on the path of devotion, Arjuna feels his doubts melt away. In a climactic moment, he asks Krishna to grant him an extremely rare boon, the ability to see Krishna in his full glory as god. Krishna gives Arjuna a divine eye with which to gaze on the god's primordial form. The passages that relate this great vision are fascinating and memorable. Vyasa, the story's narrator, describes the scene:

> If the light of a thousand suns
> Were to rise in the sky at once,
> It would be like the light
> Of that great spirit.

> Arjuna saw all the universe
> In its many ways and parts,
> Standing as one in the body
> of the god of gods.

> Then filled with amazement,
> his hair bristling on his flesh,
> Arjuna bowed his head to the god,
> [and] joined his hands in homage.[12]

J. Robert Oppenheimer, director of the Manhattan Project, said that when he saw the first atomic bomb detonated in the desert of New Mexico in 1945 he immediately recalled the first two lines of this passage, comparing the light of Krishna to a thousand suns rising at once in the sky: "We knew the world would not be the same. A few people laughed, a few people cried, most people were silent. I remembered the line from the Hindu scripture, the Bhagavad Gita. Vishnu is trying to persuade the Prince that he should do his duty and to impress him takes on his multi-armed form and says, 'Now, I am become Death, the destroyer of worlds.' I suppose we all felt that one way or another."[13]

Arjuna's response to this awesome vision is characteristic of many such experiences in the history of religions. Rudolph Otto called these events experiences of "the holy."[14] Otto said the experience of the holy is marked by a highly ambivalent reaction, just as we observe in Arjuna. He is both terrified of and fascinated with the sight. What Arjuna sees accents the absolute otherness of divinity:

I see no beginning
or middle or end to you;
only boundless strength
in your endless arms, the moon and the sun
    in your eyes,
your mouths of consuming flames,
your own brilliance
scorching the universe.

You alone
fill the space
between heaven and earth
and all the directions;
seeing this awesome,
terrible form of yours,
Great Soul,
the three worlds
tremble.[15]

Seeing the many mouths
and eyes
of your great form,
its many arms,

thighs, feet, bellies, and fangs,
the worlds tremble
and so do I.[16]

Now Krishna speaks:

I am time grown old,
creating world destruction,
set in motion
to annihilate the worlds;
even without you,
all these warriors
arrayed in hostile ranks
will cease to exist.

Therefore arise
and win glory!
Conquer your foes
and fulfill your kingship!
They are already
killed by me.
Be just my instrument,
the archer at my side![17]

After his vision, Arjuna arises and goes to battle, claiming that his doubts have been dispelled. It is not altogether clear what has resolved his misgivings. Has he been persuaded by Krishna's arguments or by the awesome vision? Is he convinced by the understanding that Krishna embraces all things in life and death, and that ultimately, from the perspective of eternity, whether one lives or dies does not really matter? What about Arjuna's initial uncertainty about fighting against his own clan? Has Krishna adequately set that issue to rest? Many have noted that much in the Gita is left unsettled, despite the fact that Arjuna himself seems to have gained clarity.

The war commences, and Arjuna and his brothers, the Pandavas, win. Significantly, the

Gita itself ends before we know the battle's outcome. The question of who wins and who loses is not the issue in the Gita. Nor does the Gita really try to solve the problem of war. The two sides are not identified as good or bad. There are no clear favorites here; the war is, by almost any standard, tragic.

Yet the context of war is significant in the Gita, because the battlefield is really a metaphor for the self and its struggle. For ordinary Hindus wrestling with issues of dharma, one's sacred duty is a much more present reality than the rarefied subjects of the Vedas or the Upanishads. As a metaphor for the self and its internal struggles, the Gita is a reminder that often there are no clear avenues of choice. Our decisions must be frequently made in ambiguity and uncertainty. This context of uncertainty makes the path of *bhakti* even more compelling. When faced with a world where choices are not always clear, where decisions often leave us unsettled and insecure, the knowledge that the supreme reality judges the purity of our hearts rather than the correctness of our actions provides a great comfort for the faithful. Such consolation comes from the conviction that god brings good out of whatever decisions a person may make.

In the end, loving devotion to god is the only thing that matters.

◆ **KEY TERMS**

adharma

Arjuna

avatar

Bhagavad Gita

bhakti

Gita Govinda

International Society for Krishna Consciousness (ISKCON)

Krishna

Mahabharata

Puranas

Radha

Rama

Ramayana

Trimurti

◆ **QUESTIONS FOR REVIEW**

1. Why might the *bhakti-marga*, the path of passionate devotion to god, be more widely followed and accompanied by more popular literature than the path of knowledge?

2. At the end of the Bhagavad Gita, Arjuna claims that his doubts about going to war have been dispelled by Krishna's teachings and manifestation as god. As a reader, do you find Krishna as persuasive as Arjuna did?

3. How does the Bhagavad Gita explore the relationships among the ways of action, knowledge, and devotion?

4. Why is Arjuna's conflict and his subsequent dialogue with Krishna so compelling to Hindus across age, caste, and gender boundaries?

5. How is *smriti* different from *sruti*? Why do you think the Gita, a work of *smriti*, is more popular and well read than *sruti* like the Vedas and Upanishads?

◆ **QUESTIONS FOR FURTHER REFLECTION**

1. What are the benefits of a religious approach that offers many avenues for spiritual fulfillment?

2. Is it possible to have a religious experience without devotion?

3. What are the advantages and disadvantages of studying a sacred text from a historical and literary standpoint, without the insights and biases of religious interpretation?

◆ **FOR FURTHER STUDY**

Bhaktivedanta, A. C. Swami. *The Bhagavad Gita as It Is*. New York: Macmillan, 1968.

Buck, William. *Mahabharata*. Berkeley: University of California Press, 1973.

———. *Ramayana*. Berkeley: University of California Press, 1976.

Dimmitt, Cornelia, and J. A. B. van Buitenen, trans. *Classical Hindu Mythology: A Reader in the Sanskrit Puranas*. Philadelphia: Temple University Press, 1978.

The Mahabharata. DVD. Directed by Peter Brook. Los Angeles: Image Entertainment, 1989.

Miller, Barbara Stoler, trans. *The Bhagavad-Gita: Krishna's Counsel in Time of War*. New York: Bantam, 1986.

———, trans. *Gita Govinda of Jayadeva: Love Song of the Dark Lord*. New York: Columbia University Press, 1997.

11. The Goddess and Her Devotees

PREVIEW

Worship of the goddess is a long-established tradition in India. In this chapter, we study the essential features of goddess worship, which is known as Shaktism. We will examine the principal manifestations of the goddess as consorts to the great gods and as the autonomous *devis*. In discussing how concepts of the divine female function in relation to divine males, we will see that the feminine energy revealed by the goddess is essential to Hindu theology. The chapter also explores the practices and concepts of Tantra, an esoteric yogic discipline usually associated with the goddess and whose origins may date to the Indus Valley Civilization.

The worship of female deities has a long history in India and remains a prominent Hindu tradition today. Archaeological and literary evidence indicates a central role for the divine female in Indian religious practices from the earliest times. Terra-cotta figurines from the Indus Valley Civilization suggest that women may have been accorded a sacred status by virtue of their capacity to create new life. Even the Vedic pantheon, dominated as it was by male deities like the hypermasculine Indra, included several goddesses such as Ushas, goddess of the dawn; Sarasvati, who appears in the Vedas as a river goddess; and Vak, the highly important personification of voice. In later classical and medieval Hinduism, worship of the goddess increased in popularity and gained (or perhaps regained) a central place in everyday religious life. Today, **Shaktism**, the worship of the goddess, is regarded as a major Hindu religion alongside Shaivism and Vaishnavism. Its followers are called Shaktas. In this chapter, we continue our exploration of the goddess tradition in Hinduism, focusing on the way goddesses are conceptualized and revered. We will also introduce Tantra, a yogic practice closely associated with goddess devotion.

Manifestations of the Goddess

When speaking of the divine female in India, it is common to refer to *the* goddess in the singular. This custom derives from the belief that all individual goddesses are forms of **Mahadevi**, or simply Devi, the great goddess. This theological view was popularized in the medieval period through the *Puranas*. In myth and in worship, of course, there are countless goddesses who are usually treated as distinct deities, particularly on the popular level. Yet just as different gods can represent the one god, so the different goddesses manifest the one great goddess. Ultimately, both goddess and god (and goddesses and gods) symbolize and reveal the transpersonal Brahman. Indeed, devotees of the goddess regard her as ultimate reality itself. To know her and receive her grace is to experience final liberation from the samsaric world (figure 11.1).

Although the name *Mahadevi* is commonly used, the goddess is even more frequently known to devotees as **Mata**, **Ma**, or **Amman**, all various ways of saying "mother." Interestingly, despite this name, none but a few of the goddesses have children, and those who do usually acquired them through unusual means. The implication, of course, is that the goddess is the mother of the world and its inhabitants are her children (box 11.1).

The many manifestations of Devi can be classified into two broad categories. First are

Fig. 11.1   Tridevi. Lakshmi, Parvati, and Sarasvati are represented in a single form, suggesting that each is only a different manifestation of an indivisible reality. (Photo courtesy of http://commons.wikimedia.org/wiki/File:Tridevi.png.)

Box 11.1   MANIFESTATIONS OF THE GODDESS

In this chapter we focus on the mythic and iconic representations of the goddess. But the goddess is manifested in other ways as well. It is common, for example, for particular aspects of nature to be seen as forms of the divine female. Rivers, such as the Ganges and the Sarasvati, are also goddesses. As rivers, the *devis* nourish the world with their water and provide a nurturing source of purification. The earth itself is a goddess, and she is named Bhudevi, literally "earth-goddess," or more loosely, "Mother Nature." In temples, Bhudevi is sometimes represented anthropomorphically as the second wife of Vishnu. The entire land of India, in fact, is a goddess known as Bharat Mata, "Mother India." A temple in Varanasi dedicated to Bharat Mata contains a map of India rather than an anthropomorphic image.

The goddess may also be embodied as human women. Such incarnations of the goddess are not uncommon. For some, an especially powerful woman, such as Indira Gandhi, one of India's prime ministers, might be regarded as the goddess in the flesh. Others consider women with extraordinary spiritual qualities to embody the goddess. Sometimes the incarnation is a lesser-known woman who is believed to personify the qualities of the mother goddess. The classic film *Devi*, by the Indian director Satyajit Ray, is a poignant study of what happens when a family patriarch becomes convinced that his own daughter-in-law is the goddess.

those goddesses who generally manifest as benevolent, gentle, and life-giving; they are regarded as **cool goddesses**. Second are those who often become malevolent, terrifying, and lustful; these are the **hot goddesses**. A similar distinction can be made for the male *devas*, but the difference is more important for understanding the *devis*, since most of the *devas* are naturally cool. The meaning of the terms *hot* and *cool* in this context ought to be fairly evident, even to non-Hindus. "Hot" is often associated with passion, anger, violence, disease, and lust, and these are precisely the qualities connected with the hot goddesses. On the other hand, "cool" describes qualities of dispassion, equanimity, control, and rationality. Because she assumes these two basic forms, the great goddess herself is both cool and hot. Accordingly, she is much like Shiva, who embodies paradox and ambiguity. She is ascetic and erotic, detached and passionate, attractive and terrifying. We will consider both sides of her character as it is expressed in the manifestations of individual goddesses.

The Cool Goddesses

We will take as the principal representatives of the cool goddesses the consorts of the great cosmic gods. Each of the cosmic *devas* is married to or intimately associated with a goddess. Brahma is married to **Sarasvati** (figure 11.2); Shiva's wife is **Parvati** (box 11.2); and Vishnu's

Fig.11.2 Sarasvati. Sarasvati, consort of Brahma, is revered as the goddess of education and the arts. In this figure, she holds a stringed instrument called a *vina* in her left hand, while her right hand forms a teaching *mudra*, or gesture. (Photo courtesy of Creative Commons, Christina Kundu.)

is **Lakshmi**. Some of Vishnu's avatars also have consorts. Rama is married to Sita, and Krishna's consort is Radha. In almost every case, the married goddesses are worshiped for their

---

Box 11.2 THE WIVES OF SHIVA

Shiva has only one wife, whose name is usually Parvati. But depending on the region, she may be worshiped as Minakshi, Sati, Lalita, Chandi, Uma, or dozens of other names. Each goddess has her own unique mythology. Each of these goddesses may be understood to be forms of Parvati, just as Parvati, Sarasvati, and Lakshmi are manifestations of Devi.

loving, compassionate, and nurturing qualities. Although they are closely associated with a male god, they are not ordinarily revered for that reason—or for that reason alone. Their independence is reflected in temple iconography. In shrines and other holy places, the *murtis* of the male deities are almost never without their female counterparts (for reasons that will be made evident shortly). But images of the goddesses—even the married ones—may appear, and frequently do, without their male consorts.

This iconographic practice derives in part from the fact that the goddesses are powerful in their own right and govern domains of particular concern to human beings. Lakshmi, for example, is not only Vishnu's wife; she is also the goddess of good fortune and wealth. Her image is ubiquitous throughout India's places of commerce (figure 11.3). At the start of a new fiscal year, businesspeople commonly worship her and pray for prosperity. The *devi* Sarasvati, goddess of education, music, and the arts, is almost always worshiped alone, without her consort, Brahma. Despite his status as one of the Trimurti, Brahma has a very small role in popular Hindu practice. Temples devoted to him are extremely rare. But because of her sphere of influence, Sarasvati is very important, especially to students. She is often venerated at school festivals and prayed to before examinations.

A notable exception to the practice of worshiping the consort goddesses independently of their husbands, however, is the female companions of Vishnu's avatars. These goddesses do not govern particular domains like Sarasvati and Lakshmi, and their religious significance is tied directly to their relationship with their husband or lover. Sita, the wife of Rama, is revered as the ideal wife because of her fidelity and obedience to her husband. Radha, Krishna's consort, is the perfect image of the devotee with a passionate love for god. These two examples are among the few instances in which a goddess provides a model for human emulation.

Fig.11.3 **Lakshmi.** Lakshmi is the goddess of prosperity and fertility. Her devotees regard her as the epitome of grace and beauty. (Photo courtesy of Creative Commons, Leon Meerson.)

The Hot Goddesses

Although they are often compassionate and tender like the goddess-consorts, the hot goddesses are also subject to terrifying manifestations. They often possess greater powers and seem less approachable than the more benign cool goddesses. Yet it is that very power, even in its awesome expression, that draws the devotee to their worship.

Durga

Because of their tremendous abilities, the hot goddesses often appear as celestial deities on a level with the great gods like Vishnu and Shiva. Many of the myths about **Durga**, for example, depict her as engaged in activities akin to those of the great male deities, such as protecting the cosmos against powerful demons. Indeed, she is sometimes portrayed as accomplishing difficult tasks that the gods cannot. In a well-known story, a powerful buffalo-demon and his minions threaten to destroy the universe, and the gods find themselves impotent to contain the menace. Finally, they appeal to Vishnu and Shiva for assistance. But even the great Vishnu and Shiva are unable to control the demon army and must resort to another tactic. Their solution is to infuse a goddess with their combined anger. Out of their fury, the goddess Durga appears in a sea of light. Durga defeats the demons and their leader in a long and vicious battle (figure 11.4). After her triumph, she promises to return whenever the demons prove too powerful for Vishnu and Shiva.[1] Durga's victory is now commemorated annually in Bengal and other parts of India with a huge festival called **Navaratri** ("Nine Nights"), one of the most popular Hindu celebrations.

Kali

Like Durga, **Kali's** great powers rival—and even exceed, according to some myths—those of the male deities. Kali, "the black one," is perhaps the most terrifying form of Devi. She is most commonly represented as having black or blue skin and four arms. Her gaping mouth reveals fangs and a lolling tongue, dripping with blood. Her eyes are red with rage, her long hair is disheveled, and she wears a garland of human skulls. Often she is depicted naked or wearing a skirt of severed human arms. She wears the corpses of children as earrings and serpents as bangles. In her hands she holds the weapons and instruments associated with other gods, an iconographic way of showing that she assimilates their powers. In her manifestation as Mahakali, she has ten arms, ten heads, and ten legs. Like the ascetic Shiva, Kali haunts the cremation grounds. She is also found on battlefields, dancing wildly, drunk on the blood of the vanquished. Although she is sometimes depicted as Shiva's wife, she is often viewed as independent of him. Accentuating that inde-

Fig. 11.4 Durga. The powerful Durga defeats the buffalo-demon as the weaker *devas* look on from behind the clouds. (Photo courtesy of http://commons.wikimedia.org/wiki/File:Durga_Mahisasuramardini.jpg.)

Fig. 11.5   Kali. This colorful head of Kali was constructed for a festival in Kolkata, a major center of goddess worship. (Photo courtesy of Creative Commons, Arnab Dutta.)

pendence, some of the medieval *Puranas* declare Kali the supreme reality, the highest manifestation of Brahman (figure 11.5).

Theologically, Kali reveals that life is inherently painful and feeds on death. In the not-too-distant past, human sacrifices were offered to Kali. At a Kali temple in Tanjore in South India, human sacrifices were performed on Fridays up until the nineteenth century. In and around Kolkata (Calcutta) in the late eighteenth and early nineteenth centuries, a group known as the **Thags** (pronounced "thugs") was known for committing crimes in the name of Kali. They murdered innocent victims by strangulation as a sacrifice to their patron goddess. The Thags were often respectable men who held regular jobs during the day and served the

goddess at night. Although the British banned the Thags in the nineteenth century, their name lives on in the English language as a synonym for unsavory and brutal criminals.

Although human sacrifices in honor of Kali have almost completely disappeared, animals are regularly offered to her at the Kalighat temple in Kolkata. The animals nonetheless are only a substitute for humans. The *Puranas* say that the goddess is pleased for a while with the sacrifice of goats or buffaloes, but a human sacrifice pleases her for a thousand years. Even today, on extremely rare occasions, there are reports of human sacrifice or self-immolation in honor of the goddess. Hot goddesses are often offered blood and meat sacrifices, but the offerings to the cool goddesses are exclusively vegetarian.

In view of Kali's love for blood and her erratic temperament, one might justly wonder what would motivate a Hindu to worship such a deity. Perhaps this hymn, written by Ramprasad Sen (box 11.3), an eighteenth-century Bengali poet and devotee of Devi, can illuminate this question:

> Though the mother beat him,
> The child cries, "Mother, O Mother!"
> And clings still tighter to her garment.
> True, I cannot see thee,
> Yet I am not a lost child.
> I still cry, "Mother, Mother."
> All the miseries I have suffered
> And am suffering, I know, O Mother,
> To be your mercy alone.[2]

To be Kali's child is to suffer, but to know the source of that suffering. The Shakta tradition holds that Kali does not always give what one wants or expects. What devotees experience as cruelty forces them to reflect on the true nature

Box 11.3 **THE POETRY OF RAMPRASAD SEN**

Ramprasad Sen was an eighteenth-century Shakta who lived in Bengal. In these poems, we see the intensity of Ramprasad's loving devotion to Kali. In the first, he proclaims how devotion to the goddess obviates the common practice of pilgrimage. In the second, he contemplates the various characteristics that make Kali so appealing to the worshiper.

Of what use is my going to Kasi [Varanasi]
    any more?
At Mother's feet lie Gaya, Ganga and Kasi.
I swim in the ocean of bliss
while I meditate on Her in my heart lotus.
O Kali's feet are red lotuses
wherein lie heaps of holy places.
All sins are destroyed by Kali's name
as heaps of cotton are burnt by fire.
How can a headless man have a headache?
People think, they will discharge their debts
to forefathers by offering them pinda at Gaya!
But, O! I laugh at him who meditates on Kali
and still goes to Gaya!
Shiva assures: Death at Kasi leads to salvation.
But devotion is the root of all;
O mind! Salvation is its maid.
Of what use is nirvana?
Water mingles in water.
O mind! becoming sugar is not desirable;
I am fond of eating sugar.

Bemused, Ramprasad says, "By the strength of
    gracious
Mother, O! Meditation on Her, the wearer of
    disheveled
hair, puts four goods into the palm of our hands.*

Who is this unique warrior woman?
Her terrifying war cry
    pervades the universal battleground.
Who is this incomparable feminine principle?
Contemplating her limitless nature,
the passion to possess and be gratified dissolves.
Who is this elusive wisdom woman?
Her smooth and fragrant body of intense awareness
    is like the petal of a dark blue lotus.

A single eye of knowledge
    shines from her noble forehead
like a moon so full its light engulfs the sun.
This mysterious Goddess, eternally sixteen,
is naked brilliance, transparent insight.
Cascades of black hair stream down her back
    to touch her dancing feet.
Perfect in the art of wisdom warfare
she is the treasury of every excellence,
the reservoir of all that is good.

Her poet sings with unshakable assurance:
"Anyone who lives consciously in the presence of
    this resplendent savioress
can conquer Death with the drumbeat
    Ma! Ma! Ma!"[†]

*Elizabeth U. Harding, *Kali: The Black Goddess of Dakshineswar*, 3rd ed. (York Beach, Maine: Nicolas-Hays, 1993).

[†]From Lex Hixon, *Mother of the Universe: Visions of the Goddess and Tantric Hymns of Enlightenment* (Wheaton, Ill.: Quest, 1994), 187.

of the phenomenal world, as well as of their own selves, and ultimately to transcend them. Thus, in Ramprasad's view, the sufferings one endures in this life are the chastisements of an ultimately loving mother, to whom one must cling in all circumstances. If she is ultimate reality, what other refuge is there?

Village Goddesses

Virtually every Indian village has its goddess, whose province and power generally extend no further than the community itself. These local deities (*grama-devatas*) are usually associated with epidemics, especially smallpox, the disease that has ravaged India more than any other. Association with disease puts most of these local goddesses in the hot category. Epidemics were frequently believed to be the result of the goddess's anger, directed toward a particular village or district because the villagers had neglected her. When epidemics broke out, worship of the Devi intensified in an effort to assuage her wrath and cool her ardor. Many Hindu villagers today still refuse smallpox and other inoculations because they believe the goddess has a greater power to prevent the disease; submitting to human science would provoke her rage. These village *devis* are usually worshiped individually and stand alone in their temples and shrines, but they might also be considered consorts of Shiva.

Accounting for the Difference between Hot and Cool Goddesses

The contrast between the cool and hot goddesses is striking. A common explanation for this dissimilarity suggests that the rage to which the goddess is subject derives from her childlessness. Without children, she is seen as not having fulfilled the central role of female existence. Hindus deem it inappropriate for the goddesses and gods to have children, except in a few rare cases, since children would suggest a loss of immortality.[3] This belief is a common one in the history of religions: humans have children instead of immortality. Being childless, and perhaps sexually frustrated, the goddess's pent-up emotional energies are easily triggered and directed toward those who might upset her in the slightest way. It is always in one's best interest to cool the goddess's hot temper with appropriate gifts and offerings.

Being childless, the consort-goddesses are also subject to rage, but their relationship to gods keeps them cool, channeling anger into nurture, as it were. A myth about one of Kali's rampages illustrates the cooling effect of the male deity. After a grand battle, in which Kali defeats all of her enemies, she begins a wild, ecstatic dance, drunk on the blood of her victims. Her dance gets out of control and threatens the very safety of the world. To cool her down, Shiva appears on the battlefield as a crying infant. Seeing the baby in distress, Kali's maternal qualities are aroused. She picks up the child and nurses the infant at her breast, effectively soothing her delirium. This story reveals both sides of Kali's character as well as the role of the god in assuaging her fury.

This theology may sound merely stereotypical of a patriarchal society that believes, to cite the Laws of Manu, that a woman is never fit for independence. Still, a complex understanding of divine nature underlies this view, one that is not wholly stereotypical. In this understanding, the female aspect of divinity is a creative and activating power. The word for this power is **shakti**, and it is the root word in the name of Shaktism, the religion in which the goddess is worshiped as supreme. *Shakti* is the active principle in Hindu thought, not unlike what the

Chinese call *yang*. But whereas yang is associated with the masculine, *shakti* is feminine. The masculine principle, or **shiva**, is by contrast passive. In fact, the masculine principle is so passive as to be lifeless. *Shiva* without *shakti*, says an old proverb, is *sava*, dead. Male deities thus require goddesses to empower and enliven them. This dynamic explains why in the temple images the gods are almost always accompanied by their consorts. The indispensable nature of *shakti* is suggested in a macabre image depicting Kali dancing on Shiva's dead body (figure 11.6). This idea is also suggested by the goddess's red forehead marking as contrasted with the white forehead marking for the gods. Red is the color of life, power, and heat; white is a cooling color, often associated with death and ashes.

While the goddesses are essential to the gods' function, at the same time goddesses require passive gods to give form to their dynamic power. Without form and restraint, the energy embodied in the goddess can become out of control and dangerous, as exemplified in the fury of the hot goddess. With too much restraint, though, the goddess may become too passive. The existence of cool and hot goddesses supports the Hindu ideal of balance in life. Power must be balanced with order; male must be balanced with female.

Tantra

Closely connected with the worship of the goddess is a yogic practice called **Tantrism**, or simply Tantra.[4] Tantrism made its appearance as a movement at the beginning of the medieval period, around the fifth century C.E. But tantric yoga may be rooted in religious traditions that long antedate India's medieval era. Some scholars argue that what is known today as Tantra derived from practices that go back as far as the Indus Civilization. According to this hypothesis, when the Indo-Aryans gained dominance in northern India in the middle of the second millennium B.C.E., the esoteric beliefs and practices later labeled "Tantra" went underground and were preserved as a secret tradition. Then in the early medieval era, this tradition (or traditions) evolved into the tantric movement, first emerging in areas least influenced by the Vedic religion of the Aryans, particularly eastern and southern India. Aspects of Tantrism, however, appear compatible with certain features of the Vedic tradition, and thus it is quite possible that tantric adepts

Fig. 11.6 Kali dancing on Shiva's corpse. Kali's dance atop the body of Shiva illustrates the identification of the divine feminine with power and the divine masculine with form. (Photo courtesy of http://commons.wikimedia.org/wiki/File:Kali_lithograph.jpg.)

integrated certain mystical elements of Aryan religion into their practices.

Whatever its provenance, it was not until the fifth century C.E. that substantial textual documentation of tantric yoga began to materialize. At this time, these secret beliefs and practices from ancient traditions were described, codified, and incorporated into a collection of writings called the **Tantras**. The term *tantra* is based on a Sanskrit word related to weaving, and it denotes "that which extends knowledge." Any understanding of tantric yoga in ancient India must be largely inferred from these medieval texts.

The Tantras were essentially technical manuals for realizing *moksha* through specific yogic practices and rituals. Tantrism was based on the idea that the world of experience manifests divine energy that can be ritually accessed, appropriated, and directed in ways that conduce to spiritual progress. In the popular Western imagination today, Tantra is widely believed to be a set of skills for improving one's sexual experience and maximizing sensual pleasure. Books and workshops offered throughout the world purport to teach paying customers how to increase sexual pleasure by using tantric methods. Whether these practices represent authentic Tantra may be debatable, but it is very clear that the purpose of Hindu Tantra is not physical pleasure but rather spiritual bliss and enlightenment. Ritual sex, among other practices, was always a means to this end and never the ultimate purpose of Tantra.

Tantrism actually encompasses a wide range of beliefs and observances, and there are a great number of branches of the tradition associated with various forms of Hinduism and other Indian religions. There are tantric sects connected to the worship of Shiva, Devi, and Vishnu, as well as Buddhist Tantra—associated mainly with Vajrayana, the Buddhism of Tibet and Mongolia—Jain Tantra, and several others.

Generally, though, Tantrism historically divided into two sorts. The variety of Tantra most typically associated with sexuality was called "left-handed" Tantra (*Vāmācāra*). So-called right-handed Tantra (*Dakṣiṇācāra*) was a worship tradition not unlike the conventional worship of one of the goddesses, except that it used the repetition of a special mantra given to an initiate by a female guru. Both varieties of Tantra were open to men and women of all castes and operated independently of the authority of the Brahmin priests. Tantra was considered by its practitioners to be an advanced form of yoga; a prospective initiate had to master other yogic practices before attempting Tantra, lest it prove spiritually dangerous.[5]

The basis of left-handed Tantra was the ritual use of certain things that were ordinarily taboo to most Hindus. These elements, called the ***Panchamakara***, or the 5 Ms, included meat (*māmsa*), fish (*matsya*), parched grain (*mudrā*), believed to be an aphrodisiac,[6] wine (*madya*), and ritual sexual intercourse (*maithuna*). Tantra was not the casual enjoyment of these activities, but rather their deliberate use for the purpose of spiritual advancement.

Tantric rituals were performed in a sacred space, in the presence of an advanced adept or guru, on a specific, astrologically auspicious day. In the first part of the ritual, male and female participants, or **Tantrikas**, would ritually bathe, dress, and apply cosmetics. Then they underwent ritual purification through meditation and the recitation of mantras. Afterward, male–female couples formed a circle around the guru and the guru's partner. As the ritual began, the female partner sat on the male's left, in the traditional position of the goddess relative to the god in temple iconography. (The name "left-handed"

Tantra derived from this practice.) The participants would then consume the meat, fish, grain, and wine and eventually conclude the ritual with sexual union. Before each of these activities, mantras would be uttered to consecrate the elements; otherwise they would be highly polluting. The pronunciation of mantras was also believed to transform the female partner into the embodiment of the goddess. Sexual union was then envisioned by the male as a form of worship and devotion to his partner as Devi.

Maithuna was a difficult and complex action. Tantrikas had to achieve a meditative state, assume intricate yogic postures, and visualize *yantras* (colorful geometric diagrams representing divine feminine energy—see page 137, figure 9.9). They attempted to stay immobile to facilitate the mental processes and prevent or delay orgasm.

Numerous accounts have been advanced to explain the theoretical beliefs underlying the practice of left-handed Tantra. The most basic explanation suggests that tantric practice directed otherwise dangerous desires into the more wholesome pursuit of liberation. This philosophy argued that trying to deny certain powerful desires only empowered them further. Rather than repress these potentially harmful impulses, Tantra tried to harness them in the service of the spirit. Ritual provided a controlled and highly structured context for channeling and disarming forbidden desires.

In addition, ritualized sex was believed to awaken in the participants a deep bodily awareness of the nonduality of the world. Dualism—thinking in absolutist terms of yes and no, black and white, good and evil—kept souls bound to the world of samsara, the cycle of rebirth. According to the Advaita Vedanta tradition, dualistic thinking prevents one from recognizing that the world is fundamentally a single, indivisible reality—Brahman—and that the essential self is actually consubstantial with this reality. To think otherwise is illusory. Tantric activities were meant to break down conventionally constructed dualities, the falsely opposed realities such as pure and impure and right and wrong, to foster realization of the true oneness of all things.

In a similar vein, ritual sex could be interpreted as a reenactment of the cosmological union of *shiva* (divine masculine form) and *shakti* (divine feminine power). *Deva* and *devi*,

Fig. 11.7 The subtle body. This nineteenth-century image reveals the various cakras, or power centers, located along the spine according to tantric theory. (Public domain.)

as noted earlier, need each other: *shiva* without *shakti* is a mere corpse; *shakti* without *shiva* is overwhelming and destructive. In *maithuna*, the male was enabled to appropriate the active feminine powers, and the female appropriated the passive masculine powers, thus transcending dualism.

A final theory explained how tantric yoga aroused the latent energies of the subtle body. This conception told of a vast power source that resided, coiled up like a serpent, near the base of the human spine. Hindus call this energetic resource the **kundalini**. Enlightenment could be attained by stimulating the dormant *kundalini*

energy and allowing it to flow upward through various centers of the subtle body called *cakras* (figure 11.7). *Cakras* ("circles") were believed to be power centers along the spine from its base to the top of the head. Releasing *kundalini* allowed spiritual energy to flow upward, enabling practitioners to experience oneness with the highest reality.

Tantrism thus relies on human embodiment and sexuality as metaphors for understanding spiritual reality. But sexuality is not merely a trope; in Tantra, it is a literal means of apprehending the fundamental but veiled reality known as Brahman.

◆ **KEY TERMS**

cool goddess

Durga

grama-devata

hot goddess

Kali

kundalini

Lakshmi

Mahadevi

Mata, Ma, Amman

Navaratri

Panchamakara (the Five Ms)

Parvati

Sarasvati

shakti

Shaktism

shiva

Tantras

Tantrika

Tantrism

Thags

◆ **QUESTIONS FOR REVIEW**

1. What are the distinguishing features of "cool" and "hot" goddesses, respectively?

2. Why do images of *devis* often appear alone, while *devas* are rarely depicted without their female counterparts?

3. What is *shakti*? How is this principle related to *shiva*?

4. What is "left-handed" Tantra? How is this practice used to inspire spiritual growth?

5. How is tantric ritualized sex a form of worshiping the goddess?

6. Why are the goddesses' manifestations often more powerful than those of the gods?

◆ **QUESTIONS FOR FURTHER REFLECTION**

1. What are the potential dangers and benefits of indulging in sensual pleasure for spiritual purposes?

2. How might a goddess's childlessness affect her image as a mother of all creation?

3. What purposes are served by venerating the destructive and monstrous manifestations of divine power, in addition to the creative and benevolent aspects?

◆ **FOR FURTHER STUDY**

Brooks, Douglas Renfrew. *The Secret of the Three Cities: An Introduction to Hindu Sakta Tantrism.* Chicago: University of Chicago Press, 1998.

Coburn, Thomas B. *Encountering the Goddess: A Translation of the Devī-Māhātmya and a Study of Its Interpretation.* Albany: State University of New York Press, 1991.

Devi (The Goddess). DVD. Directed by Satyajit Ray. Brighton, U.K.: Mr Bongo Films, 2009 (originally released 1960). Bengali with English subtitles. 93 min.

Hawley, John Stratton, and Donna Marie Wulff. *Devi: Goddesses of India.* Berkeley and Los Angeles: University of California Press, 1996.

Kinsley, David. *Hindu Goddesses: Vision of the Divine Feminine in the Hindu Religious Traditions.* Berkeley and Los Angeles: University of California Press, 1988.

Pintchman, Tracy. *The Rise of the Goddess in the Hindu Tradition.* Albany: State University of New York Press, 1994.

Yeshe, Thubten. *Introduction to Tantra: The Transformation of Desire.* 3rd ed. Boston: Wisdom, 2001.

PART IV

MODERN CHALLENGES

12. The Modern Period

PREVIEW

The greatest challenges for the Hindu traditions in the modern era have come as the result of forces from beyond India's borders. Islam, which was introduced into India in the medieval period, has had a long and highly ambivalent relationship with the indigenous Hindu traditions. Likewise, Hindus' interactions with the British, who colonized India in the eighteenth century, have been both positive and negative. Now that Hindu perspectives and practices have begun to move beyond the subcontinent into the West, they have been met with a similar ambivalence.

The modern era brought great challenges to the Hindu traditions through the advent of Islam and Western culture in India. Both incursions left profound and lasting imprints. In many ways, twenty-first-century Hindus continue to struggle with issues associated with Islam and **westernization**. This chapter will delve into these challenges. We will first discuss Islam in India and the history of its relationship with the Hindu traditions. Then we will explore the effects of the British colonization of India and the various religious responses to the British presence. Finally, we will examine the movement of Hinduism beyond the borders of South Asia.

The Advent of Islam

Westerners generally associate Islam with the Middle East and North Africa and are often unaware that the majority of Muslims live in South Asia and eastward.[1] The country with the largest Islamic population today is Indonesia, followed by Pakistan, Bangladesh, and India. The last three nations, of course, comprised India prior to its partition in 1947.

Islam first came to the Indian Subcontinent in the late seventh and early eighth centuries c.e. by way of Arab merchants who traded and eventually settled on India's western and southern coasts. For the next several centuries, Muslims were few in number and hardly a force to be reckoned with. But beginning in the eleventh century, military conquests led by sultans from Central Asia greatly intensified the Muslim presence in northern India. The Islamic influence in India, however, was not consolidated until several centuries later, when Muslim leaders established their capital at **Delhi** (now Old Delhi). By the fifteenth century, Muslim sultans ruled most of India, but their power was concentrated in the northern regions. Today, Muslims live throughout India, but the north still has the highest density of Muslims, and the south is considered the most Hindu region of the nation.

In some respects, it is hard to imagine two religions that contrast as starkly as Hinduism and Islam. As we have seen, Hinduism embraces both polytheism and monotheism. Islam, however, is fervently and emphatically monotheistic. It has even criticized Judaism and Christianity for not being sufficiently monotheistic. Most Hindus venerate images of the divine, but Muslims abhor visual representations of God (box 12.1). In Islam, the greatest sin is **shirk**, or idolatry, and from the Muslim perspective, images are, ipso facto, idols. Although controversial even to Muslims, the Taliban's destruction of ancient Buddha statues in the Bamyan Valley of Afghanistan in 2001 is a vivid reminder of this component of Islamic theology (figure 12.1a,b). When Islam began to spread during India's medieval period, its proponents often destroyed Hindu temples and temple images. Hindus accept the belief that god may incarnate in human and other forms, but Muslims categorically deny this possibility. Hindus think the self endures an infinite number of rebirths until it attains liberation, but Muslims believe that

---

Box 12.1   ISLAM ON MONOTHEISM AND IMAGES

Islam declares that the basic character of ultimate reality is *tawhid*, or unity. In an early revelation, Muhammad is told, "Say, 'It is God, unique, God the eternal, not begetting or begotten, not having any equal.'"* This statement from the Qur'an reveals that *tawhid* implies not just singleness but singularity, in the sense that Allah is incomparable, utterly unlike anything else in human experience. To suggest that Allah is a deity like Zeus or Indra would imply that God can be imagined, envisioned, or understood like other beings. That, Muslims believe, would diminish the majesty and mystery of the ultimate reality. Precisely to avoid this assumption, Allah was never to be represented with images and icons like the members of the Arabian pantheon. The Qur'an also prohibits thinking of god as having children or co-equals:

God never begot any offspring,	God is beyond
and there are no coexistent deities,	anything they describe,
for each deity would have taken	knowing the hidden
away what it created,	and the manifest,
and some of them would surely gain	transcendent beyond any
ascendancy over others.	association they impute.†

Despite clear theological differences, the similarities between Hindu and Muslim theologies should not be overlooked. Like Muslims, most Hindus adamantly affirm the oneness and mysterious nature of ultimate reality through the concept of *nirguna* Brahman.

*Thomas Cleary, trans., *The Qur'an: A New Translation*, Sura 112 (Baltimore, Md.: Starlatch, 2004), 301.
†Ibid., Sura 23:91–92, 169.

Fig. 12.1a,b Buddha figures in Afghanistan. The Taliban's destruction of ancient Buddha images in Afghanistan recalls Islam's traditional iconoclasm. (A: Photo courtesy of http://commons.wikimedia.org/wiki/File:Tall-Buddha-Bamiyan_F.Riviere.jpg. B: Photo courtesy of http://commons.wikimedia.org/wiki/File:BigBuddha.jpg.)

human beings live one life, during which their worthiness for paradise is assessed. Hindus have an ages-long practice of cow reverence, honoring the animal's life-giving and life-sustaining qualities, but Muslims have no reservations about eating properly slaughtered beef. Today, much of the butchering in India is performed by Muslims. In short, the theological and religious differences between Hinduism and Islam have primed these two religions for conflict.

Still, Muslims and Hindus coexisted in India for centuries. At the level of ordinary life, relations between Hindus and Muslims were often peaceful and even cordial. Sometimes,

Hindus and Muslims intermarried and interdined (that is, took meals together). Occasionally, Muslims and Hindus even came together for religious purposes. There were times when Hindu *bhaktas* and Islamic mystics known as Sufis worshiped together at a *mazār*, the tomb of a Sufi saint. They sometimes shared spiritual heroes, such as Lalla, the Kashmiri *bhakta* discussed earlier. **Kabir** (1440–1518), a medieval poet from Vanarasi who is revered by both Muslims and Hindus, provided inspiration for the development of Sikhism, a prominent religious tradition that incorporates elements of both Hinduism and Islam (box 12.2). Many

Indians, particularly those in the lower strata of society, found no need to identify themselves as either Hindu or Muslim and practiced aspects of both traditions.[2] Such individuals might celebrate both Holi and **Ramadan** and worship Allah as their *ishta-devata*. The Hindu-Muslim

---

Box 12.2 KABIR

The religious identity of the mystical poet Kabir (1440–1518) has long been the subject of debate. Today, both Muslims and Hindus claim him as one of their own, although during his lifetime, both Muslims and Hindus tried to silence him, sometimes violently. His legacy is also claimed by the Sikhs, who include many of his poems in their scripture, the Adi Granth. A religious community called the Kabir Panth ("Path of Kabir"), comprising persons of both Hindu and Muslim heritage, embraces him as its founder and inspiration.

Kabir's name is Muslim, one of Islam's ninety-nine "beautiful names" of Allah. But his poetry seems to suggest a greater affinity for Hindu practices, such as his recitation of Ram as the name of god and his apparent belief in rebirth. Many scholars think that Kabir belonged to a caste of weavers from the holy city of Varanasi who had recently (and perhaps cursorily) become Muslims. No matter how he identified himself, Kabir leveled scathing criticisms at both Hindus and Muslims.

In the following verse, Kabir condemns the ascetics who think renunciation and celibacy will bring them closer to the divine.

> Go naked if you want,
> Put on animal skins.
> What does it matter till you see the inward Ram.
> If the union yogis seek
> Came from roaming about in the buff, every
>   deer in the forest would be saved.
> If shaving your head
> Spelled spiritual success, heaven would be
>   filled with sheep.
> And brother, if holding back your seed
> Earned you a place in paradise, eunuchs would
>   be the first to arrive.
> Kabir says: Listen brother,
> Without the name of Ram who has ever won
>   the spirit's prize?*

In the next poem, Kabir takes on the Brahmins:

> The pandit got lost
> in Vedic details
> but missed the mystery
> of his own self.
> Worship, prayers,
> six sacred activities,
> four ages teaching Gayatri,
> I ask you: who's got liberty?
> You splash yourself
> if you touch somebody,
> but tell me who
> could be lower than you.
> Proud of your quality,
> great with authority,
> such pride never brought anyone good.

Box 12.2 continues on the following page

Box 12.2 (continued)

He whose name is Pride-Breaker—
how will he tolerate pride like yours?
Drop family, drop status,
seek the non-existent space,
destroy the shoot, destroy the seed,
reach the unembodied place.[†]

And then the Muslims:

Qazi [the title of an Islamic scholar and jurist],
what book are you lecturing on?
Yak, yak, yak, day and night.
You never had an original thought.
Feeling your power, you circumcise—
I can't go along with that brother.
If your God favored circumcision,
Why didn't you come out cut?
If circumcision makes you a Muslim,
What do you call your women?[‡]

While Kabir condemns the rituals and sacred traditions of his contemporaries, he invites them to turn inward to seek the divine in their hearts.

The creatures are like you Allah-Ram.
Lord be kind to them.

Why bump that shaven head on the earth,
why dunk those bones in the water?

Parading as a holy man,
you hide yourself, and slaughter.
Why wash your hands and mouth, why chant
with a heart full of fraud?
Why bow and bow in the mosque, and trudge
to Mecca to see God?
Twenty-four days for the Hindus,
thirty days for the Turks—
a month each year for fasting,
eleven for other works.
Does Khuda live in the mosque?
Then who lives everywhere?
Is Ram in idols and holy ground?
Have you looked and found him there?
Hari in the East, Allah in the West—
so you like to dream.
Search in the heart, in the heart alone:
there live Ram and Karim!
Which is false, Koran or Veda?
False is the darkened view.
It's one, one in every body!
How did you make it two?
Every man and woman born,
they're all your forms, says Kabir.
I'm Ram-and-Allah's foolish baby,
he's my guru and pir.[**]

pir = Muslim spiritual guide

*John Stratton Hawley and Mark Juergensmeyer, *Songs of the Saints of India* (New York: Oxford University Press, 1988), 50.
[†]Linda Hess and Shukdev Singh, trans., *The Bijak of Kabir* (Delhi: Motilal Banarsidass, 1983), 85–86.
[‡]Ibid., 69.
[**]Ibid., 73–74.

relationship thus was frequently tense, although not always and everywhere.

Although early Muslims in India were usually openly antagonistic to non-Muslims, Hindu beliefs and practices survived because they were so deeply rooted in the everyday routine of India. India's other major religion at the time was Buddhism. Buddhism did not survive the coming of Islam, as it was in decline by that time and the era of its dominance in India had long passed (box 12.3). Eventually, Muslim rulers granted Hindus a religious toleration similar to the sort granted to Christians and Jews in other Muslim countries, although it may have been more out of political expediency than genuine respect.

The Hindus first considered the Muslims merely another caste, not another religion. In this way, Hindus could generally ignore the challenges Islam presented to their religious ways of life. And at first, the Muslim rulers ignored Hindu challenges. They did not try to proselytize Hindus. Later, however, Sufis succeeded in converting great numbers of Hindus to Islam. The Sufis were successful in part because their version of Islam was much like the *bhakti* religion already well established among Hindus. The Sufi **shaykh**, or teacher, was also a familiar religious type to Hindus, appearing to them like a guru figure. The *shaykhs* used the vernacular language and taught in parables. Islam thus began to appeal to many Hindus, particularly

Box 12.3   THE DECLINE OF BUDDHISM IN INDIA

For a significant part of Indian history, Buddhism was the dominant religion on the subcontinent. Beginning with Emperor Ashoka (304–232 B.C.E.), Buddhism often enjoyed royal patronage. The rulers of India frequently supported the *sangha* (the Buddhist monastic community), built temples and *stūpas* (reliquaries), and sent Buddhist missionaries to other parts of Asia. But by the medieval period, Buddhism was in severe decline in the land of its birth and had all but disappeared by the beginning of the twentieth century. Several factors may have contributed to its decline, but the ultimate reason for its demise remains a mystery.

Some texts suggest that Buddhist practitioners suffered persecution at the hands of partisans of Hindu orthodoxy in the Epic and Early Puranic era, but the extent of such mistreatment is unknown. That the Buddha was designated as an avatar of Vishnu whose purpose was to lead the faithful astray may reflect a historical tension between Hindus and Buddhists.

The decline of Buddhism also coincided with the resurgence of certain Hindu traditions in various regions of India during the medieval period. This Hindu revival may in fact have been stimulated by the assimilation of Buddhist ideas and practices into Hindu theology. Shankara, the great philosopher of Advaita Vedanta and Hindu reformer, has been interpreted as both a harsh critic of Buddhism and a covert Buddhist. It is hard to resist the conclusion that Shankara's philosophy was strongly influenced by Buddhism. Buddhism may have been simply absorbed by Hinduism.

In any event, by the advent of Islam in India, Buddhism retained only vestiges of its former glory. The suppression of Buddhism by the first Islamic conquerors of India only completed a process that had begun centuries earlier.

those of lower caste, who were attracted to the Muslim message of human equality and who had little real investment in the caste system. Islam also appealed to others who aspired to upward social mobility; adopting the religion of one's rulers has frequently helped people to gain social power. It is not altogether clear, however, that these converts actually regarded themselves as switching religions. It is just as likely that they saw themselves as accepting a new *ishta-devata*.

Despite the tensions, there have been many bright moments in Hindu Muslim relations. The rise of **Mughal** emperor **Jalāl ud-Dīn Muhammad Akbar** (1542–1605) in the sixteenth century was certainly one. In his early years as emperor, Akbar sought to extend the borders of his empire and eventually brought most of northern and central India under his control. Over time, Akbar began to develop a respect for the Hindus' worship practices, which he had disliked earlier in his life. Some historians think the shift in Akbar's attitude was fostered by his marriages to Hindu princesses, which he had made to consolidate political alliances with the powerful Rajput caste. Whatever the cause of this new outlook, Akbar began to make it easier for Hindus to practice their traditions, and he took a personal interest in Hindu theology. He abolished a tax levied on Hindu pilgrims as well as the *jizyah*, the tax imposed on the non-Muslim population. He sponsored and participated in religious and philosophical discussions involving Muslims, Hindus, Sikhs, Christians, Jews, and atheists, and he made trips to visit with saints and scholars of those traditions. Today, Akbar is remembered by many as one of India's greatest rulers. Despite the tolerance of emperors like Akbar, however, friction between Hindus and Muslims continued and even increased. This tension has been the background noise in the history of modern India.

In 1947, the centuries-long stresses came to a head when India was partitioned into India, West Pakistan, and East Pakistan (later Bangladesh) at the moment of its independence from Great Britain. **Mohandas K. Gandhi** (1869–1948) strongly resisted the creation of Pakistan. **Muhammad Ali Jinnah** (1876–1948), the Muslim leader who was a driving force for the separate state of Pakistan, argued that the differences between Islam and Hinduism are profound and irreconcilable (figure 12.2). In his presidential address to the All India Muslim League, given at Lahore in 1940, Jinnah articulated the Two-Nation Theory, the ideological basis for the 1947 Partition of India:

> The Hindus and Muslims belong to two different religious philosophies, social customs, and literature[s]. They neither intermarry nor interdine together, and indeed they belong to two different civilisations which

Fig. 12.2 Two giants of modern South Asia. Muhammad Ali Jinnah and Mohandas K. Gandhi appear together in Mumbai in 1944, a few years before Pakistan and India won their independence from Great Britain. (Photo courtesy of http://commons.wikimedia.org/wiki/File:Gandhi_Jinnah_1944.jpg.)

are based mainly on conflicting ideas and conceptions. Their aspects on life, and of life, are different. It is quite clear that Hindus and Mussalmans [Muslims] derive their inspiration from different sources of history. They have different epics, their heroes are different, and different episode[s]. Very often the hero of one is a foe of the other, and likewise their victories and defeats overlap. To yoke together two such nations under a single state, one as a numerical minority and the other as a majority, must lead to growing discontent, and final destruction of any fabric that may be so built up for the government of such a state.[3]

Jinnah argued that Muslims needed a separate state to be true to Islam, since Islam does not distinguish between religious and political law. Jinnah's view carried the day.

The partition of India, however, did not end Hindu-Muslim hostilities. Immediately following the creation of Pakistan, widespread violence erupted as millions of Muslims from India fled to Pakistan and Hindus from Pakistan left for India. The fighting caused the deaths of about one million people and the dislocation of at least eleven million. Early in the twenty-first century, tensions between India and Pakistan remained extremely high as the two nations continued a longstanding dispute over the region of Jammu and Kashmir. Within the Republic of India, Hindu-Muslim friction often erupts in violence, as happened in 1992 when Hindus destroyed Babri Masjid, a mosque that had long stood in the village of Ayodhya on the site reputed to have been the birthplace of the god Rama, the avatar of Vishnu. That riot sparked a wave of Hindu-Muslim violence throughout India that killed thousands.

The British Raj

After nearly eight hundred years, Muslim rule of India ended in the eighteenth century, when Muslim leaders were defeated by British forces, thus inaugurating the period of British colonialism. As the British incorporated India into their empire, they tended to treat Hindus and Muslims differently. This practice effectively generated a perception that the British rulers favored one group over the other. The perception of favoritism, of course, aggravated hostilities that were never far from the surface.

In many ways, British colonialism in India was more significant than Muslim rule, even though the British governed India for a shorter period (1757–1947). The British brought with them Western folkways and culture, and many Indians sought to imitate them by speaking English, playing cricket, taking afternoon tea, and converting to Christianity. Yet the effects of the British Raj were deeper and more complicated than just the adoption of behavioral patterns. The British introduced into India Western values and social dynamics, elements that were disruptive to traditional Hindu culture.

Britain's initial and foremost interest in India was commercial. The East India Company was Britain's first established involvement on the subcontinent. The British developed the cities of Kolkata (which the British called Calcutta), Mumbai (which they called Bombay), and Chennai (formerly Madras) into large, industrialized trading centers. Industrialization and urbanization combined to uproot traditional Indian society. Old restrictions imposed by caste and family could be more easily disregarded in urban areas. Traditional practices and beliefs were called into doubt and reevaluated.

The establishment of these market-based, industrial economies increased people's expectations of material gain. India had for millennia explicitly favored the transcendent over the material world. *Artha* and *kama*, wealth and pleasure, were goods to be sure, but *moksha*, the bliss of ultimate release, had been the supreme good. Now, under the influence of the Western focus on the material world, many Hindus began to reassess *this* world's significance, spurring a greater interest in the realm that had been historically regarded as *maya*, a veil hiding what was truly real and important. Many Hindus began to consider that the way to happiness and freedom from suffering was perhaps not to transcend the world, but rather to transform it.

The British also encouraged literacy. Learning to speak and read English was—and often still is—regarded by Indians as an avenue to success. Nevertheless, only about 66 percent of the Indian population over age fifteen can read and write in any language today.[4] The encouragement of literacy and the English language was sufficient, however, to generate interest among many Indians in reading the Western classics, including the Bible. As Indians became more acquainted with the literature of the Western traditions, they were exposed to Western values, such as the liberal democratic principle of the equality of all persons, that stood in direct contrast to traditional Hindu beliefs. As we shall see, the leaders of India's liberation movements were able to use their knowledge of Western values to win their freedom from the British Empire.

The reactions of Hindus to the Raj were mixed. Two important Hindu movements, both founded in the nineteenth century, illustrate different Hindu responses to westernization. The first is the **Brahmo Samaj**, or the Society of Believers in Brahman. The Brahmo Samaj was founded in 1828 by **Rammohun Roy** (1774–1833), an important Hindu reformer regarded by many as "the father of modern India" (figure

12.3). Roy, who was born just as the American colonies were beginning their own revolution against the British, was educated by Muslims and early in his life developed an intense aversion to the British occupation. As a young man, however, Roy began to work for the East India

Fig. 12.3   The father of modern India. This statue of Rammohun Roy stands in Bristol, England, in commemoration of the nineteenth-century Hindu scholar and reformer. In addition to his many accomplishments in India, Roy served as ambassador to Great Britain. He died in Bristol in 1833. (Photo courtesy of http://en.wikipedia.org/wiki/File:Ram_Mohan_Roy.jpg.)

Company. He learned English and came to appreciate Western ways. Eventually, he came to champion British rule and to value Western education.

The movement he initiated, the Brahmo Samaj, reflected Roy's critical appreciation of the West. The Brahmo Samaj might be described as traditional Hinduism transformed by an encounter with Christianity. Roy studied the Bible and admired Jesus, but he could not accept the idea of Jesus' divinity. Yet he saw much of value in Christianity. He was troubled by the polytheism of popular Hinduism and denounced it. He also criticized the veneration of divine images, calling it idol worship. Roy preferred the Upanishads to all other Hindu scriptures, and he contended that the Vedantic perspective taught a simple monotheism. He adopted what might be called a liberal approach to scripture, arguing that the Vedas are authoritative only when they are shown to be reasonable or conscionable. In this respect, Roy's view paralleled that of liberal nineteenth-century Christians, who made the same argument about the Bible. Roy even established weekly congregational worship services like those of the Christians. But he may be best remembered for his efforts to improve the treatment of women in India, especially widows. He was instrumental in the abolition of *sati*, which the British outlawed in 1829.

Whereas the Brahmo Samaj took a liberal approach to traditional Hinduism, the **Arya Samaj**, another religious movement begun in the nineteenth century, had a more fundamentalist outlook. We are, of course, using Western labels here, but perhaps these adjectives may help us understand the Indian situation, because "liberal" and "fundamentalist" designate two responses to modernity itself. The Arya Samaj was fundamentalist in its approach

to the Hindu collection of scriptures. It not only regarded the Vedas as the *only* authoritative Hindu text, thus undercutting the importance of popular books like the Gita and the *Puranas*; it also maintained that the Vedas are the source of *all* truth, scientific and spiritual. This view was not unlike Christian fundamentalism, which considered the Bible historically and scientifically accurate. And just as Christian fundamentalists considered the Bible open and accessible to anyone, the Arya Samaj maintained that the Vedas should be available to all for study.

The Arya Samaj was founded by Swami **Dayananda Sarasvati** (figure 12.4) in the late

Fig. 12.4   Dayananda Sarasvati. Dayananda Sarasvati was the founder of the Arya Samaj, a conservative reform movement. (Public domain.)

nineteenth century, about the time Christian fundamentalism got its start in the United States. Like the more liberal Rammohun Roy, Swami Sarasvati criticized much that he saw in the popular Hindu practices of his day, especially *puja* and pilgrimage. He regarded much of popular religion as mere superstition. Sarasvati even went so far as to deny the divinity of the avatars Rama and Krishna and to reject the idea of *jatis*—the hereditary birth classes—because the word *jati* does not appear in the Vedas. Again like Roy, Sarasvati was an advocate for the fairer treatment of women. He contended that women should be educated and widows allowed to remarry. He also held that Hinduism was superior to other religions and that all religions attempt to approximate what is clearly evident in Hinduism. Many Christians have argued the same point about the superiority of their faith.

The Brahmo Samaj and the Arya Samaj were both responses to the disrupting effects of westernization. They exemplified the complex encounters between Hinduism and Western culture and values. The Brahmo Samaj demonstrated a critical openness to Christianity and the values of reason and human equality. The Arya Samaj, like other fundamentalisms, reacted with suspicion toward the agents of change, and it sought to restore authority to a single text and maintain the superiority of its own perspective.

Naturally, the British presence in India had political as well as religious ramifications. The Western idea of nation-state sovereignty helped stimulate a nationalist spirit that eventually led to the movement to establish India as an independent nation. Christianity itself lent to nationalist Indians some of the ideas they used to achieve independence. Gandhi, for instance, was greatly impressed by Jesus' Sermon on the Mount and the writings of Leo Tolstoy. It may well be that the British unwittingly planted the very seeds of the independence movement within the soul of India.

Gandhi (figure 12.5) was the most important figure in that movement, and his life illustrates the best of modern Hindu practice and belief. Gandhi was above all a devout Hindu. Although he was educated in England as a

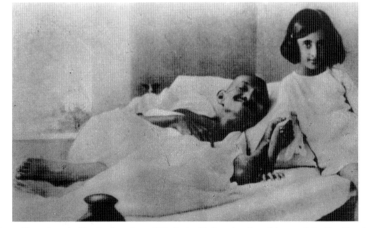

Fig. 12.5   Two leaders of modern India. During one of his fasts, Mohandas Gandhi was visited by the daughter of Jawaharlal Nehru, the first prime minister of India. Indira Nehru would later become Indira Gandhi by marriage (her husband, Feroze, was not related to Mohandas Gandhi). Like her father, Mrs. Gandhi served as India's prime minister. (Photo courtesy of http://commons. wikimedia.org/wiki/File:Gandhi_and_Indira_1924.jpg.)

barrister, Gandhi's politics were based less on jurisprudence and more on his religious values and convictions.

The title by which Gandhi was known in India and throughout the world emphasized the spiritual foundations of his life. He was called *mahatma*, or "great soul," an epithet reserved for only the most spiritually accomplished Hindus. Yet Gandhi was not a Brahmin or even a Kshatriya; he was a Vaishya. Neither was he a theologian or systematic religious thinker. His political vision and practice, however, were deeply rooted in his understanding of sacred scriptures from many of the world's religions, especially the Bhagavad Gita and the New Testament. This kind of openness to spiritual truth, regardless of where it is found, is a widespread Hindu quality (box 12.4). Indeed,

---

Box 12.4 GANDHI'S HINDUISM

Gandhi understood himself as first and foremost a seeker of god. His political activity was the natural and ineluctable consequence of his spiritual quest. In these passages from his autobiography, first published in his native Gujarati in 1927, Gandhi underscores the relationship between his religion and his political practices and reveals his indebtedness to the Hindu traditions.

What I want to achieve,—what I have been striving and pining to achieve these thirty years,—is self-realization, to see God face to face, to attain *Moksha*. I live and move and have my being in pursuit of this goal. All that I do by way of speaking and writing, and all my ventures in the political field are directed to this same end.

[…] for me, truth is the sovereign principle, which includes numerous other principles. This truth is not only truthfulness in word, but truthfulness in thought also, and not only the relative truth of our conception, but the Absolute Truth, the Eternal Principle, that is God. There are innumerable definitions of God, because His manifestations are innumerable. They overwhelm me with wonder and awe and for a moment stun me. But I worship God as Truth only. I have not yet found Him but I am seeking after Him. I am prepared to sacrifice the things dearest to me in pursuit of this quest. Even if the sacrifice demanded be my very life, I hope I may be prepared to give it. But as long as I have not realized this Absolute Truth, so long must I hold by the relative truth as I have conceived it.

[…] Often in my progress I have had faint glimpses of the Absolute Truth, God, and daily the conviction is growing upon me that He alone is real and all else is unreal.

[…] The instruments for the quest of truth are as simple as they are difficult. They may appear quite impossible to an arrogant person, and quite possible to an innocent child. The seeker after truth should be humbler than the dust. The world crushes the dust under its feet, but the seeker after truth should so humble himself that even the dust could crush him. Only then, and not till then, will he have a glimpse of truth.*

*Mohandas K. Gandhi, *An Autobiography: The Story of My Experiments with Truth,* trans. Mahadev Desai (Boston: Beacon, 1957), ii–xiv.

Gandhi had an appreciation of all the major religious traditions and did not want religion to become divisive. This was one of the reasons behind his opposition to the partition of India and Pakistan.

Gandhi called his philosophy *satyāgraha*, a term that means "grasping for and holding on to truth." It might also be thought of as grasping for and holding on to god, because for Gandhi, "God is Truth." He believed that truth is more important than political expediency. While others in the independence movement argued that India's freedom from Britain should be gained through armed conflict or other coercive means, Gandhi maintained that just ends should never be attained through evil means.

This conviction spurred the development of his philosophy and practice of nonviolent resistance, a notion that also owed much to the Jains. As a child, Gandhi frequently interacted with Jains in his community and learned from them the practice of *ahimsa*, the doctrine of not harming living beings. The result of these many religious influences in Gandhi's life was a political vision of achieving justice by revealing the truth of oppression to the oppressor. Nonviolent resistance endeavored to demonstrate in a powerful and vivid way the oppressor's own brutality. Gandhi believed that when injustice was clearly pointed out to those who were responsible for it, the oppressor's own sense of fairness and truthfulness would force an end to tyranny. In order to demonstrate the brutality of oppression, however, one must be willing to endure the brunt of the tyrant's force without retaliation. For that, one needed great courage and the discipline of a yogi. In a sense, Gandhi opened a new avenue of *karma-marga* by making the political sphere an acceptable arena for the practice of spirituality.

In 1948, shortly after India had gained independence and been partitioned, Gandhi was assassinated by a fellow Hindu who believed that he had conceded too much to the Muslims. Once again, Hindu-Muslim hostilities had come to tragic expression.

Hinduism Comes West

Thus far, we have examined the incursion of the West into Hindu life on the Indian Subcontinent. We turn now to discuss the reciprocal direction, the movement of Hindus and the Hindu traditions into the West. The history of this movement is much briefer.

Prior to the late nineteenth century, the main vehicle for the transport of Hindu beliefs and practices to the West was literary. By then, many of the most important Hindu scriptures had been translated into European languages and were available to Western intellectuals. Because Western impressions were principally based on these translations from the Hindu scriptural traditions, most Western thinkers had a rather skewed understanding of the Hindu traditions that neglected their more popular expressions. Those Westerners who actually visited India saw a different side of Hindu beliefs and practices—the many colorful festivals and *murtis*, the astrologers and fortune-tellers, the caste system and the rituals—and were, more often than not, repelled by what they saw. To these Western visitors, "Hinduism" smacked of superstition, idolatry, and cultural backwardness.

These impressions—based on the translations of some of its philosophy on the one hand, and on the observations of its popular practices on the other—contributed to an extremely ambivalent Western view of the Hindu traditions. Some who knew Hinduism through its

scriptures regarded it as morally and spiritually superior to the Western traditions. Many of those who knew it from popular practice regarded it as vastly inferior to Western ways.

It was into this context of ambivalence that the first significant Hindu representative came to the West. Swami **Vivekananda**, whom we mentioned in chapter 1, is sometimes known as the first Hindu missionary to the West (figure 12.6). He appeared in Chicago in 1893 at the first **World's Parliament of Religions**. Vivekananda's address to this international gathering of delegates from the major religious traditions was extremely well received and widely

Fig. 12.6   Swami Vivekananda. Swami Vivekananda is sometimes regarded as the first Hindu missionary to the West. His visits to the United States and Europe helped galvanize the West's early impressions of "Hinduism." (Photo courtesy of Creative Commons, Ramakrishna Mission Delhi.)

Box 12.5   SWAMI VIVEKANANDA'S ADDRESS TO THE WORLD'S PARLIAMENT OF RELIGIONS

What follows is the text of Swami Vivekananda's first address to the World's Parliament of Religions in Chicago on September 11, 1893.

Sisters and Brothers of America. It fills my heart with joy unspeakable to rise in response to the warm and cordial welcome which you have given us. . . . I thank you in the name of millions and millions of Hindu people of all classes and sects. . . . I am proud to belong to a religion which has taught the world both tolerance and universal acceptance. We believe not only in universal toleration but we accept all religions as true. I am proud to belong to a nation which has sheltered the persecuted and the refugees of all religions and all nations of the earth. I am proud to tell you that we have gathered in our bosom the purest remnant of the Israelites who came to Southern India and took refuge with us in the very year in which their holy temple was shattered to pieces by Roman tyranny. I am proud to belong to the religion which has sheltered and is still fostering the remnant of the grand Zoroastrian nation. From a hymn which I remember from my earliest childhood: "As the different streams having their sources in

Box 12.5 continues on the following page

different places all mingle their water in the sea, so, O Lord, the different paths which men take through different tendencies, various though they appear, crooked or straight, all lead to Thee."

The present convention is in itself a vindication of the wonderful doctrine preached in the Gita: "Whosoever comes to me, through whatsoever form, I reach him; all men are struggling through paths which in the end lead to me." Sectarianism, bigotry, and its horrible descendant, fanaticism, have long possessed this beautiful Earth [and] have filled the earth with violence. . . . But their time is come; and I fervently hope that the bell that tolled this morning in honor of this convention may be the death-knell of all fanaticism, of all persecutions with the sword or with the pen, and of all uncharitable feelings between persons wending their way to the same goal.*

*Available at http://www.ramakrishna.org/chcgfull.htm.

celebrated. Vivekananda subsequently toured the United States and established centers for the study and practice of Advaita Vedanta, the monistic Hindu philosophy he embraced and which was taken by many to be the essence of "Hinduism" (box 12.5).

In the path pioneered by Swami Vivekananda there followed many other Hindu gurus. Many of their names or the names of their orders are familiar to Westerners today. We have already noted Swami **A. C. Bhaktivedanta** in connection with the founding of the International Society for Krishna Consciousness (ISKCON). **Maharishi Mahesh Yogi** became well known in the 1960s as the spiritual guide of the Beatles and as the promoter of a spiritual practice called Transcendental Meditation, or TM. In the 1970s and 1980s, many in the West were attracted to the teaching of **Bhagwan Sri Rajneesh** (later known as Osho), an Indian of Jain background who taught a monistic philosophy combining elements of

Hinduism, Buddhism, and Christianity. The names of these modern teachers continue to evoke ambivalent feelings among many in the West. Many celebrate these teachers and their messages, and many others revile them and consider their practices cultish and dangerous (box 12.6 and figure 12.7 on the following page).

It is unclear, at this point, what the future of Hinduism will be beyond the Indian Subcontinent. In India and the surrounding area, Hinduism remains firmly established and its future seems secure. How Hinduism will negotiate the challenges of westernization, however, is not certain. Nor is it clear how the West will negotiate the challenges of the Hindu traditions. But already, Western culture is beginning to accommodate Hindu immigrants as great numbers of temples and Hindu societies multiply throughout the United States and Europe. And it is evident that many Westerners find much in Hinduism worthy of adoption and admiration.

Box 12.6 **YOGA IN THE WEST**

Perhaps the greatest influence the Hindu traditions have had in the Western world has been through the practice of what is known as "yoga." What Westerners understand as yoga, however, constitutes only a small part of what that term means in the Hindu traditions. In the West, most people think of yoga as a form of exercise and relaxation—what Hindus know as hatha or asana yoga. In Hinduism, "yoga" of course means much more. It is one of the six schools of orthodox philosophy, as well as a generic term meaning any sort of spiritual discipline, used synonymously with the term "marga."

Restricting "yoga" to exercise, neglecting its richer sense as a particular Hindu philosophy and as a generic term for religious practice, has made it more acceptable in the West. Today, it is not uncommon to find yoga taught not only in special yoga centers, but also in churches and synagogues in the United States and Europe. Many of these Western religious institutions would find the wider sense of yoga to be incompatible with their theology, so it is only by emphasizing the physical dimensions that they can offer yoga practice. The more conservative religious institutions, however, ban yoga altogether precisely because they are unable to separate the physical and spiritual aspects of the practice. Those religious institutions that forbid yoga, interestingly, may have a better grasp of its broader meaning than those who seek to embrace it only as exercise.

Fig. 12.7 Yoga at a Methodist church. Yoga as physical exercise has now become widely accepted in the West and is even offered in some Christian churches. (Photo: Mark W. Muesse.)

◆ KEY TERMS

Akbar, Jalāl ud-Dīn Muhammad

Arya Samaj

Bhaktivedanta, A. C.

Brahmo Samaj

Delhi

Gandhi, Mohandas K.

Jinnah, Muhammad Ali

Kabir

Maharishi Mahesh Yogi

Mughals

Rajneesh, Bhagwan Sri

Ramadan

Roy, Rammohun

Sarasvati, Dayananda

satyāgraha

shaykh

shirk

Vivekananda

westernization

World's Parliament of Religions

◆ QUESTIONS FOR REVIEW

1. Why have the Muslim and Hindu communities often been in tension with one another throughout India's history? Are there any notable exceptions to this conflict?

2. Why were the Sufis so successful in converting Hindus to Islam?

3. Are you convinced by the Two-Nation Theory, as presented by Muhammad Ali Jinnah? Why or why not?

4. How did industrialization and urbanization under British colonialism challenge traditional Hindu practices and beliefs?

5. What are the Brahmo Samaj and the Arya Samaj? How do these Hindu movements represent different responses to the British presence in India?

6. How has Hindu influence been received in the West?

◆ QUESTIONS FOR FURTHER REFLECTION

1. Is it possible for vastly different religious communities truly to understand one another?

2. What are the advantages and disadvantages for a state that encourages the separation of religious and political affairs? What are the advantages and disadvantages for a state in which religion and politics are inseparable?

3. Do you agree or disagree with Gandhi's belief that the end never justifies evil means?

4. What are the consequences of a fundamentalist interpretation of sacred scripture?

5. Westernization has had a profound impact on the world's religious, cultural, and political landscape. Do you think Western influence has been primarily positive or negative?

◆ FOR FURTHER STUDY

Easwaran, Eknath. *Gandhi the Man: The Story of His Transformation.* 3rd ed. Tomales, Calf.: Nilgiri, 1997.

Gandhi, Mohandas K. *An Autobiography: or The Story of My Experiments with Truth.* Translated by Mahadev Desai. Boston: Beacon, 1957.

———. *The Way to God.* Berkeley, Calif.: Berkeley Hills, 1999.

Islam, Sirajul. *Sufism and Bhakti: A Comparative Study.* Washington, D.C.: Council for Research in Values and Philosophy, 2004.

Nikhilananda, Swami. *Vivekānanda: A Biography.*
New York: Ramakrishna-Vivekananda Center,
1989.

Zastoupil, Lynn. *Rammohun Roy and the Making of Victorian Britain.* Palgrave Studies in Cultural and Intellectual History. Basingstoke, U.K.: Palgrave Macmillan, 2010.

Introduction: Hinduism in Time and Space

1. The earliest published usage of the term appears to be from 1811, in William Ward, *A View of the History, Literature and Religion of the Hindoos*. Ward (1769–1823) was a Baptist missionary to India from Derby, England. I am indebted to my colleague Prof. Lynn Zastoupil for bringing this reference to my attention.

2. *Sthāna* is Old Persian for "place."

3. David Lorenzen, "Who Invented Hinduism?" in *Comparative Studies in Society and History* 41:4 (Oct. 1999): 631.

4. For more details on Swami Vivekananda's appearance at the World's Parliament of Religion, see chapter 12.

5. This point is well illustrated in the difficulty of formulating a legal definition of *Hindu*. The constitution of the Republic of India (adopted January 26, 1950) indicates that *Hindu* includes members of the Jain, Sikh, and Buddhist traditions. Constitution of India, Article 25 (available at http://www.unesco.org/most/rr3indi.htm). More recently, the Indian Supreme Court has ruled that Jainism is not a part of Hinduism.

6. Klaus K. Klostermaier, *Hinduism: A Short Introduction* (Oxford: Oneworld Publications, 1998), 3.

7. E. M. Forster, *A Passage to India* (1924; repr., New York and London: Harcourt Brace Jovanovich, 1952), 292.

8. *Rig-Veda* 1.164.46, in Wendy Doniger, trans., *The Rig-Veda: An Anthology* (London: Penguin, 1981), 80.

9. Forster, *Passage to India*, 261.

10. The name *India* derives from *Sindhu*, the same Sanskrit word from which the word *Hindu* is derived. *India* was first used by outsiders to refer to the land surrounding the Indus River and then later applied to most of the subcontinent.

11. United Nations estimate, February 24, 2005.

12. The major language groups of these languages include Indo-Aryan, Dravidian, Austro-Asiatic, and Tibeto-Burman.

13. Some Sikhs have identified themselves as Hindu-Musalman (Muslim), and Sikhism itself (along with Buddhism and Jainism) has sometimes been regarded as a Hindu religion. These facts point once again to the fluidity of Hindu identity.

1. The Indus Valley Civilization

1. The Indus Valley Civilization is considered to be one of the four great cultures of the ancient world, all of which were situated on large river systems. The other three are Egypt on the Nile, Mesopotamia on the Tigris and Euphrates, and China on the Yellow.

2. Prabhat Kumar Mukherjee's modern short story *"Devi"* ("The Goddess") is an intriguing study of what happens when the patriarch of a Bengali family becomes convinced that his own daughter-in-law is a divine incarnation. Director Satyajit Ray turned the story into a classic film by the same name.

3. These other images were discovered in ritual settings and bore traces of red ochre, an indication that they served as divine symbols.

4. See, for example, Riane Eisler, *The Chalice and the Blade: Our History, Our Future* (New York: Harper, 1988); and Monica Sjöö and Barbara Mor, *The Great Cosmic Mother: Rediscovering the Religion of the Earth* (New York: Harper, 1987).

5. For a balanced, even-handed analysis and assessment of the issues at stake and the arguments on all sides of the question, see Edwin Bryant, *The Quest for the Origins of Vedic Culture: The Indo-Aryan Migration Debate* (Oxford and New York: Oxford University Press, 2001).

2. The Noble Ones

1. The Mazda automobile company was so named for three reasons: first, to honor the god Mazda; second, because Mazda means "wisdom" in Persian; and third, because the family name of the Japanese manufacturer is Matsuda, which when anglicized sounds much like Mazda.

2. Yasna 39.1–2, quoted in Mary Boyce, *Zoroastrians: Their Religious Beliefs and Practices* (New York: Routledge, 2001), 5.

3. *Rig-Veda* 8.48, in Wendy Doniger, trans., *The Rig-Veda: An Anthology* (London: Penguin, 1981), 134–35.

4. *Rig-Veda* 10.119 in ibid., 131–32.

3. The World of the Vedas

1. Hymn 10.129 in Wendy Doniger, trans., *The Rig-Veda: An Anthology* (London: Penguin, 1981), 25–26.

2. Hymn 10.16 in ibid., 49–50.

3. Hymn 10.16.3 in ibid., 49.

4. "He" may refer to a creator god or to the Purusha himself.

5. Hymn 10.90 in Doniger, *Rig-Veda*, 30–31.

6. James George Fraser, *The Golden Bough* (Sioux Falls, S.D.: NuVision Publications, LLC, 2006), chap. 3, §1, 15 (Available at http://www.nuvisionpublications.com/eBooks.asp?ISBN=1595473831).

4. Rebirth and Karma

1. Alfred North Whitehead exaggerated only slightly when he said, "The safest general characterization of the European philosophical tradition is that it consists of a series of footnotes to Plato." Alfred North Whitehead, *Process and Reality* (New York: Free Press, 1979), 39.

2. Karl Jaspers, *The Origin and Goal of History*, trans. Michael Bullock (New Haven, Conn.: Yale University Press, 1953), 51.

3. Karl Jaspers, *The Way to Wisdom: An Introduction to Philosophy*, trans. Ralph Manheim (New Haven, Conn.: Yale University Press, 1951), 98.

4. Juan Mascaró, trans., *The Upanishads* (New York: Penguin, 1996), 56–57.

5. Hymn 10.14.2 in Wendy Doniger, trans., *The Rig-Veda: An Anthology* (London: Penguin, 1981), 43.

6. *Brhadāranyaka Upanishad* 4.4.3–4 in Patrick Olivelle, trans., *Upanisads* (New York: Oxford University Press, 1996), 64.

7. *Chandogya Upanishads* 5.10.5–6 in ibid., 142.

5. Dharma and Caste

1. The Laws of Manu X.97 in Sarvepalli Radhakrishnan and Charles Moore, eds., *A Sourcebook in Indian Philosophy* (Princeton, N.J.: Princeton University Press, 1957), 184.
2. The Laws of Manu I.87 in ibid., 176.
3. The Laws of Manu VIII.353 in ibid., 177.
4. The Laws of Manu X.74–76 in ibid., 184.
5. The Laws of Manu X.3 in ibid., 176.
6. The Laws of Manu VII.2 in ibid., 186.
7. The Laws of Manu VII.87, 88, 89 in ibid., 187.
8. The Laws of Manu VII.20, 22, 24 in ibid., 186.
9. The Laws of Manu IX.326, 328–330 in ibid., 188.
10. The Laws of Manu IX.334, 335; VIII.414 in ibid., 188–89.
11. For a fascinating study of the consequences of an illicit sexual relationship between a Brahmin man and an untouchable woman on the community in which they live, see the popular novel *Samskara* by U. R. Anantha Murthy (Delhi: Oxford University Press, 1978).

6. Men, Women, and the Stages of Life

1. The Laws of Manu III.78 in Sarvepalli Radhakrishnan and Charles Moore, eds., *A Sourcebook in Indian Philosophy* (Princeton, N.J.: Princeton University Press, 1957), 179.
2. The Laws of Manu III.55, 56 in ibid., 189.
3. The Laws of Manu IX.2, 3 in ibid., 190.
4. The Laws of Manu III. 56 in ibid., 189.

7. The Way of Action

1. Thomas Hobbes, *Leviathan*, pt. I, chap. 13., (London: Oxford University Press, 1947), 97.
2. Swami Nikhilananda, trans., *The Gospel of Sri Ramakrishna* (Chennai: Sri Ramakrishna Math, n.d.) chap. 25, n.p. Available at http://www.belurmath.org/gospel/index.htm.
3. Mircea Eliade, *The Sacred and the Profane: The Nature of Religion*, trans. Willard R. Trask (New York: Harcourt Brace Jovanovich, 1987), 73–85.

8. The Way of Knowledge

1. Hermann Kulke and Dietmar Rothermund, *A History of India*, 3rd ed., (London: Routledge, 1986), 49.
2. Bhikkhu Ñāṇamoli and Bhikkhu Bodhi, trans., *The Middle Length Discourses of the Buddha: A New Translation of the Majjhima Nikāya* (Boston: Wisdom Publications, 1995), 335.
3. Juan Mascaró, trans., *The Upanishads* (Harmondsworth, U.K.: Penguin, 1965), 75.
4. Ibid., 123.
5. *Katha Upanishad* 2.18–19 in ibid., 279–80.

6. *Kaushitaki Upanishad* in ibid., 107.

7. Valerie J. Roebuck, trans., *The Upaniṣads* (New York: Penguin, 2003), 7–9.

8. *Kena Upanishad* 1.3–9 in ibid., 263–64.

9. Thomas Aquinas, *Summa contra gentiles* I.14.2, trans. Anton C. Pegis (Notre Dame, Ind.: University of Notre Dame Press, 1975), 96. Emphasis in original.

10. *Kena Upanishad* 2.3 in Roebuck, *Upaniṣads*, 265.

11. Mascaró, *The Upanishad*, 114.

12. *Chandogya Upanishads* in ibid., 117.

13. Psalm 8:3–4 (Revised Standard Version).

14. *Maitri Upanishad* 3.2 in Mascaró, *Upanishads*, 101.

15. *Chandogya Upanishad* in ibid., 121.

16. "Supreme Teaching" in ibid., 136.

9. Seeing God

1. Aristotle, *De Anima*, bk. 3, chap. 7 in *The Basic Works of Aristotle*, ed. Richard McKeon (New York: Random House, 1941), 594.

2. *Brihad Aranyaka Upanishad* III.9 in Valerie J. Roebuck, trans., *The Upaniṣads* (New York: Penguin, 2003), 53–55.

3. Reginald Heber, "From Greenland's Icy Mountains" (1819). Available at www.cyberhymnal.org/htm/f/r/fromgrim .htm.

4. Ludwig Feuerbach, *The Essence of Christianity*, trans. George Eliot (New York: Harper Torchbooks, 1957), 6, 7.

5. Wendy Doniger, *Śiva: The Erotic Ascetic* (New York: Oxford University Press, 1981).

6. Paul Tillich, *Dynamics of Faith* (New York: HarperOne, 2001), 48.

10. The Way of Devotion

1. Swami Nikhilananda, trans., *The Gospel of Sri Ramakrishna* (Chennai: Sri Ramakrishna Math, n.d, chap. 26, n.p.). Available at http://www.belurmath.org/gospel/index.htm.

2. Although the incorporation of the Buddha into the mythology of Vishnu aptly exemplifies the Hindu tendency toward assimilation, his inclusion as an avatar is not unambiguous. According to some stories in the *Puranas*, Vishnu's appearance as the Buddha was a test designed by the great god to delude the faithful and divert them from the true dharma. Those whose devotion to god was steadfast were able to resist the allure of the Buddha's false teachings. In other Hindu sources, the Buddha is presented favorably as a teacher of yoga and a champion of animal protection.

3. The Laws of Manu VII.87, 88, 89 in Sarvepalli Radhakrishnan and Charles Moore, eds., *A Sourcebook in Indian Philosophy* (Princeton, N.J.: Princeton University Press, 1957), 187.

4. Barbara Stoler Miller, trans., *The Bhagavad-Gita: Krishna's Counsel in Time of War* (2.34) (New York: Bantam, 1986), 34.

5. Ibid. (2.19, 20), 32.

6. Ibid. (2.47–49), 36.

7. Ibid. (3.8–9), 42.

8. Ibid. (3.2), 41.

9. Ibid. (9.22), 86.

10. Ibid. (9.26–28), 86–87.

11. Ibid. (9.23), 86.

12. Ibid. (11.12–14), 99.

13. From an interview in the television documentary, *The Decision to Drop the Bomb*, NBC White Paper, 1965. Produced by Fred Freed.

14. Rudolf Otto, *The Idea of the Holy: An Inquiry into the Non-rational Factor in the Idea of the Divine and Its Relation to the Rational*, trans. John W. Harvey (Oxford: Oxford University Press, 1966).

15. Miller, *Bhagavad-Gita* (11.19–20), 100.

16. Ibid. (11.23), 101.

17. Ibid. (11.32–33), 103–4.

11. The Goddess and Her Devotees

1. Thomas B. Coburn, *Encountering the Goddess: A Translation of the Devī-Māhātmya and a Study of Its Interpretation* (Albany: State University of New York Press, 1991).

2. Quoted in Sister Nivedita, *Kali the Mother* (n.p., 1899), 53, Vivekananda Library Online, http://www.vivekananda .net/PDFBooks/KaliTheMother.pdf.

3. Among the few gods and goddesses with children, the most prominent are Shiva and Parvati (or one of her forms), who have two sons, Ganesha and Murugan (also known as Skanda). The stories about these sons, however, suggest they were conceived and delivered in something other than the conventional way.

4. This section is adapted from Mark W. Muesse, "Ancient India," in *The Greenwood Encyclopedia of Love, Courtship, and Sexuality through History*, vol. 1, The Ancient World, ed. James W. Howell (Westport, Conn.: Greenwood, 2008), 185–206.

5. Word to the wise: do not attempt to practice tantra at home! Tantra is best left to the professionals!

6. The significance of parched grain may also be related to the fact that it was used as an offering to the gods by the lower castes, suggesting a form of impurity.

12. The Modern Period

1. About 62 percent of the world's Muslims live in Asia. Almost one-third of all Muslims live in South Asia—the Indian Subcontinent. By comparison, only 20 percent of the Muslim population live in the Middle East and North Africa. *Mapping the Global Muslim Population: A Report on the Size and Distribution of the World's Muslim Population* (Washington, D.C.: Pew Research Center's Forum on Religion & Public Life, 2009), 15, 19.

2. Jyotsna Singh, "Islam and Hinduism's Blurred Lines," *BBC News*, July 14, 2008, http://news.bbc.co.uk/2/hi/7473019.stm.

3. Quaid-i-Azam Mohammad Ali Jinnah, address at Lahore Session of Muslim League, March 1940 (Islamabad: Directorate of Films and Publishing, Ministry of Information and Broadcasting, Government of Pakistan, 1983), para. 23. Available at http://www.pakalumni.com/profiles/blog/show?id=1119293%3ABlogPost%3A57587.

4. This figure is based on 2009 statistics. United Nations Population Fund, "Monitoring ICPD Goals," *State of World Population 2009*, available at http://www.unfpa.org/swp/2009/en/pdf/EN_SOWP09_ICPD.pdf. At the end of the Raj, only 12 percent of the Indian population was literate.

GLOSSARY

Abrahamic traditions. The religions that trace their lineage to the biblical patriarch Abraham, namely Judaism, Christianity, and Islam.

adharma. The absence of dharma; chaos.

Advaita Vedanta (*Advaita Vedānta*). The subschool of Vedanta philosophy that argues a monist (or more precisely, nondual) view of reality.

Agni. Vedic god of fire and mediator between human and divine realms. According to the Vedas, Agni dwells in the fires of the hearth, the sacrifice, and cremation.

ahimsa (ahimsā). The practice of not harming living beings.

ahuras. The Avestan word for the gods or spirits aligned with the principle of good.

airyana waējah. "The land of the noble" in the ancient Iranian language; the name from which "Iran" is derived.

Akbar, Jalāl ud-Dīn Muhammad. Often known by the redundant phrase "Akbar the Great"—"Akbar" means "the great"—Akbar (1542–1605) was the third Mughal ruler of India. A devout Muslim, Akbar, later in life, developed a great respect for other religions and instituted laws (and repealed others) to promote religious toleration in the empire.

Ambedkar, Bhimrao Ramji. Ambedkar (1891–1956) was a prominent Dalit and leader of the Dalit liberation movement.

aniconic image. A non-anthropomorphic representation of the divine.

animism. The belief that spiritual realities reside in the nonhuman realms.

apophatic theology. Based on the view that ultimate reality is ineffable, apophatic theology attempts to indicate the absolute by noting what it is not. Contrast with cataphatic theology.

apotropaic. Concerned with warding off evil.

arati (also arathi, aarthi). Waving a camphor flame or lighted lamp before an image of a deity or a person as an expression of reverence.

Ardhanarishvara (*Ardhanārīśvara*). "The Lord Who Is Half-Woman"; androgynous image of Shiva-Parvati depicted as one-half male, one-half female.

ariya. "Noble."

Arjuna. One of the five sons of Pāndu in the *Mahabharata.* Arjuna's dialogue with his charioteer Krishna comprises the Bhagavad Gita.

Arya Samaj (*Ārya Samāj*). A Hindu sect begun in the nineteenth century by Swami Dayananda Sarasvati, who disliked popular Hindu practices such as *puja* and pilgrimage. The Arya Samaj held the Vedas as the source of all truth—scientific, historical, and spiritual—and denied the authority of the Gita and the *Puranas.*

"Aryan question." The current debate about the origins of the Aryans.

Aryans (*Āryans*). According to the majority of scholars, the Aryans were originally Central Asian pastoral nomads who migrated into northwestern India in the middle part of the second millennium B.C.E., bringing with them the Vedas in oral tradition.

Aryavarta (Āryāvarta). "The land of the noble"; the Indo-Aryan name for their homeland in northern India.

asceticism. The practice of training for spiritual purposes, often involving restricting bodily and mental desires and activities.

asha (aša). The Iranian principle of right and order; opposed to *druj*, the principle disorder and chaos.

ashram. An ascetic community.

ashrama (āśrama). Stage, or order, of life.

asuras. Sanskrit term for a class of divinities opposed to the *devas*; usually demonic in character.

Atharvan. A shamanic priest of the Vedic era whose work included healing and conducting rites of passage for Aryans. The term is also used to indicate the rituals performed by this priest.

Atharva-Veda. Division of the Vedas containing instructions and formula for *Atharvan* ceremonies.

atheism. The denial of the existence of gods or god.

atman (ātman). The human essence. Initially understood as the breath in the early Vedic era, the *atman* is later regarded by Hindus as immortal and transmigratory.

aum (or om). The primordial mantra, or *Prāvnava*. Aum is the syllable that encompasses all syllables; the word out of which the whole world is created; the oral embodiment of Brahman.

avatar (avatāra). An earthly manifestation of god. Avatars are usually associated with Vishnu, who "descends" at critical times in the world's history.

Avesta. The central scripture of Zoroastrianism. The most sacred sections of the Avesta are the *Gathas*, or Hymns of Zoroaster.

Avestan. The Indo-European language in which the Zoroastrian Avesta was originally written.

Axial Age. Term coined by philosopher Karl Jaspers to denote the era of exceptional religious and philosophical creativity between 800 and 200 B.C.E. that gave rise to the major world religions.

Bhagavad Gita (Bhagavad Gītā). Much beloved Hindu text recounting the dialogue of Lord Krishna and Arjuna prior to the war between the Kauravas and the Pāndavas.

bhakti. Devotion to god.

bhakti-marga (bhakti-mārga). The way of devotion.

Bhaktivedanta, A. C. Swami Bhaktivedanta (1896–1977) was a Vaishnavite teacher who founded the International Society for Krishna Consciousness (ISKCON) in 1966. He was inspired by the teachings of Sri Caitanya Mahaprabhu, a fifteenth-century saint and religious reformer.

Bhārata. The Sanskrit name for India.

bindi. Ornamentation often used by women and girls worn as a mark between the eyebrows.

Brahma (Brahmā). One of the Trimurti, usually associated with cosmic creation.

brahmacarya. The first *ashrama* for an upper-caste male in which he practices celibacy and studies with a guru. The term *brahmacarin* can also refer to anyone who practices celibacy for spiritual purposes.

Brahman. The absolute, ultimate reality. Originally, Brahman was the Indo-Aryan word for the power inherent in ritual; later, the term comes to designate the highest reality.

Brahmin. The *varna* of priests and intellectuals.

Brahmo Samaj. A Hindu movement founded in the nineteenth century by Rammohun Roy. The Brahmo Samaj, or Society of Believers in Brahman, denounced polytheism and *puja*, criticized the mistreatment of women, and held the Vedas to be authoritative only when consistent with reason.

Buddha. Siddhattha Gotama, the Buddha (c. 490–410 B.C.E.), was a former *shramana* who gave up extreme asceticism in favor of what he called the "Middle Way." His teachings became the basis of Buddhism.

caste. Derived from the Portuguese term *casta*, caste refers to the stratification of Hindu society based on occupation and purity. In its simplest sense, caste refers to the *varna* system, the fourfold classification of Brahmins, Kshatriyas, Vaishyas, and Shudras.

cataphatic theology. The effort to describe ultimate reality by giving it positive attributes and characteristics. Contrast with apophatic theology.

cool goddess. The manifestation of the goddess as benign and nurturing.

daeva. Avestan cognate of *deva*, a "shiny one"; considered by Zoroaster to be a class of malevolent divinities; the word from which *devil* derives.

Dalits. Self-designation for the outcastes of India. *Dalit* means "oppressed one."

darshan (darśan). A vision or sighting of the sacred; also the term for any school of Hindu philosophy.

Delhi. City in North India established by the Mughals as India's capital.

deva. Sanskrit term for god; literally, "shiny one."

dharma. Sacred duty according to caste; the principle of cosmic order; variously translated as "religion," "duty," and "Truth."

Dharma-Shastras (Dharma-Śāstras). The genre of literature that prescribes the duties of castes.

dowry. The money, property, or other forms of wealth that are negotiated and given to the groom and his family by the family of the bride prior to the wedding.

Durga (*Durgā*). A terrific form of the goddess.

Dyaoš, Dyaus-Pitr. Ancient names for the high god in the Avesta and the *Rig-Veda*, respectively; cognates of Zeus and Jupiter.

ethicization. The process by which objects, events, or activities are accorded a moral significance.

evil eye. The belief that certain individuals have a conscious or unconscious power to cause injury or misfortune to other individuals whom they envy. This belief is found in cultures throughout the Mediterranean region, the Middle East, and South Asia.

Five Ms. See *Panchamakara.*

Five Tribes. A term often used by the Indo-Aryans to refer to themselves.

forest dweller/hermit. The third stage of life for an upper-caste male Hindu. The forest dweller stage indicates increasing withdrawal from society and preparation for the fourth stage, complete renunciation (*sannyasa*).

four goods of life. An ancient Hindu belief that life has four beneficial aims: dharma (duty), *artha* (prosperity), *kama* (pleasure), and *moksha* (liberation).

fruiting of karma. The return of karma to the agent.

Gandhi, Mohandas K. As the leader of the Indian Independence movement, Gandhi's (1869–1948) vision of liberation was deeply influenced by his Hindu piety and informed by his appreciation for many religious traditions.

Ganesha (*Ganeśa*). The elephant-headed god who is the remover of obstacles.

Ganga (*Gaṅgā*). The goddess who manifests as the river Ganges.

gayatri-mantra (gāyatrī-mantra). A verse from *Rig-Veda* 3.62.10 often recited at sunrise and sunset as part of daily Hindu ritual.

ghee. Clarified butter, used for cooking and rituals.

girlhood. The first stage in the female life cycle, from birth to marriage.

Gita Govinda. Poetic work composed by Jayadeva (twelfth century C.E.) relating the story of Krishna and female cowherders of Vrindavan.

grama-devata. The patron deity of a village.

griha **rites.** Vedic rituals conducted within the home.

guru. Teacher.

Haoma. The Avestan name for the god whose manifestation as a particular plant produced visions and a sense of well-being for those who ingested it. Sanskrit: Soma.

Harappa (*Harappā*). One of the two largest cities of the Indus Valley Civilization. The size and centrality of Harappa suggests that it functioned as the capital of this culture, which is sometimes called the Harappan Civilization.

Hare Krishnas. Colloquial term for members of the International Society for Krishna Consciousness.

harijans. "Children of God." Coined by Mohandas Gandhi to refer to the untouchables of India. Today, the name Dalits is generally preferred.

henotheism. The religious practice in which a multiplicity of gods and goddesses is affirmed but only one is worshiped.

Hindoo. Archaic spelling of Hindu.

Hindustan (Hindustān). Name derived from Old Persian to designate the region surrounding the Indus River. Depending on the context, Hindustan can refer to the northwestern part of the Indian Subcontinent, the Republic of India, or the entire Indian Subcontinent.

Hindūtva. "Hinduness."

Holi. The "Festival of Colors" celebrated principally in North India.

hot goddess. The manifestation of the goddess as destructive and angry.

House of Clay. The underworld, occasionally mentioned in the Vedas.

householder (*grīhastha*). The second stage of life for both men and women of caste. At the householder stage, Hindus marry, raise children, work, and contribute to the good of family and society.

iconic image. Anthropomorphic representation of the divine.

idolatry. Confusing the ultimate reality with what is less than ultimate.

Indo-Aryans (*Indo-Āryans*). Modern designation for the Central Asian people who eventually settled in India in the second millennium B.C.E., according to the dominant theory.

Indo-Iranians. According to the dominant theory, the Indo-Iranians were a Central Asian people who migrated southward from the steppes and eventually split, with some going to Iran (the Iranians or Irano-Aryans) and some to India (the Indo-Aryans).

Indra. The war god of the Aryans; the ascendant deity of the *Rig-Veda*; the *deva* who also controlled the waters.

Indus Valley Civilization. Also known as the Harappan Civilization. One of the great cultures of the ancient world, the Indus Valley Civilization existed approximately 3300–1400 B.C.E. in northern India along the Indus River system.

International Society for Krishna Consciousness (ISKCON). The International Society for Krishna Consciousness was founded in 1966 as a Vaishnavite sect by Swami A. C. Bhaktivedānta. Also known as the "Hare Krishnas."

Irano-Aryans. Modern designation for the Central Asian people who eventually settled in Iran. The dominant scholarly theory suggests the Irano-Aryans were a branch of the Indo-Iranians.

ishta-devata. One's favorite deity; the god or goddess to whom one is personally devoted.

Jainism. A small but highly influential religious and philosophical tradition based on the teachings of Vardhamāna Mahāvīra (c. 540–468 B.C.E.).

jati (jāti). One's birth group. *Jati* determines social standing, occupation, marital possibilities, diet, and other practices. Often translated as "subcaste," there may be as many as 3,000 jatis throughout India.

Jinnah, Muhammad Ali. As a leader in the Indian Independence movement, Jinnah (1876–1948) was president of the All India Muslim League and Pakistan's first governor-general.

jñana. The deep or esoteric knowledge that liberates. *Jñana* is etymologically related to the Greek word *gnosis*.

jñana-marga (jñana-mārga). The way of liberating knowledge.

Kabir (*Kabīr*). Kabir (1440–1518) was an early modern mystic-poet from the city of Varanasi and revered by Muslims, Hindus, and Sikhs.

Kali (*Kālī*). A terrific form of the goddess.

karma. Action and its consequences. In the Hindu view, karma is a principle of justice, ensuring that the effects of one's actions return to the agent. Karma is what binds the self to the cycle of endless existence and determines its station in future existences.

karma-marga (karma-mārga). The way of action.

kolam. The handmade geometrical designs made on or in front of homes to attract favorable spirits or good fortune.

Kolkata (Calcutta). City in the state of Bengal; former capital of India under the British Raj.

Krishna (Kṛṣṇa). One of the principal avatars of Vishnu and central character in the Bhagavad Gita.

Kshatriyas (Kṣatriyas). The varna of warriors and administrators.

Kubera. Vedic god of wealth.

kundalini (kundalinī). The source of energy located at the base of the spine, often imagined as a coiled serpent.

Lakshmi (Lakṣmī). Goddess of good fortune and consort of Vishnu. She is also known as Śrī.

Lalla (Lalleshwari, Lal Ded). Kashmiri woman of the fourteenth century (1320–1392) who left an unhappy marriage to wander about North India as an itinerant teacher and poet.

Laws of Manu. One of the earliest and most important codifications of dharma, attributed to Manu, the ancestor of all human beings.

libation. The ritual pouring of a drink as an offering to the gods.

lingam. The most common aniconic representation of Shiva.

Mahabharata (Mahābhārata). One of the two grand epics of Hinduism. The *Mahabharata*, probably the world's longest poem, comprises eighteen books and details the conflict between the Kauravas and the Pāndavas.

Mahadevi (Mahādevī). The "great goddess"; a term to refer to the divine feminine of which all particular goddesses are manifestations.

Maharishi Mahesh Yogi. Twentieth-century Hindu guru (1914–2008) who developed and taught the technique known as Transcendental Meditation.

Mahāvīra, Vardhamāna. Mahāvīra (c. 540–468 B.C.E.) was the twenty-fourth Tirthankara of Jainism.

Mahayogi (Mahāyogi). The great yogi; epithet for Shiva in his aspect as practitioner of meditation and austerities.

manas. Vedic word for that which animates the body; translates as "mind," "heart," or "life-force."

mantra. A sound or phrase embodying sacred power.

Mata, Ma, Amman. Various words for "mother" that are often used to refer to the goddess.

Mazda. An *ahura* of early Iranian religion; according to Zoroaster, Mazda was the principal (and perhaps sole) benevolent deity, locked in combat with the Evil One until the end of time.

Mitra. One of the major gods of Indo-Iranian religion initially associated with promise-keeping.

Mohenjo-daro. One of the two major cities of the Indus Valley Civilization. Mohenjo-daro, or the "Mound of Death," takes its name from a later city built atop the Indus Valley site. What Indus Valley dwellers called this city is not known.

moksha (mokśa). Release or liberation from the wheel of samsara. Pursued and conceptualized in a variety of ways, *moksha* is the ultimate goal of Hindus.

monism. The philosophical position that reality comprises only one thing.

monotheism. The belief that the ultimate reality is a single personal deity.

mother goddess. Female deity associated with birth, motherhood, creation, and nature.

Mughals. Muslim emperors who ruled northern India, beginning with the reign of Zahīr ud-Dīn Muhammad Babur (1483–1531). The Mughals remained in power in the north until the establishment of British rule in the eighteenth century.

murti (also murthi). The visible form of the divine.

Nachiketas. Young Brahmin in the Upanishads who inquires into the nature of postmortem existence.

namkaran. The naming ceremony.

Nanak, Guru. Nanak (1469–1539) was the founder of Sikhism.

Nandi. The bull associated with Shiva; Nandi usually appears with representations of Shiva as *lingam*.

Nataraja (*Natarāja*). Literally, the "Lord of the Dance"; iconic depiction of the Mahadeva Shiva as a cosmic dancer.

Navaratri. Popular festival lasting "nine nights" to celebrate Devi.

negative theology. See apophatic theology.

nirguna. "Without qualities or characteristics"; a term applied to the concept of Brahman to indicate its utter incomprehensibility.

once-born (*advija*). Those who do not undergo the ritual initiation reserved for members of the three upper castes, i.e., the Shudras and Dalits.

Out of India theory. The idea that the Aryans originated in India and migrated to other parts of the world.

outcaste. One who does not have caste. Also known as an untouchable or Dalit.

Pakistan. Name of the modern state in the northwestern region of the subcontinent that was part of India until 1947.

Panchamakara **(the Five Ms).** The elements of left-handed Tantra yoga—meat (*māmsa*), fish (*matsya*), parched grain (*mudrā*), wine (*madya*), and ritual sexual intercourse (*maithuna*).

pandit. One skilled in law, religion, philosophy, and other intellectual endeavors, particularly matters concerning the Vedas.

panentheism. The theological position that god pervades and transcends the created world.

pantheism. The theological position that god pervades the created world.

Parsis (also Parsees). Descendants of the Persian Zoroastrians who began to migrate to India in the eighth century to flee religious persecution.

Parvati (*Pārvatī*). Benign form of the goddess; wife of Shiva.

Pashupati (*Paśupati*). The "Lord of the Animals"; one of the epithets for the Hindu god Shiva.

polytheism. The theological view that posits the existence of many gods and goddesses.

prashad **(*praśad*).** Food offered to the gods and then shared by devotees.

Prāvnava. The primordial mantra, *aum*; the word out of which the whole world is created; the oral embodiment of Brahman.

puja **(*pūjā*).** The ritual worship of a god, goddess, or object representing sacred reality.

Punjab (*Panjab*). Region in the northwestern part of the India Subcontinent. Also the name of provinces in both Pakistan and India.

Puranas **(*Purāṇas*).** Composed between 300 and 1700 c.e., the *Puranas* are the main source of mythology about the great gods of Hinduism, especially Shiva, Vishnu, and Devi.

Purusha (*Puruśa*). The primordial human being. According to a prominent creation myth of the *Rig-Veda*, the world and society are created by the gods' sacrificial dismemberment of the Purusha's body.

Radha (*Rādhā*). The childhood friend and consort of Krishna.

Rajneesh, Bhagwan Sri. A controversial guru, Rajneesh (1931–1990) originated the Rajneesh movement and influenced the New Age movement in the West; also known as Osho.

Ramadan (*Ramadān*). The holy month of Islam that commemorates the beginning of Muhammad's reception of the Qur'an. Observing Ramadan is now considered one of the Five Pillars of Islam.

Ramakrishna. Ramakrishna (1836–1886) was a Bengali mystic and teacher of Advaita Vedanta.

Ramanuja (*Rāmānujācārya*). Ramanuja (c. 1077–1157) was a philosopher and proponent of the Vishishtadvaita subschool of Vedanta.

Ramayana **(*Rāmāyana*).** One of the two great epics of India, the *Ramayana* relates the adventures of Rama and his wife Sita.

redeath. The idea that the individual might ascend to heaven but later die again as a consequence of exhausting the merits that led there.

reincarnation. The process whereby the self assumes a new bodily form.

Rig-Veda. Comprising over 1,000 hymns of praise, the *Rig-Veda* is the oldest and most important collection of Vedic scripture.

rishis (ṛṣis). Seers; one of many Hindu words to denote a holy person. Often used especially to refer to the ancient sages to whom the Vedas were revealed.

rita (ṛtá). The Vedic principle of order and harmony.

ritual purity and pollution. The concern with one's fitness to approach the sacred.

Roy, Rammohun. The founder of the Brahmo Samaj, Roy (1774–1833) took an appreciative, but not uncritical, approach to Christianity and Western values. His movement sought to reform Hinduism by eliminating image veneration and the practice of *sati*.

Rudra. Terrifying Vedic god known as "the Howler," enemy of gods and humans alike. It is possible that Rudra was a prototype for the Hindu god Shiva.

sacred. Holy, worthy of veneration and devotion.

saguna **Brahman.** That aspect of Brahman that can be conceptualized and discussed.

Sama-Veda. Collection of the Vedas concerned with sacrificial melodies.

samhitas (samhitās). The four "collections" of the Vedas, including the *Rig-Veda*, the *Sama-Veda*, the *Atharva-Veda*, and the *Yajur-Veda*.

samsara (*samsāra*). The phenomenal world of change and transience. Samsara denotes the situation in which the *atman* sequentially incarnates in different bodies at different levels of existence.

samskara (*samskāra*). A sacrament; one of the rituals performed as a rite of passage in many Hindu communities.

sanātana dharma. The "eternal Truth."

sannyasa (sannyāsa). Renunciation; the final *ashrama*, or stage, for upper-caste Hindu males.

sannyasin (sannyāsin). One who renounces family, home, possessions, and all markers of previous identity in order to seek final liberation.

Sanskrit. Indo-European language in which the Vedas were composed.

saptapadi (saptapadī). A wedding ritual in which the bride and groom take seven steps around (or circumambulate seven times) a fire altar.

Sarasvati, Dayananda. Swami Sarasvati (1824–1883) disliked much that he saw in the popular Hindu practice of his day, especially *puja* and pilgrimage. He advocated a return to the singular authority of the Vedas and founded the Arya Samaj to promote his cause.

Sarasvati (*Sarasvatī*). Benign goddess of education, music, and the arts; wife of Brahma.

sati (*satī*; also suttee). Ritual act in which a widow burns with her husband's corpse on his funeral pyre. Abolished by the British in the nineteenth century, the act is extremely rare today. The ritual takes its name from Sati, a name for the wife of Shiva, who self-immolated in anger at her father's snubbing of her husband.

satyāgraha. Literally, "grasping for the truth." *Satyāgraha* was Gandhi's term for his philosophy and practice of nonviolent resistance to injustice.

shakti (śakti). Divine power; usually depicted as a goddess.

Shaktism. The religion centered on goddess worship; one of the three major religions of the Hindu traditions along with Shaivism and Vaishnavism.

shaman. Cross-cultural term to refer to an individual with special access to the spirit world.

Shankara (*Śankarācārya, Ādi*). Shankara (c. 788–820) was a Hindu reformer and philosopher in the Advaita Vedanta school.

shaykh. Islamic scholar or teacher.

shirk (śirk). The Arabian word meaning "association"; often translated as "idolatry."

shiva. The principle of order, form, and restraint.

Shiva (*Śiva*). One of the Trimurti, usually associated with cosmic destruction.

shraddha (śrāddha). The rituals associated with honoring one's ancestors, particularly one's deceased parents.

shramana. "Striver." One who seeks *moksha* by specific physical and spiritual disciplines.

shrauta (*śrauta***) rites.** Ordinarily complex Vedic ceremonies using the verses of the Vedas for the purpose of maintaining divine-human relations.

shruti (*śruti***).** Sacred literature of the highest authority in Hinduism. Believed to have been revealed to the ancient *rishis*, *shruti* includes the Vedas and the Upanishads.

Shudras (*Śūdras***).** The lowest of the four *varnas*; the caste of peasants and servants.

Sikhism. An indigenous Indian religion inspired by Kabīr, a mystic-poet from Varanasi, and founded by Guru Nanak, a Hindu from Punjab. Both men condemned Hindu and Muslim sectarianism and sought to establish authentic worship of the one true God. The name *Sikh* means "disciple."

Sindhu. The Sanskrit name for the Indus River.

sindura. The streak of red powder placed in the part of the bride's hair by the groom during the wedding.

smriti (*smṛti***).** Secondary sacred literature in Hinduism. Whereas *shruti* is literature of the highest authority, the authority of *smriti* derives from *shruti*. *Smriti* includes such popular texts as the *Puranas* and the Bhagavad Gita. *Smriti* means "recollection" or "tradition."

Soma. The Sanskrit name for the god whose manifestation as a particular plant produced visions and a sense of well-being for those who ingested it. Avestan: Haoma.

Soul of the Bull (Geush Urvan). The divine being in ancient Indo-Iranian religion who sustained and nurtured animal life.

stridharma (*strīdharma***).** The duties governing the life of a woman, particularly in her role as wife and mother.

Surya (*Sūrya***).** One of the Vedic Hindu sun deities.

Svarga. Heaven in the Vedic *triloka*.

swastika (*svastika***).** Ancient Indian design signifying auspiciousness.

sympathetic magic. The belief that a person or object can be affected by using another object (or a name) to represent it.

Tantras. A collection of manuals describing yogic techniques for realizing *moksha*.

Tantrika. A tantric practitioner.

Tantrism. The esoteric yogic practice closely associated with worship of Devi.

tarpana. Water ritual to honor the gods and ancestors.

Thag. Literally, "thief." Some Thags were devotees of Kali or Durga who sought to provide her with human sacrifices.

Thai Pongal. Harvest festival celebrated mainly in South India.

tilak. Forehead marking that may indicate one's religious affiliation.

transmigration of the self. The postmortem movement of the self from one body to another.

triloka (*trīloka***).** The Vedic conception of the world as tripartite, divided into heaven, atmosphere, and earth.

Trimarga (*Trīmārga***).** A traditional typology denoting three different spiritual orientations, including the paths of action, knowledge, and devotion.

Trimurti (*Trimūrti***).** The three gods associated with the cosmic life span. Brahma is the creator, Vishnu the sustainer, and Shiva the cosmic destroyer.

twice-born (*dvijas***).** A term for members of the three upper castes, so called because they undergo a ritual initiation or second birth (*upanayana*).

untouchable. A Dalit.

upanayana (*upanāyana***).** The ritual that initiates study of the Vedas and marks entry into studenthood for upper caste members. The initiate is given a sacred thread, worn over the left shoulder, to indicate his new status.

Upanishads (*Upaniṣads***).** Composed between 800 and 200 b.c.e., the main Upanishads represent an evolution in Vedic thought, bringing together speculation about the nature of the self and ultimate reality in the insight that Brahman and *atman* are identical.

Ushas (*Uṣas*). Vedic goddess of the dawn.

Vaishyas (*Vaiśyas*). The varna of farmers, cattle herders, artisans, and businesspeople.

Vak (*Vāk* or *Vāc*). Vedic goddess of speech.

***varna*.** Literally, "color"; usually rendered as caste. *Varna* designates the fourfold classification of Brahmins, Kshatriyas, Vaishyas, and Shudras.

Varuna. Indo-Iranian god associated with promise-keeping.

Vedanta (*Vedānta*). The "end of the Vedas." Vedanta is one of the most important and influential of the Hindu philosophies. Deriving inspiration particularly from the Upanishads, the last part of the Vedas, Vedanta emphasizes unity of the self and the Absolute.

Vedas. The collection of ancient texts that provides the oldest and highest authority for most Hindu traditions.

Vishishtadvaita Vedanta (*Viśiṣṭādvaita Vedānta*). Subschool of Vedanta philosophy that subscribes to "qualified" nondualism.

Vishnu (*Viṣṇu*). One of the Trimurti, usually associated with cosmic maintenance. Vishnu is often worshiped as one of his many avatars.

Vivekananda. The foremost disciple of the nineteenth-century saint Ramakrishna, Swami Vivekananda (1863–1902) created a sensation at the first World's Parliament of Religions in Chicago in 1893. His speech at the Parliament marked the beginning of Hindus coming to the West to represent their religion. Vivekananda began a worldwide network known as the Vedanta Society.

westernization. The process by which modern Western values, beliefs, and practices exert influence on non-western cultures.

World's Parliament of Religions. Meeting held in Chicago in 1893 to encourage dialogue among the world's religions.

***yajña*.** Sanskrit term for "sacrifice." Avestan: *yasna*.

***Yajur-Veda*.** Collection of the Vedas concerned with sacrificial instructions.

Yama. The god of death.

***yantra*.** A geometric design that functions as an aniconic image representing the presence of the divine.

***yasna*.** See *yajña*.

***yatra* (*yātrā*).** Pilgrimage.

Zoroaster. The Greek transliteration of Zarathustra, an Iranian prophet and founder of the religion of Zoroastrianism, or Mazdaism. There is no consensus on when Zoroaster lived. Some scholarly estimates suggest he lived as early as the fifteenth century B.C.E. and as late as the sixth century B.C.E. Zoroaster was a priest who felt called to urge his contemporaries to worship Ahura Mazda exclusively.

Zoroastrianism. Dualist religion based on the teachings of Zoroaster.

Note: Page numbers in italics represent photographs and illustrations.